W9-DCF-774

JOURNAL FOR THE STUDY OF THE NEW TESTAMENT
SUPPLEMENT SERIES

264

Executive Editor
Stanley E. Porter

Editorial Board
Craig Blomberg, Elizabeth A. Castelli, David Catchpole,
Kathleen E. Corley, R. Alan Culpepper, James D.G. Dunn,
Craig A. Evans, Stephen Fowl, Robert Fowler, George H.
Guthrie, Robert Jewett, Robert W. Wall

The Polemic of the Pastorals

A Sociological Examination of the
Development of Pauline Christianity

Lloyd K. Pietersen

T & T CLARK INTERNATIONAL
A Continuum imprint
LONDON • NEW YORK

Copyright © 2004 T&T Clark International
A Continuum imprint

Published by T&T Clark International
The Tower Building, 11 York Road, London SE1 7NX
15 East 26th Street, Suite 1703, New York, NY 10010

www.tandtclark.com

British Library Cataloguing-in-Publication Data
A catalogue record for this book is available from the British Library

Library of Congress Cataloging-in-Publication Data
A catalogue record for this book is available from the Library of Congress

Typeset by CA Typesetting, Sheffield
Printed on acid-free paper in Great Britain by The Cromwell Press, Trowbridge, Wiltshire

ISBN 0-567-08183-4

CONTENTS

PREFACE

This volume is a thoroughgoing revision of a doctoral thesis accepted by the University of Sheffield in December 2000. I conducted my research under the able supervision of Dr Loveday C.A. Alexander. I would like to thank her for encouraging me to attend the research induction programme for postgraduate students in sociology at the University of Sheffield. It was in this programme that I learned to think sociologically in a more rigorous way. I am grateful to her too for her careful critique of my work.

In revising my thesis for publication I have attempted to interact with the most relevant secondary literature that has appeared since I submitted my thesis for examination in August 2000. In addition, I have attempted to address the criticisms of my doctoral examiners, Dr R. Barry Matlock of the University of Sheffield (internal examiner) and Dr David G. Horrell of the University of Exeter (external examiner). I am grateful to the latter for taking the trouble to offer an extensive critique in addition to his comments on the examiners' report. Their critique has served to sharpen my own thinking and writing and this volume has been considerably strengthened as a result.

During the writing of my thesis and the subsequent writing of this book I have received much support. I would like to thank, in particular, the elders of Bristol Christian Fellowship for releasing me from eldership duties to pursue further studies and for providing me with initial financial support. I have learned much from members of staff and colleagues in the Department of Biblical Studies at the University of Sheffield. Apart from the debt owed to both Dr Alexander and Dr Matlock, I would especially like to thank Dr Margaret Davies for her friendship, encouragement and stimulating conversations concerning the Pastorals.

My academic friends Fiona Black, Mark Blackwell, Helen Bond, James Harding, John Lyons, Ruth Anne Reese and Andy Reimer have been a constant source of encouragement. I have greatly appreciated their friendship, the collegial chats and the malt whisky. John Lyons, in particular, has been both a regular source of constructive critique of my work and a fellow dedicated malt whisky drinker.

I cannot thank enough my regular dinner companions and great friends Hilary Deering, John and Katie Lyons and Steve and Nettie Matthews. Our dinner parties have been truly remarkable demonstrations of the pursuit of culinary and oenological excellence. Thanks too to my special friend and work colleague, Karen Chelton, whose friendship and support have been invaluable.

Over the last few years I have been privileged to be involved in a great training programme called Workshop. I am grateful to the programme director, Noel Moules, for giving me the opportunity to teach on this exciting course. His friendship and encouragement mean a lot to me as do those of my teaching colleagues Cherryl Hunt, Jill Ogilvy, Rosemary Pike and Simon Scott. However, I must single out my erstwhile colleague and current member of the London Workshop team, Sue Haines. She has become a special friend and spent some time with me helping me with my German translation. For that I will forever be extremely grateful.

Special mention too must be made of my good friends Alan and Ellie Kreider whose wisdom, insight and peaceful presence have been greatly valued. Alan has been a particular source of intellectual stimulation in relating my work on the Pastorals to Mennonite history and praxis. I thank too my other colleagues on the Anabaptist Network Steering Group, especially Dr Stuart Murray Williams, for giving me the opportunity to express some of my thoughts on the Pastorals in the journal *Anabaptism Today*.

Finally, all my love and appreciation go out to my family who have had to put up with long periods of my absence in the study. I dedicate this book, therefore, to my children Beth, Keren, Kez and Jed and my wife Sheila. I thank them all for their patience.

Lloyd K. Pietersen

ABBREVIATIONS

AB	Anchor Bible
AnBib	Analecta biblica
ANF	Anti-Nicene Fathers
BDF	Friedrich Blass, A. Debrunner and Robert W. Funk, *A Greek Grammar of the New Testament and Other Early Christian Literature* (Cambridge: Cambridge University Press, 1961)
BJRL	*Bulletin of the John Rylands University Library of Manchester*
ConB	Coniectanea biblica
Ebib	Etudes bibliques
EKKNT	Evangelisch-Katholischer Kommentar zum Neuen Testament
FRLANT	Forschungen zur Religion und Literatur des Alten und Neuen Testaments
HTR	*Harvard Theological Review*
HR	*History of Religions*
ICC	International Critical Commentary
JBL	*Journal of Biblical Literature*
JHC	*Journal of Higher Criticism*
JRelS	*Journal of Religious Studies*
JSNT	*Journal for the Study of the New Testament*
JSNTSup	*Journal for the Study of the New Testament*, Supplement Series
JSSR	*Journal for the Scientific Study of Religion*
NICNT	New International Commentary on the New Testament
NIGTC	The New International Greek Testament Commentary
NovT	*Novum Testamentum*
NovTSup	*Novum Testamentum*, Supplements
NTS	*New Testament Studies*
OTP	James Charlesworth (ed.), *Old Testament Pseudepigrapha*
RB	*Revue biblique*
SBLDS	SBL Dissertation Series
SBLMS	SBL Monograph Series
SBLSBS	SBL Sources for Biblical Study
SBLSP	SBL Seminar Papers
SNTSMS	Society for New Testament Studies Monograph Series
TDNT	Gerhard Kittel and Gerhard Friedrich (eds.), *Theological Dictionary of the New Testament* (trans. Geoffrey W. Bromiley; 10 vols.; Grand Rapids: Eerdmans, 1964–)
WBC	Word Biblical Commentaries
WUNT	Wissenschaftliche Untersuchungen zum Neuen Testament

INTRODUCTION

Speaking of the Pastorals, Dunn (1975: 349) states:

> Clearly then the vision of charismatic community has faded, ministry and author-
> ity have become the prerogative of the few, the experience of the Christ-Spirit
> has lost its vitality, the preservation of the past has become more important than
> openness to the present and future. *Spirit and charisma have become in effect
> subordinate to office, to ritual, to tradition* – early Catholicism indeed![1]

The view that the Pastorals represent an institutionalised form of Pauline Christianity has a long pedigree.[2] This conclusion, which represents the scholarly consensus,
is based on Weber's concept of the routinisation of charisma and the institutionalisation of charismatic authority. In this thesis I wish to present an alternative model
which leads to a different conclusion. Utilising insights from the sociology of
deviance, I argue that the function of the Pastorals is to provide a literary version
of a status degradation ceremony whereby previously influential insiders in the
communities addressed are transformed into outsiders. Drawing on Wilson's (1973)
typology of sectarian responses to the world, I seek to refine Weber's approach by
defining a developmental model which suggests that both institutionalisation and
the potential subversion of that institutionalisation through thaumaturgical demand
characterise charismatic communities[3] over time. I then utilise this model to argue
that the Pastorals reflect this process and that the opponents addressed advocate a
form of spirituality informed by a view of Paul as primarily a thaumaturge. The
author of the Pastorals seeks to combat the opponents by appealing to Paul as primarily a teacher and by claiming to represent authentic Pauline tradition.

At the outset it is important to define terms. I am using *thaumaturgy* in Wilson's
(1973) sense of 'the demand for miracles and oracles'. In describing Paul as a
thaumaturge I therefore draw attention to Paul's wonder-working, prophecies,
glossolalia and visionary experiences. I use *charismatic community* throughout in
Dunn's sense as described in note three. I also use the phrase 'intensification of

---

1.   Italics in the original. Dunn continues to hold this view some twenty years later. Dunn
(1998: 598) states that in the Pastorals 'we see the familiar second-generation pattern of routinization of charisma and institutionalization of authority'.
2.   See especially Sohm (1892), Harnack (1910), Schweizer (1961), Käsemann (1964) and von
Campenhausen (1969). Dunn (1998: 567 n. 8) admits that the last three considerably influenced his
approach in *Jesus and the Spirit*.
3.   In Dunn's sense of Christian communities in which charismata are indispensable to the
community and in which every member of the community is a charismatic through whom the Spirit
may be manifested in various ways at any time. See Dunn (1975: 260–65).

charisma' as the binary opposite of Weber's 'routinisation of charisma' and, as such, I use the phrase in a way which is synonymous with thaumaturgical demand.

In Chapter 1 I give an overview of the history of scholarship concerning the opponents in the Pastoral Epistles. I conclude that there are real problems with viewing the opponents as Gnostics and that the view that they represent 'a Gnosticizing form of Jewish Christianity'[4] is far too vague. On the other hand, those who argue that the opponents and the resulting polemic are primarily literary devices do not pay sufficient attention to the sociological reality of conflict in Christian communities. In Chapter 2, therefore, I describe various approaches in the sociology of deviance and conclude that, given the author resorts to name-calling in connection with the opponents, the most useful sociological approach is that of 'labelling theory'.

In Chapters 3 to 5 I expound my developmental model of the simultaneous routinisation and intensification of charisma in charismatic communities. Chapter 3 describes Weber's approach to institutionalisation and refinements of Weber when applied to the Pauline communities. In this chapter I examine Wilson's analysis of sect development.[5] The second half of the chapter considers the conditions for persistence of charisma utilising the work of MacMullen (1984) on Christianising the Roman Empire, Lewis (1989) on ecstatic religion and Wilson (1973) on the thaumaturgical response to the world. In Chapter 4 I extend Wilson's analysis (which was based on his research on tribal and other people groups from the two-thirds world) to the western world by examining the development of one Christian, charismatic group over a period of some thirty years. This chapter provides empirical evidence for my model. In Chapter 5 I argue that a close reading of Ignatius, utilising the model as a sensitising concept, leads to the conclusion that the scholarly consensus (that by the time of Ignatius the church had clearly institutionalised) needs to be revised. My conclusions, from a sociological perspective, support those of Trevett (1992). This is further borne out by the emergence of Montanism in the second half of the second-century CE.

Having argued that my model makes sense of second-century developments, I finally turn to the text of the Pastorals in Chapter 6. In this chapter I argue that the Pastorals are polemical documents in which paraenesis serves the overall purpose of the polemic. I suggest that the opponents were enthusiasts, some of whom had previously been leaders within the community. I conclude that the Pastorals are engaged in a battle for the memory of Paul between the author, who regards Paul as the great teacher, and the opponents who consider him to be the great thaumaturge.

4.   Kelly (1963: 12).
5.   Wilson (1967).

Chapter 1

THE OPPONENTS IN THE PASTORAL EPISTLES

1. *Introduction*

The Pastoral Epistles have traditionally been thought of as providing a manual of church order. Consequently, the question of the opponents in the Pastorals has usually arisen primarily in the context of the debate over authenticity. Those who regard the Pastorals as inauthentic have argued either that the opponents are drawn from a developed second-century Gnosticism or that the polemical passages are merely a literary device designed to warn readers against heresy in general. Supporters of authenticity, on the other hand, have argued that the opponents are real and represent a much less developed form of Gnosticism[1] compatible with a date within the lifetime of Paul. On the other hand, an increasing number of scholars have come to see the significance of the polemical nature of the Pastorals and argue that this is fundamental to their interpretation, and not just to the question of authenticity. Fee, for example, believes that the impact of false teachers at Ephesus provides the reason for the writing of 1 Timothy; these false teachers also form the background to 2 Timothy, and reflection on the nature of the opposition at Ephesus encouraged Paul to write to Titus in order to deal with similar, though less threatening, opposition in Crete.[2] Towner states:

> There is general agreement that the heresy reflected in the Pastoral Epistles is the most important aspect of the background of these letters. At almost every turn it forms the backdrop to the author's parenesis and theological expression, and one must assume that the letters are intended in some sense as a response to this dangerous situation (1989: 21).

However, although the importance of the polemical nature of the Pastorals is now widely recognised, there is no scholarly consensus as to the identity of the opponents nor the extent or manner of their influence on the communities addressed. It is my contention that the Pastoral Epistles were written largely to combat a view of Paul widely circulating in the post-Pauline communities – namely Paul as primarily a charismatic miracle worker. In this chapter I will trace the history of scholarship concerning the identity of the false teachers. I shall argue that the lack of consensus leaves room for a fresh approach using social-scientific analysis.

---

1. For the definitional problems associated with the use of the term 'Gnosticism' see Rudolph (1983).
2. Fee (1988: xiii–xiv, 5–14).

2. *The Opponents as Real*

If it is accepted that the opponents in the Pastorals posed a real historical threat to the communities addressed then the following factors need to be taken into account in any scholarly reconstruction of their identity.[3]

(i)   They came from within the Christian community. They are accused of having suffered shipwreck in the faith (1 Tim. 1.19); having renounced the faith (1 Tim. 4.1); having missed the mark as regards the faith (1 Tim. 6.21); and having swerved from the truth so as to upset the faith of some (2 Tim. 2.18). It may be that certain elders in the community were involved (1 Tim. 5.19–20). They appear to have been a significant threat to the writer (1 Tim. 4.1–4; 2 Tim. 3.1–5; Tit. 1.10–11), and have been particularly effective at the household level (2 Tim. 3.6; Tit. 1.11), apparently targeting women (2 Tim. 3.6–7).

(ii) There was a clear Jewish element.[4] The opponents are accused of wanting to be teachers of the law (νομοδιδάσκαλοι), a term used elsewhere in the New Testament only in Lk. 5.17 (where they are linked with the Pharisees) and Acts 5.34 (with reference to Gamaliel). Those 'of the circumcision' are especially numbered amongst the rebellious, idle talkers and deceivers in Tit. 1.10. The false teaching involved the use of Jewish myths (Tit. 1.14) and quarrels over the law (Tit. 3.9).

(iii) There was also an ascetic element which included the forbidding of marriage and abstinence from foods (1 Tim. 4.1–3).

(iv) The opponents' teaching, according to the writer of the Pastorals, involved myths (1 Tim. 1.4; 4.7; 2 Tim. 4.4; Tit. 1.14); genealogies (1 Tim. 1.4; Tit. 3.9); speculations (1 Tim. 1.4; 6.4; 2 Tim. 2.23; Tit. 3.9); disputes about words (1 Tim. 6.4; 2 Tim. 2.14); profane chatter (1 Tim. 6.20; 2 Tim. 2.16); the concern for γνῶσις (1 Tim. 6.20); and a belief that the resurrection had already taken place (2 Tim. 2.18). The opponents are described as having rejected conscience (1 Tim. 1.19) and as teaching for financial gain (1 Tim. 6.5; Tit. 1.10).

The problem arises in trying to combine the above elements and, to date, there has been no decisive scholarly consensus. Gunther (1973: 4–5) summarised this lack of consensus concerning the identity of the opponents in the history of scholarship up until the time of writing his monograph. Gunther's summary of the opponents can be analysed under four broad headings: 'Jewish'; 'Gnostic'; 'Jewish-

---

3.   The term 'the opponents' in the following summary is used as a shorthand expression to denote everything that is opposed in the Pastoral Epistles. This is not meant to imply that the opponents addressed represent a single homogeneous group; this question must remain open at this stage of the discussion.

4.   Quinn (1990a: 13) suggests that the communities addressed may have consisted of several 'house churches' some of which were entirely Jewish-Christian in composition.

Gnostic' and 'Others' ('Proto-Montanists', 'Cerinthians' or 'Marcionites influenced by Valentinianism').[5]

His analysis suggests there is a prevailing view in scholarship, although clearly contested, that the opponents most likely came from a Jewish-Gnostic context. Gunther's own thesis is that the opponents addressed in the entire Pauline corpus form a basic unity. He proposes that they were:

> believers whose background was a mystic-apocalyptic, ascetic, non-conformist, syncretistic Judaism more akin to Essenism than to any other well-known 'school' or holiness sect (1973: 315).

a. *Jewish-Christian Emphasis*
Gunther (1973: 314–17) concludes that Paul's opponents were drawn from 'apocalypticists, Nazirites and Essenes (in the broad sense)' who were first attracted to John the Baptist, then to Jesus and/or the early Jerusalem Christian community led by James. Because they did not fully share the Qumran community's preoccupation with priestly purity and exclusiveness, Gunther speculates that they were largely town dwellers who did not isolate themselves from the wider world. Consequently, they were able to welcome Christian evangelists and eventually sent out their own missionaries. In Greek-speaking areas these workers would, out of necessity, use some Hellenistic terminology. However, this does not mean that they should be regarded as Gnostics. 'Paul's adversaries were syncretists, gnostics and pneumatics in the same sense that the terms are applicable to the Essenes and Qumranians; their pneumaticism, of course, was enriched as the result of their Christian conversion' (1973: 317). Nevertheless, Gunther himself concedes that the Pastorals provide evidence for an organised antinomian group distinct from this Judaizing group. He argues that this group was led by Hymenaeus and Philetus (2 Tim. 2.17) and finds evidence of their activities in 1 Tim. 1.19–20; 2 Tim. 2.11–4.8. The writer of the Pastorals was thus facing opposition on two fronts: an organised antinomian group and Judaizers similar to those faced earlier by Paul.

However, it is not at all clear that the opponents in the Pastorals can be divided as neatly as Gunther suggests. For example, profane chatter (βεβήλους κενοφωνίας), mentioned in 2 Tim. 2.16 which Gunther assigns to the antinomians, is also mentioned in 1 Tim. 6.20 which Gunther regards as referring to the Judaizers. Similarly, Gunther's antinomians are engaged in controversies (ζητήσεις) and myths (μῦθοι) (2 Tim. 2.23; 4.4), but so are the Judaizers according to 1 Tim. 1.4; 4.7; 6.4; Tit. 1.14; 3.9. The antinomians disrupt households (2 Tim. 3.6–7), but so do the Judaizers (Tit. 1.10–11). Gunther is, of course, aware of this but simply states that both antinomians and Judaizers could be accused of the same things 'for such was the nature of the Pastor's general polemics' (1973: 13). However, this brief statement does not do justice to the question as to whether there are two groups of opponents addressed in the Pastorals.

Gunther argues that the rest of the polemical passages in the Pastorals, apart from those relating to the organised antinomian group, are concerned with the

---

5. These headings are, by no means, mutually exclusive. Gunther adds the names of the leading proponents of the various views listed.

Judaizers found elsewhere in Paul's letters. Gunther does not believe that Paul wrote the Pastorals but he is happy that there is a 'historical connection between the Judaizing of Paul's day and that of the Pastor's day' (1973: 17). He argues that the νομοδιδάσκαλοι of 1 Tim. 1.7 were exegetes of the Torah who were interested in legal traditions (Tit. 1.14), hidden mysteries of the law (1 Tim. 1.7; 6.4; Tit. 3.9), and Jewish myths (Tit. 1.14). He suggests that ἐκζητήσεις (1 Tim. 1.4), ζητήσεις (1 Tim. 6.4; Tit. 3.9), ματαιολογία (1 Tim. 1.6; cf. Tit. 1.10), and λογομαχίαι (1 Tim. 6.4) refer to their disputes over rabbinic exegesis of the Torah (1973: 65–66). Gunther further states that μῦθοι (1 Tim. 1.4; Tit. 1.14) are 'non-revealed, legendary, allegorical, imaginative Haggadah [*sic*], fables, tales, sagas and folklore concerning the creation story, Adam and Eve, Satan's fall and glorified Jewish "history"', and that γενεαλογίαι concern 'the origin and relationships of listed groups and pedigrees of peoples, tribes, patriarchs and priests'. Together myths and genealogies 'were components of biographical legends which purported to be didactic and edifying sacred history supplementing and reconciling Scripture' (1973: 77–78).

For Gunther, the asceticism opposed in 1 Tim. 4.1–5 and suggested by Tit. 1.14–15 reflects Jewish concern for distinction between clean and unclean things (1973: 101). Asceticism, for the opponents, was an expression of εὐσέβεια so that for them 'true εὐσέβεια was manifested by obeying ascetic laws after growth in knowledge and understanding of the myths and genealogies of the law-giving spirits' (1973: 131). Gunther goes on to suggest that the 'ἀντίθεσις of the false γνῶσις (1 Tim. 6.20) may have referred to the contrast of clean and unclean or of flesh and the spirit, as they did for Marcion' (1973: 136). He further suggests that the use of the emphatic prefix ἐπι- in ἐπίγνωσις (1 Tim. 2.4) may indicate that the false teachers claimed that γνῶσις was not available for all Christians; this is met with a firm rebuttal by the Pastor who insists that God 'desires *everyone* to be saved and to come to the knowledge of the truth' (1973: 278). Finally, Gunther argues that the opponents denied that Paul was appointed as a herald and an apostle (1 Tim. 2.7; 2 Tim. 1.11). They were strongly opposed to the Pauline message (2 Tim. 4.15) (1973: 304–305).

Gunther's analysis clearly sets out the view that the opponents encountered in the Pastorals were real and that they formed two distinct groups – an organised antinomian group, and a Judaizing group in historical continuity with the Judaizers faced by Paul. He is not particularly interested in the former faction – he deals with this group in just two pages (1973: 12–13). For Gunther the main opposition came from the Judaizers whom he regards as opposed to the Pauline message. As his thesis is that there was a basic unity among Paul's Judaizing opponents, it is not surprising that the data of the Pastorals is read by him through this lens. This leads, in my view, to some sweeping generalisations, in particular concerning the nature of myths, genealogies, and speculations. Furthermore, Gunther pays insufficient attention to the opponents' opposition to marriage (1 Tim. 4.3). This does not appear to be a feature of the Judaizing opposition faced by Paul. Most significantly, Gunther does not even entertain the view that the polemic of the Pastorals is so strong because the opponents themselves claimed to be representing Paul. He is apparently insensitive to the possibility that there may have been competing claims for the memory of Paul in the post-Pauline communities.

Kelly (1963: 10–12), writing some ten years before Gunther, also believes that the Pastorals are combating real, historical opponents. Kelly is convinced both of the Pauline authorship of the Pastorals and their historical setting in Ephesus and Crete. Unlike Gunther, Kelly does not see two different groups of opponents in the Pastoral Epistles; he suggests that there is a single heresy which took somewhat different forms in Ephesus and Crete. This heresy combined Jewish and Gnostic ingredients. For Kelly these Judaizers were not those that Paul had to combat in his earlier ministry; unlike the earlier Judaizers, the ones encountered in the Pastoral Epistles had an ascetic outlook which included the renunciation of marriage (1 Tim. 4.1–3). They disparaged the material creation (1 Tim. 4.4–5), spiritualised the resurrection of the body (2 Tim. 2.18), and boasted of a higher, esoteric γνῶσις (1 Tim. 6.20). Kelly suggests the possibility that they may also have practised magic,[6] but dismisses this as 'on the whole unlikely' (1963: 11).

Kelly insists that the Pastoral Epistles are not combating the fully developed Gnosticism of the second century CE. In a discussion of the meaning of the 'myths and endless genealogies' of 1 Tim. 1.4, which he describes as coming 'tantalizingly near disclosing the content of the heresy' (1963: 44), Kelly rightly notes that the myths are specifically described as 'Jewish' in Tit. 1.14; furthermore Kelly states that the Valentinian Gnostic notion of systems of aeons was never referred to as 'genealogies'. Kelly is careful, however, to note that an emphasis on the Jewish character of the opponents must not overlook the Gnostic elements. Although this is not second-century Gnosticism, Kelly states that the very phrase μῦθοι καὶ γενεαλογίαι 'which had been a Greek cliché from Plato's time, confirms its syncretistic character' (1963: 45). Consequently, Kelly concludes that the heresy 'is perhaps best defined as a Gnosticizing form of Jewish Christianity' (1963: 12).

In view of the difficulties with Gunther's position that there are two groups of opponents in the Pastoral Epistles, Kelly is right, in my view, to suggest that there is only one broad heresy in view. He also correctly points out the difficulties of identifying the Judaizers in the Pastorals with those encountered earlier by Paul. The burden of this present monograph is to examine whether his conclusion that the opponents represent a 'Gnosticizing form of Jewish Christianity' can stand the test of further analysis.

Fee, who like Kelly argues for the Pauline authorship of the Pastoral Epistles, also suggests that the opponents are drawn from Hellenistic Jewish Christians involved in syncretising their faith with Jewish and Hellenistic elements (1988: 9). He too is convinced that the heresy does not reflect second-century Gnosticism. Fee is, however, more specific than Kelly; he notes the affinities of the views countered in the Pastorals with the over-realised eschatology Paul encountered at Corinth (1 Cor. 7.1–7; 15.12), and with the syncretistic Hellenistic Judaism found at Colossae (Col. 2.3–8, 16–23) (1988: 9). Furthermore, Fee argues (in the light of Acts 20.30 and the fact that the opponents are described as teachers in 1 Tim. 1.3,

---

6. 2 Tim. 3.8 and the mention of γόητες in 2 Tim. 3.11.

7; 6.3), that the church at Ephesus was being led astray by some of its own elders. These elders had been particularly successful among women, particularly younger widows (1 Tim. 2.9–15; 5.3–16; 2 Tim. 3.6–9). The fact that the church at Ephesus probably consisted of a number of house-churches (1 Cor 16.19; 1 Tim. 2.8) each led by one or more elders, suggests the possibility that the problem was not that of a single church being split down the middle but rather that of various house-churches defecting *in toto*. This, Fee believes, is the reason for the degree of urgency in 1 Timothy (1988: 7–8). Fee argues that the opposition was similar in Crete but had not reached the advanced stage there that it had at Ephesus; consequently, there is less urgency concerning the opponents in Titus (1988: 10–12).

Knight, in his commentary, also believes that the false teaching opposed in the Pastoral Epistles arises from one broad group of opponents 'since similar errors or tendencies are mentioned and similar terminology used, though not in every mention of them' (1992: 11). Like Fee he notes the similarities with the heresy at Colossae (1992: 12). Knight quotes with approval Kelly's definition of the nature of the opposition as a 'Gnosticizing form of Jewish Christianity' (1992: 28).

Towner, however, notes that this general tendency among scholars, who believe that real opponents are addressed in the Pastoral Epistles, to regard the heresy as a mixture of Judaizing and Gnosticizing elements obscures significant differences between them. He notes that there is still plenty of discussion concerning the precise meaning of 'myths and genealogies,' the meaning of γνῶσις, the nature of the resurrection doctrine in 2 Tim. 2.18, and the question of ascetic practices. He concludes:

> And disagreement persists over the matter of how the false teaching affected the communities. Even at the point of final identification the pendulum of opinion seems to swing freely from an emphasis on the judaizing nature of the movement to the gnosticizing (1989: 23).

Towner insists that the polemical language in the Pastorals, whilst widespread and harsh, remains rather general in nature. He is impressed with the work of those who argue that the polemic in the Pastorals is primarily a literary device,[7] but 'would not want to go as far as some who conclude that the polemic reflects nothing (or very little) of the actual situation' (1989: 25). Towner believes that there were real opponents and that, although the writer did use 'stock' forms, he moulded them to fit the actual situation. Like Fee, Towner is convinced that the opponents came from within the church and that they found openings among some of the Christian households. He does not consider, however, the evidence to be sufficiently strong to support the claim that the opponents primarily targeted women. Towner's major contribution to the debate is that he considers the opponents' emphasis on γνῶσις to be directly linked to their 'over-realised eschatology',[8] and that this is paralleled by the situation Paul faced in 1 Corinthians.

---

7. See the next section below.
8. Schlarb (1990: 121–22) also connects the opponents' γνῶσις with 2 Tim. 2.18. He suggests that the opponents described their knowledge of baptism, spirit, death and life/resurrection as γνῶσις and that their 'antitheses' consisted of statements about the overwhelming reality of

Towner begins by noting the similarity between 1 Tim. 6.20–21 and 2 Tim. 2.15–18.[9]

1 Tim. 6.20–21	*2 Tim. 2.15–18*
Ὦ Τιμόθεε, *τὴν παραθήκην φύλαξον* ἐκτρεπόμενος **τὰς βεβήλους κενοφωνίας** καὶ ἀντιθέσεις τῆς ψευδωνύμου γνώσεως, ἥν τινες ἐπαγγελλόμενοι *περὶ τὴν πίστιν* ἠστόχησαν. Ἡ χάρις μεθ᾽ ὑμῶν.	σπούδασον σεαυτὸν δόκιμον παραστῆσαι τῷ θεῷ, ἐργάτην ἀνεπαίσχυντον, *ὀρθοτομοῦντα τὸν λόγον τῆς ἀληθείας.* **τὰς δὲ βεβήλους κενοφωνίας** περιΐστασο· ἐπὶ πλεῖον γὰρ προκόψουσιν ἀσεβείας καὶ ὁ λόγος αὐτῶν ὡς γάγγραινα νομὴν ἕξει. ὧν ἐστιν Ὑμέναιος καὶ Φίλητος, οἵτινες *περὶ τὴν ἀλήθειαν* ἠστόχησαν, λέγοντες τὴν ἀνάστασιν ἤδη γεγονέναι, καὶ ἀνατρέπουσιν τήν τινων πίστιν.

For Towner the presence of the phrase τὰς βεβήλους κενοφωνίας in both passages is highly significant as the phrase occurs nowhere else in the New Testament.

> Through this descriptive phrase, *gnōsis* in 1 Tim. 6.20 is linked to 'their message' (*ho logos autōn*) in 2 Tim. 2.17 and, hence, to the perverted doctrine of the resurrection mentioned in v. 18. Reference to Hymenaeus in 1 Tim. 1.20, who there is said to have 'suffered shipwreck of the faith' and to have been turned over to Satan to receive chastisement for his blasphemy, seems to support further that the resurrection heresy was within the purview of 1 Timothy. The situation in Crete is less clear in this respect. Some think that the denunciation in Tit. 1.16 ('they profess to know [*eidenai*] God, but deny it with their deeds') indicates that the false teachers there also made a claim to possess special knowledge. But if so, the brevity of the author's treatment would suggest that the situation in Crete was probably much less developed (1989: 30–31).

Towner rightly states that the phrase λέγοντες ἀνάστασιν ἤδη γεγονέναι in 2 Tim. 2.18 does not amount to a denial of the resurrection of believers but rather to some form of 'spiritualising' of the event. For Towner this amounts to an over-realised eschatology based, most probably, on a misunderstanding of Pauline baptismal teaching (1989: 31–33). In this respect, Towner argues, the situation addressed in the Pastorals is analogous to the situation Paul faced at Corinth. He believes that the parallels with 1 Corinthians are closer than the Gnostic ones usually made. Drawing primarily on the work of Thiselton,[10] Towner notes the link between an 'over-realised eschatology' in Corinth, and 'emancipatory activism' there. He argues that this 'over-realised eschatology' was embraced by enthusiasts at Corinth and that this eschatological outlook 'pervaded the community and affected various aspects of community life' (1989: 36).

---

salvation in the present contrasted with the Pastorals' insistence on the future dimension of salvation.

9. In the comparison which follows matching phrases are in bold type and similar concepts are in italics.

10. Thiselton (1978).

In the light of the parallels with Corinth, Towner concludes:

> Thus the major social problems addressed by the author are capable of being explained consistently as related to the over-realized eschatology. The parallel situation in Corinth seems to support the reconstruction of the situation in Ephesus offered here. The very limited amount of information about the Cretan community does not allow the same degree of certainty in reconstructing the background there. However, the similar descriptions of the opposition and the similar concerns registered by the author (for example, for the stability of the household) suggest that he may have anticipated that the situation in Crete would develop along the same lines as the situation in Ephesus (1989: 42).

Towner, like Thiselton, too readily equates an enthusiastic view of the Spirit with an 'over-realised eschatology'.[11] As I shall show in a subsequent chapter, enthusiasm can be combined with a thoroughly millenarian eschatology as numerous sociological studies have demonstrated. Furthermore, Deming has recently provided a powerful counter-argument to the view that an over-realised eschatology lies behind the discussion of celibacy in 1 Cor. 7.[12] His analysis highlights the fact that scholars can all too easily use the notion of an over-realised eschatology as something which explains everything. This makes Towner's use of the presence of an over-realised eschatology as the overarching category of the opponents in the Pastorals problematic. Nevertheless, his argument that there are significant parallels between the situations addressed in the Pastorals and 1 Corinthians is persuasive.

Although Towner argues strongly for his view of the opponents in the Pastorals as having a consistent over-realised eschatology as a result of misunderstanding Paul, he recognises that this does not ultimately solve the problem of the relation of the opponents to Gnosticism. For an over-realised eschatology coupled with ascetic tendencies also existed within Gnosticism. In the end he is content to state that 'it seems safer to say only that both situations [Corinth and the Pastorals] reflect elements vital to the later Gnosis-constellations and lack others of equal importance' (1989: 44). In the next section I shall highlight the position of those who regard the opponents in the Pastorals as thoroughly Gnostic.

Schlarb (1990) is also convinced of the Jewish-Christian background of the opponents. He takes seriously the location of 1 and 2 Timothy in Ephesus and, in his introductory chapter, argues that the Lukan account of the Pauline mission to Ephesus in Acts 19–20 (especially Paul's speech to the Ephesian elders at Miletus in Acts 20.17–38) is shaped by Luke's awareness of the problems affecting the Ephesian community as addressed in the Pastoral Epistles. Schlarb insists that 2 Tim. 2.18 is the key text in evaluating the teaching of the opponents. After noting parallels with problems faced by the Christian communities in Corinth and Colos-

---

11. Thiselton (1978: 512) states: 'distortions or imbalance in the area of eschatology stand in direct causal relationship to errors about the gifts and work of the Holy Spirit... In specific terms, *an over-realized eschatology leads to an "enthusiastic" view of the Spirit*'; (his emphasis). The problem is that the reverse does not necessarily hold true: the presence of an enthusiastic view of the Spirit does not automatically imply an over-realised eschatology.

12. Deming (1995: 21–32).

sae, he concludes that the underlying conviction of the opponents 'zeigte sich in einem massiven präsentischen Heilsverständnis' (1990: 132). This understanding was drawn from a particular view of baptism and the gifting of the Spirit accompanying baptism. For Schlarb the opponents were pneumatics and enthusiasts who, as well as their experience of the Spirit, drew on Pauline statements concerning new creation, new life, sonship and heirship to argue that the resurrection had already taken place.

Marshall (1999) is a commentary written with the collaboration of Towner (1999: xiii). Marshall is persuaded that real opponents are being addressed and that '[o]n the whole [the view that similar opponents are addressed in all three letters] appears to be the more likely interpretation of the evidence' (1999: 41). He recognises that the opposition represented a real threat to the communities addressed and that it included active proponents within those communities. He notes its considerable success, particularly among women, and therefore rightly concludes that the Pastorals were largely written to combat the opponents. The opponents, according to Marshall, pose such a threat because they are largely engaged in teaching, both in public and private contexts. Marshall draws attention to the fact that the author of the Pastorals regards this teaching as foolish and speculative (1 Tim. 6.3–5; 2 Tim. 2.14–16; 2.23; Tit. 1.10; 3.9) and helpfully suggests parallels with the speculations of the door-to-door representatives of some modern cults.

Marshall is prepared to accept the charges of immorality, particularly greed, levied at the opponents at face value (1 Tim. 6.5–10; 2 Tim. 3.1–5; Tit. 1.11–15). He does not believe, unlike Karris (1973), that these are simply stock charges typical of ancient polemic. This leads him to the unlikely conclusion that the opponents preached asceticism but practised sexual immorality.[13] He notes the Jewish character of the opposition but is cautious about simply identifying them with some form of Judaizing Christianity due to the teaching about the resurrection and the freedom given to women, neither of which, he notes is particularly Jewish (1999: 46). In addition, Marshall rightly states that there is no specific attack on either circumcision or dependence on 'works of the law' in the Pastoral Epistles.

Marshall, following Thiessen (1995), completely rejects the view that the opponents embraced an early form of Gnosticism, but does accept that they were attracted to asceticism. He concludes:

> A combination of the Jewish, Christian and ascetic elements suffices to explain the nature of the opposition in the PE. We have to do with a group of Jewish Christians, perhaps travelling teachers with an ascetic streak, who were active within the Pauline mission area (1999: 51).

Marshall's analysis of the opposition is, on the whole, exemplary. However, two further conclusions of his need modifying in my view. First, Marshall believes that the fact that the author accuses the opponents of rejecting the truth (1 Tim. 6.5; 2 Tim. 3.8; 4.4; Tit. 1.14) suggests that they were openly opposed to Paul and his teachings. This would be true if Pauline authorship of the Pastorals is accepted.

---

13. Marshall (1999: 43 n. 51), citing Lucian, *Fugitivi* 18ff.

However, if the Pastorals post-date Paul,[14] we can only say that the opponents' teaching is regarded as opposed to that of Paul as constructed by the author. This leaves open the question as to whether the opponents themselves were 'anti-Paul' or advocated a very different view of Paul to that of the author. Second, Marshall is unconvinced by Schlarb's arguments that the opponents also claimed to have a special endowment of the Spirit and so were, in this sense, 'enthusiasts' (1999: 45, 51). He too easily dismisses this view as 'somewhat speculative'. It is this particular question that this study seeks to address further.

Mounce (2000) also accepts that there are real opponents and concludes his discussion:

> One point is clear. The opponents' teaching was not developed Gnosticism and was much closer to the errors at Colossae and Corinth, mixed with portions of aberrant Judaism, speculative superstition, and possibly magic (2000: lxxv).

b. *Gnostic Emphasis*

Hanson believes that the Pastorals were written shortly after the turn of the first century CE primarily in order to challenge the rise of incipient Gnosticism. This challenge was so great that the writer of the Pastoral Epistles was compelled to use the authority of Paul to combat it. For Hanson

> The author of the Pastorals is also faced with a situation where some have made what he believes to be a wrong choice: these are the Christians in his congregations who have fallen for the attraction of incipient Gnosticism. This is nothing less than a catastrophe (the exact word which he uses in [2 Tim.] 2.14) (1981: 408–409).

Hanson, unfortunately, in his paper provides no evidence for his assumption that the opponents were Gnostic. Rudolph (1983) has sought to demonstrate the importance of Gnosticism for an understanding of the New Testament. He is unimpressed by attempts to trace historical development from a 'pre-gnosis' in the first century CE to full blown Gnosticism in the second century CE. He is critical of the view that Gnosticism in the first century was primarily a pervasive atmosphere rather than a definite system. Instead he argues that the basic features of Gnosticism must have:

> existed already in the first century if we are going to understand at all the great systems of the second (which were no longer only anonymous). It is hard to find 'doctrines' of any sort that lack any semblance of system in the sense of an inner logical coherence (1983: 31).

Consequently, Rudolph states that it is difficult to imagine a huge leap from a merely Gnostic atmosphere to Gnosticism as such.

> Rather we will see a smooth transition, more or less completely attested by the New Testament writings: we will see a world-view alien to the (Synoptic) Jesus-traditions entering and engaging Christian thinking in increasing measure; the latter could only resist by adapting itself (formation of a Christology) and rejecting

14. A position which, with appropriate modifications, Marshall himself holds.

theologoumena which attacked or undermined the central Christian message (contained in the Jesus-tradition and its Pauline representation); these included the doctrines of creation and sin, the historicity of the Redeemer, justification, etc. This process cannot be illustrated in detail (the literary remains we have attest only some conclusions to, or crossroads in, its paths), but it largely determined the early history of Christianity. It is already detectable, I think, in Paul's writings, in the Corinthian church and his reaction to it (1983: 32).

However, it is Schmithals who has been the outstanding proponent of the view that Paul consistently encountered Gnostic opposition. He is unconvinced by the view that Paul was fighting on two fronts – against Gnostic enthusiasts on the one hand, and Judaizers on the other. In his opinion Paul does not provide us with any direct evidence of such a situation and there is no historical evidence of a Judaizing world mission among the Gentiles in the first century CE (1983: 109). Like Gunther, Schmithals believes in the basic unity of Paul's opponents but emphasises their Gnostic rather than their Jewish character. He regards the opponents in the Pastorals as 'representatives of a Jewish-Christian Gnosis in the broadest sense' (1983: 115). He argues that the emphasis in the Pastoral Epistles on teaching in general, correct teaching, the tradition of teaching, and the office of teacher is designed to combat a Gnostic enthusiasm which promotes 'the authority of the free *pneuma*' (1983: 115–16). Unlike Fee and Towner, Schmithals regards the opponents as coming from outside the Christian community. He describes them as 'intruders' and 'imposters' (cf. 2 Tim. 3.13) (1983: 116). He argues that, although they appealed to Jewish tradition, they should not be regarded as Judaizers; for Schmithals 'all the other characteristics of the false teaching are against this last suggestion' (1983: 116). He regards the claim to possess 'Gnosis' as decisive for his view that the opponents take up an 'enthusiastic and spiritualistic' position. This is reinforced by the spiritualising of the idea of resurrection and implied by the ascetic tendencies of the false teachers.[15]

Schmithals has difficulty with the references to 'myths and genealogies'. He suggests that:

---

15.   A similar position is taken by Roloff (1988: 228–39). For Roloff, the opponents' asceticism derived from a hostile view of creation, their esoteric speculations and their use of 'gnosis' as a catchword. These strongly suggest to him that they were Gnostics. He links the false teaching of the Pastorals with the Colossian heresy and also with problems encountered in the communities addressed in Revelation. Roloff suggests that the teachings of the Nicolaitans (Rev. 2.6, 15), Balaam (Rev. 2.14) and the prophet Jezebel (Rev. 2.20) were broadly similar in nature and largely identical to the false teaching addressed in the Pastoral Epistles. He recognises that the lack of an ascetic element in the false teaching in Revelation is problematic for this identification but suggests that the group opposed had both ascetic and libertine elements. This seems highly unlikely.

Roloff also downplays the Jewish-Christian dimension to the opposition in a way that does not do justice to the evidence. For example, Roloff (1988: 71–72) rightly states that we should not hastily draw parallels with Galatians from the author's description of the opponents as those who desire to be νομοδιδάσκαλοι but immediately cautions that we should also not conclude that they were law-abiding Jewish-Christians. It seems to me that Tit. 1.10, 14; 3.9, together with 1 Tim. 1.7, conclusively point to a Jewish-Christian dimension to the false teaching.

the false teachers used Old Testament passages (e.g. Genesis 4.17ff.; 5.1ff.; 6.1ff.) to present mythical speculations on the aeons like those attested so plentifully in extant Gnostic texts. Jewish Gnostics, who could not postulate an absolute dualism, tried by means of these to explain the emanation of evil from the unity of God (1983: 117).[16]

However, in the final analysis, Schmithals admits that the Gnosis combated in the Pastorals does not reflect any of the second-century Gnostics actually known to us. Consequently, he contends that the Gnosis opposed is 'truly mythical' (1983: 117). This admission in the end makes the whole Gnostic thesis highly problematic. In this respect Schmithals ends up closely allied to the view which will now be discussed, namely that the opponents in the Pastorals are a literary construct representing heresy wherever and whenever it should be encountered.

3. *The Polemic as (Primarily) a Literary Device*

a. *Dibelius and Conzelmann*
Dibelius and Conzelmann[17] argue that the combination of the prohibition of marriage, abstinence from certain foods, and enthusiasm including the spiritualising of the idea of resurrection 'must always be attributed to a kind of Gnosticism' (1972: 65–66). However, they recognise that the particular heresy attacked in the Pastorals cannot be identified with any known Gnostic sect. Noting the very general nature of the polemic of the Pastorals they conclude that there are two possible ways of explaining why a particular group is not more clearly identified. The first is to take an historical approach and suggest that no particular group is identified because the writer tackles a number of diverse opponents.[18] The second is to take a literary approach; this is the solution which they adopt.

Dibelius and Conzelmann note that the style of the polemic in the Pastorals is very different from that of the genuine Pauline epistles. Unlike Paul, the writer does not engage in any substantial argument with his opponents. The general nature

---

16. See too Roloff (1988: 64) who links 'myths' with cosmogonic and anthropological Gnostic teachings and 'genealogies' with speculative interpretations of the genealogies in the early chapters of Genesis.

17. This is the English translation of Hans Conzelmann's revision of the second edition of *Die Pastoralbriefe* by Martin Dibelius. Dibelius' second edition was published in 1931. Conzelmann's revision was first published in 1955 some eight years after Dibelius' death, and was itself revised in 1966. Conzelmann himself states in his foreword to the third and fourth German editions that his revision involved numerous changes to Dibelius' commentary, but that only the most important instances have been specifically noted. In view of the fact that it is not possible in the majority of cases in the English translation to distinguish Conzelmann's revisions from Dibelius' original comments, this monograph constantly refers to 'Dibelius and Conzelmann' in the plural, although I am fully aware that the commentary was not actually co-authored.

18. This is the position adopted by Collins (2002: 11–12) who, after noting that various issues are addressed such as 'a misreading of the law (1 Tim. 1.7; see Tit. 1.14), a misunderstanding of the resurrection (2 Tim. 2.18), an elite sectarianism (1 Tim. 2.1–6), and the worship of divinized emperors (1 Tim. 6.15–16)', concludes that it is unlikely that such a variety of errors came from a single source.

of the polemic means that it is difficult to reconstruct a picture of the opponents (1972: 2). Furthermore, the polemic frequently uses the techniques with which philosophers attacked the sophists[19] (1972: 20–21, 66). The catalogues of vices also yield no historical information, and should not be taken as pointing to the antinomianism of the opponents. An antinomian tendency, in any case, would contradict the clear ascetic references in 1 Tim. 4.1–5. These vice catalogues should be treated purely as 'products of a literary convention' (1972: 67). Consequently, Dibelius and Conzelmann conclude:

> The author attempts to characterize his opponents as broadly as possible, in order to create an apologetic *vademecum* for all sorts of anti-Gnostic conflicts… The forms which the polemic takes correspond to a concept of heresy just being developed (1972: 66).

b. *R.J. Karris*

Karris (1973)[20] takes up in detail the claim of Dibelius and Conzelmann that the Pastorals frequently employ the weapons with which philosophers attacked the sophists. He notes that the polemic of philosophers against sophists dates back to Plato but was very common in the Graeco-Roman period, particularly between 70 CE and the second century CE. Karris' thesis is that there is a schema[21] which can be discerned behind this polemic, and that this schema is employed by the author of the Pastorals. He identifies the following elements of the schema (1973: 552–54):

- The charge that the opponents are greedy. They teach for the sake of financial gain. This charge can be found in 1 Tim. 6.5; Tit. 1.11.
- The charge that the opponents are deceivers (go&htej); cf. 2 Tim. 3.13.
- The charge that the opponents do not practise what they preach (cf. 2 Tim. 3.5; Tit. 1.16; 3.8–9).
- The charge that the opponents simply engage in verbal disputes and quibbles (cf. 1 Tim. 1.4, 6; 4.2; 6.4; 2 Tim. 2.14, 16, 23; Tit. 1.10; 3.9).
- Catalogues of vices are employed to describe the opponents (cf. 1 Tim. 1.9–10; 2 Tim. 3.2–4).
- Occasionally reference is made to the opponents' success among women (cf. 2 Tim. 3.6).

Karris is sensitive to the charge that the elements of the schema outlined above could be used by anyone in any kind of polemical rhetoric. He argues that there is hardly any evidence to suggest that writers used the schema to oppose anybody and everybody. Rather, the controlling factor in the use of the schema was whether the

19. This point is specifically developed by Karris (1973: 549–64).
20. Quinn also notes the 'typological character' of the opponents (1990a: 15).
21. This is defined by Karris as 'the convergence of items that regularly occur in the presentation of a particular topic. It is distinguished from a form in that it is not invariable (one or the other item may be missing) and in that it does not contain the items in a set sequence with item one following item two, etc. It is also distinguished from a random occurrence of items in the presentation of a particular topic by the fact that the items occur with measurable regularity' (1973: 551 n. 10).

opponent was considered a teacher of one sort or another. Where the opponents cannot be classified generally as teachers the schema was not employed; for example, the schema is not typical of the polemic used by pagans against Jews (1973: 555).

Karris notes that the schema was employed in a variety of situations. Plato originated it in his controversies with the sophists of his day. Philo used it to demonstrate the soundness of Judaism. Dio Chrysostom and Lucian employed it against sophists and against self-professed, wandering Cynics respectively. Christian apologists such as Tatian and Athenagoras used it to champion Christianity as the true philosophy, or to demonstrate that Christianity fostered sound morals (1973: 555–56). The schema had a threefold use. First, it was intended to produce aversion for the opponents and sympathy for the writer's position among the readers. Second, it served to disassociate the writer's teachings from those of the opponents. Thirdly, and most significantly for Karris, it demonstrated 'who had the right to and actually did impart genuine wisdom and truth' (1973: 556).

Having identified the schema and having demonstrated to his satisfaction that it was employed by the author of the Pastorals, Karris then uses redaction criticism on the polemical passages of the Pastorals. His purpose in doing this is to highlight those aspects of the description of the opponents which depart from the traditional schema. Methodologically, he argues, 'stock' descriptions drawn from the schema should be disregarded in any reconstruction of the opponents whereas unique elements probably do point to real aspects of the opponents' teaching. His analysis highlights the following elements which do not occur in the traditional schema:

- Endless genealogies (1 Tim. 1.4; Tit. 3.9).
- Teachers of the law (1 Tim. 1.7).
- Forbidding of marriage and abstention from certain foods (1 Tim. 4.3).
- The claim that the resurrection has already taken place (2 Tim. 2.18).
- In view of the fact that reference to success among women is only occasionally part of the schema, Karris argues that the redaction of this theme in 2 Tim. 3.7, together with the emphasis on the proper role of women elsewhere in the Pastorals (1 Tim. 2.11–15; 5.13; Tit. 2.5), suggest that the opponents did enjoy some success among women.
- The Jewish character of the opposition (Tit. 1.10–16).
- Disputes over the law (Tit. 3.9).
- This analysis allows Karris to conclude:

> The opponents are Jewish Christians who are teachers of the law (1 Tim. 1.7; Tit. 3.9; cf. Tit. 1.14). They teach Jewish myths (Tit. 1.14; cf. 1 Tim. 1.4; 4.7; 2 Tim. 4.4) and genealogies (1 Tim. 1.4; Tit. 3.9). They forbid marriage and enjoin abstinence from food (1 Tim. 4.3–5). They teach that the resurrection has already occurred (2 Tim. 2.18). They may have had significant success among the womanfolk, especially because of their teaching about emancipation (2 Tim. 3.6–7; cf. 1 Tim. 2.11–15; 5.13; Tit. 2.5) (1973: 562–63).

Karris thus finally comes down in favour of the position that there are real, historical opponents but that only the elements deduced above apply to them. All the other accusations in the Pastorals derive from the traditional schema which the author employed for similar reasons to other writers who utilised the schema. In other words, the author's use of the schema suggests that:

> the author views his teaching as genuine wisdom, philosophy, truth, and that he views the teachings of his opponents as false wisdom, as sophistry. More specifically, he wants to disassociate his teaching from that of the heretics, for his teaching is 'the sound teaching', 'the truth', 'the faith', 'the deposit'. Moreover, it is the author's desire to show that he alone has the right to and actually does impart the truth, that he and his disciples alone have the power to teach correctly. Furthermore, by using this schema, the author wants to cause aversion for his opponents in the minds of his readers and to establish a strong alternative to their view of Pauline tradition. This strong alternative can be seen in the office of the bishop and in the sound teaching which the bishop is commissioned to impart (1973: 563–64).

c. *L.T. Johnson*

Johnson (1978/79) is sympathetic to Karris' approach but is sharply critical of his above conclusion. Johnson argues that, although Karris' threefold definition of the function of the schema outlined above is broadly correct, 'there are instances where the function is quite plainly different' (1978/79: 3). Johnson believes that Karris and others such as Dibelius and Conzelmann pay too little attention to the literary form of the writings in which the polemical language appears. In the case of the Pastorals Karris' conclusion simply does not correspond to their actual literary shape (1978/79: 4). They provide no evidence that the author used the polemic to convince readers of his own credentials. Everywhere the authority of the author is assumed. Johnson's contention is that the function of the polemic has to be derived from the literary form in which it is embedded. In his article, therefore, he begins by examining the literary form of 2 Timothy which he regards as a personal paraenetic letter. He then examines parallel examples drawn from Hellenistic paraenetic letters, and finally he looks at paraenesis and polemic in 1 Timothy and Titus.

Johnson notes from the epistolary handbooks[22] that the paraenetic letter form was designed to exhort the reader to follow something and to avoid something else. Role models are a crucial element; the reader is not simply to follow instructions but is urged to be an imitator of a particular model and to avoid other models. Good conduct is encouraged in the hope that a good reputation will be gained. 2 Timothy follows this form closely: 'Paul is presented as a model to Timothy, and Timothy's mode of teaching is presented by means of antithesis to false teachers. He is to pursue certain things and to avoid others' (1978/79: 14). In this context, therefore, the polemic against false teachers functions as the antithesis to the ideal that Timothy is exhorted to follow. 'The false teachers are not spoken of or addressed, except in relation to Timothy. They serve entirely as contrast' (1978/79: 12). Johnson highlights a number of examples[23] from Hellenistic paraenesis where the use of polemical language against false teachers serves not to establish the authority of the writer

---

22. He cites the example of the handbook of Ps-Libanius.

23. Ps-Isocrates, *Ad Demonicum*; Epictetus, *Diatribes* III; Lucian, *Demonax*; Lucian, *Nigrinus*; Dio, *Oration* 77/78.

but to act as a 'negative foil to the ideal, so that hearers will know what to avoid as well as what to follow' (1978/79: 20).

In connection with 2 Timothy, Johnson divides the body of the letter into two sections. The first section, 1.3–2.13, presents Paul as a model of sound teaching and faithful suffering whom Timothy is to follow. Timothy is reminded to rekindle the gift of God within and exhorted to remember Jesus Christ. In this section, according to Johnson, there is no mention of false teachers; the entire focus is on Timothy's need to gain confidence in the face of suffering. In the second section, 2.14–4.8, the author elaborates on the model of Paul as the ideal teacher by a series of longer and shorter antitheses. A characteristic feature is the singular imperative addressed to Timothy, alternating with third person plural descriptions of the false teachers. Thus, for Johnson, 2 Timothy fits the genre of the personal paraenetic letter and so he is able to conclude, 'the characteristics of the false teachers function simply as contrast to the image of the ideal Christian teacher' (1978/79: 11).

In a brief examination of 1 Timothy and Titus Johnson notes that in these letters too the function of the polemic against false teachers is to provide an anti-type to the ideal teacher. For Johnson, therefore, the polemic is clearly in the service of paraenesis. Thus he is able to conclude that for the Pastoral Epistles as a whole the function of polemical language is to provide a contrast to the ideal Christian teacher. Nevertheless, although recognising the largely stereotypical language of the polemic, Johnson too does not want to suggest that there were no real opponents. He rightly notes that, although stereotypical language is used in disputes between philosophical schools, such disputes and such schools were nonetheless real. He deplores the idea that 'the false teachers were just 'straw men' propped up only to be demolished. The anxious tone of the letters does not permit such a purely literary understanding' (1978/79: 26).

Johnson expands on this in his subsequent commentary on 1 and 2 Timothy (2001). He argues that each letter has to be examined in its own right rather than constructing a composite picture of the opponents derived from all three letters.[24] In connection with 1 Timothy he is prepared to accept that, once the stock accusations are peeled away, the opposition 'represents an intellectual elite that demands performance measured by law and asceticism rather than by grace and conscience'

---

24. He notes that in 1 Tim. there is: no reference to the resurrection having already happened (2 Tim. 2.18); no concern for circumcision, or purity regulations or Jewish 'myths' (Tit. 1.10, 14, 15); no mention of the progress being made by the opponents, especially in connection with upsetting households (2 Tim. 3.6; Tit. 1.11); a clear indication that the opponents come from within the Christian community, unlike Titus where this is not clear according to Johnson; no call for the correction of the opposition (2 Tim. 2.25; 4.2) or for their rebuke and silencing (Tit. 1.13; 3.10); no hope for their conversion (2 Tim. 2.25–26); finally, like Titus but unlike 2 Tim., a theological engagement with the opponents' position (2001: 146). Johnson overstates the case as 1 Tim. is clearly concerned about those who are occupied with 'myths and genealogies' and desire to be 'teachers of the law' (1 Tim. 1.4, 7) and thus connects with Titus in this respect. It is also unclear to me as to how Titus can be exhorted to rebuke the opponents 'so that they may become sound in the faith' if they are not envisaged in Titus as arising from within the community. Finally, as I will seek to demonstrate in chapter 6 below, a clear connection can be made between the ascetism of the opponents in 1 Tim. 4.1–4 and their success with households in 2 Tim. 3.1–9 and Tit. 1.11.

(2001: 146). He also acknowledges, in the case of 2 Timothy, that 'it may be possible to cut beneath the rhetoric' to reveal two instances of the opponents' actual
belief and practice: the belief that the resurrection has already happened (2 Tim. 2:
18) and the charge in 2 Tim. 3.6 that ἐκ τούτων γάρ εἰσιν οἱ ἐνδύνοντες εἰς τὰς
οἰκίας καὶ αἰχμαλωτίζοντες γυναικάρια (2001: 411).

d. *B. Fiore*

Fiore (1986) provides one of the most detailed literary analyses of the Pastorals.
Fiore argues that the Pastorals are 'hortatory pieces and not polemical writings'
(1986: 197). After a very brief examination of the history of scholarship, Fiore
spells out the hortatory character of the Pastorals. He then turns to the use of example in early rhetorical theory, in discourses to young officials and kingship trea-
tises, and in epistolary exhortation. This is followed by a major chapter on example
in the Socratic letters for it is Fiore's thesis that these provide an important parallel
to the Pastorals. Following a brief look at how example functions in the undisputed
Pauline letters, Fiore turns finally to the use of example in the Pastorals. In this
chapter he lists twelve substantial points of comparison between the Pastorals and
the Socratic letters.[25] This detailed comparison allows him to conclude that the Pastorals are works of epistolary paraenesis which blend two particular paraenetic
traditions: first, 'hortatory instructions addressed to young officials on the conduct
and attitudes expected of them and their constituencies;' and second, 'epistolary
exhortations to a way of life consistent with the traditions of a philosophical school'
(1986: 232). For Fiore the negative examples in both the Pastoral and Socratic
Epistles function as a foil for the proper way of life advocated in the letters. The
use of similar rhetorical features suggests that the author of the Pastorals was
acquainted with rhetorical theory and that at least some of the audience would have
been able to appreciate the rhetorical merits of the letters. Fiore suggests that the
Socratic Epistles arose in the setting of a 'school of a grammaticus or rhetor of the
early Empire' (1986: 229). He rightly cautions that the similarities in rhetorical
features between the Socratics and the Pastorals do not justify the conclusion that
the Pastorals arose in a scholastic community. Nevertheless, he is prepared to suggest that the hortatory features of the Pastorals indicate a settled community in

---

25. First, they both use the full range of hortatory language, devices and techniques. Second, in
both cases the variety of devices sometimes falls into the arrangement proper to the development of
the chria. Third, they are both concerned to preserve a tradition of teaching and practice. Fourth, in
both cases the examples are varied but are often simple sketches found in conjunction with virtue
and vice lists and precepts. Fifth, although they both have principal examples (Socrates and Paul
respectively), others also join in fully exercising that function. Sixth, the Socratic Epistles utilise
the founding fathers of the Socratic and Cynic traditions as examples and the Pastorals use examples of the same stature (Paul's associates). Seventh, they both use examples to promote a particular mode of conduct. Eighth, they both use negative examples in antithetical relationship. These
negative examples are largely unnamed, indefinite or typical. Ninth, they both urge their readers to
avoid harmful associations. Tenth, they both emphasise growth in virtue and use athletic imagery
to express this. Eleventh, they both contain a broad range of widely applicable teachings intended
for a broad audience. Twelfth, in both cases the letters stand as a substitute for face-to-face
dialogue (1986: 224–26).

unbroken continuity with Paul and his associates. The community is encountering some difficulty in areas such as asceticism, legalism, Jewish influence, and resurrection faith. However, these difficulties are not perceived as a major threat to the community. Heresy is perceived as a perennial problem for the church and not as an immediate threat. Fiore thus locates the Pastorals in the late first or early second century CE before Gnosticism became a real threat.

e. *Summary*

Dibelius/Conzelmann, Karris, and Johnson all rightly recognise the stereotypical nature of the polemical language in the Pastorals. Consequently, they regard attempts at detailed reconstruction of the opponents from the polemical passages as misguided. As Johnson states:

> The picture of rigorist, mythically-oriented, quasi-gnostic Judaizers results from pushing the few concrete hints to their limit, and sometimes beyond, and still lacks any convincing specificity (1978/79: 1–2).

Nevertheless, neither Karris nor Johnson are prepared to go as far as Dibelius/Conzelmann; they do not see the opponents purely as a literary construct to provide paradigmatic material for countering heresy wherever and whenever it should crop up. Karris and Johnson are, in my view, correct. They rightly realise that the urgency of the language in the Pastorals points to some real, rather than imaginary, opposition. Consequently, any reconstruction of the opponents has to take into account both the fact that the language used is stereotypical and that real opponents are addressed. If this is taken seriously then the polemical language will contain both 'stock' language and specific references to the opponents. The major difficulty lies in trying to distinguish the two. Karris makes an interesting attempt by using redaction criticism. However, by making a rigid distinction between 'stock' language and 'unique' language he takes his analysis too far. For example, in 1 Tim. 1.4 he notes that 'myths' belongs to the schema but 'endless genealogies' does not, and consequently ascribes teaching about genealogies to the heretics but not teaching concerning myths. It does not seem to me that 'myths and genealogies' can be split in this way, especially as the two terms are found together elsewhere.[26] Similarly, Karris splits out 'genealogies' and 'quarrels about the law' as unique in Tit. 3.9, whereas they seem inextricably linked to 'stupid controversies' and 'dissensions' in the text. In other words, some of the 'stock' language may well point to actual features of the opposition. The fact that stereotypical language is being used should make us rightly cautious, but the use of such language does not necessarily mean that some of the 'stock' charges do not apply in any particular instance.

Johnson avoids this problem entirely with his thesis that the polemical language serves as a negative contrast to the ideal teacher. However, this conclusion does not help at all when attempting to discern the identity of the false teachers. This is unfortunate if one accepts, as I do, Towner's basic statement that 'the heresy reflected in the Pastoral Epistles is the most important aspect of the back-

---

26. See Dibelius and Conzelmann (1972: 16).

ground of these letters' (1989: 21). Furthermore, Johnson makes much of the material in Ps-Isocrates' *Ad Demonicum* which certainly fulfils the criteria for paraenesis. However, unfortunately for Johnson, the negative contrasts to the positive ideal are couched in very general language. Even Johnson's clearest example of the negative contrast (*Ad Demonicum*, 38) simply states:

> Put yourself in a position in which you have the power to take advantage, but refrain when you have your fair share, so that men may think that you strive for justice, not from weakness, but from a sense of equity. Prefer honest poverty to unjust wealth; for justice is better than riches in that riches profit us only while we live, while justice provides us glory even after we are dead, and while riches are shared by bad men, justice is a thing in which the wicked can have no part.

No specific 'bad men' are named, unlike Hymenaeus and Philetus in 2 Tim. 2.17 and Alexander in 2 Tim. 4.14. Nowhere is there anything like the catalogue of vices found in 2 Tim. 3.2–5. Johnson rightly draws attention to the stereotypical nature of some of the polemic in the Pastorals but fails to recognise the significance of the naming of opponents in 1 Timothy as well as 2 Timothy.[27] Indeed Johnson, in his conclusion, appears to acknowledge that he may have overstated his case. Having consistently argued that polemical language simply serves as a foil for the model of the ideal teacher, Johnson (1978/79: 25–26) finally admits:

> By accepting the position that the polemical language is to a large extent stereotyped and that identifying the opponents is hazardous, I do not suggest there were no real opponents. The polemic against false teachers in the hellenistic materials is stereotyped, but there is more than enough evidence that the disputes between philosophic schools and teachers of all sorts were real and bitter. Nor does the position that these polemical passages in the Pastorals serve the Paraenetic function I have suggested lead to the inference that the false teachers were just 'straw men', propped up only to be demolished. The anxious tone of the letters does not permit such a purely literary understanding.

It is my conviction that the 'anxious tone of the letters' is precisely what undermines the literary attempts of Johnson and others to view the Pastorals as simply paraenetic letters.

Fiore's analysis is both detailed and compelling. Indeed Davies concurs with Fiore. She states:

> Fiore…therefore, is correct in arguing that [the opponents] represent the antithesis of the positive examples endorsed by the epistles, and that these references serve a hortatory rather than a polemical purpose. Against Karris (1973) and most other

---

27. Quinn (1990a: 15) recognises that the naming of opponents is unusual but simply asserts that this 'underscores their typological function'. On the contrary, it is precisely this naming of some of the opponents which suggests that real opponents are being addressed and that they do not merely 'have a typological character'. Schlarb (1990: 131) rightly recognises the significance of named opponents. He notes that the naming of contemporaries of Paul suggests that these opponents could gain entrance into the communities precisely because of their connections with Paul. Their teaching, based on certain emphases in Paul's proclamation, found acceptance 'weil sie eben ihre Legitimierung von diesem Apostel her beanspruchte'.

interpreters, Fiore demonstrates this hortatory purpose, and suggests that the epistles were not occasioned by the immediate threat of an opposing system, but by
the commonly felt need to provide both positive and negative examples in this
kind of literature (1996: 99).

However, despite Fiore's detailed analysis, I remain unconvinced that the polemical language in the Pastorals really only serves a hortatory purpose. For example, I
do not think Fiore deals adequately with 1 Tim. 1.20. He sees this simply as strong
censure of opponents which is part of the method of paraenesis in order to make
clear harmful alternatives (1986: 201 n. 27). However, he nowhere deals with the
actual language used here: οὕς παρέδωκα τῷ Σατανᾷ. This echoes the language
of 1 Cor. 5.5: παραδοῦναι τὸν τοιοῦτον τῷ Σατανᾷ. This seems to me to be
more than a rhetorical device and suggests real conflict in the community requiring
drastic action in a way parallel to that advocated by Paul in Corinth. Furthermore,
Fiore mentions 1 Tim. 4.3 only once in the entire monograph. He relegates this
verse to a footnote elaborating his assertion that the content of the opponents'
teaching is not clearly specified. He merely states that 1 Tim. 4.3 refers to 'a false
asceticism' (1986: 3 n. 5). However, the verse specifically states that the opponents
'forbid marriage and demand abstinence from foods'. It seems sufficiently clear to
me that real opponents are in view here (and to Karris also for he includes this in
his list of features of the real opponents). Finally, Fiore's concentration on literary
parallels means that he pays too little attention to the sociological reality of community conflict. The bulk of his thesis compares the Pastorals with the Socratic
letters. He suggests that, as the latter arose in a school context, the literary parallels
indicate that the Pastorals also arose in a settled community in unbroken continuity
with Paul and his associates (1986: 234). But at what point can we speak of 'settled'
Pauline communities? We know that there was real conflict in the communities
within Paul's lifetime from the undisputed Pauline letters. We know of real conflicts
early in the second century through the letters of Ignatius. Can we, with any degree
of confidence, state, therefore, that the Pastorals were written in a period marked
by the absence of any real conflict in the communities addressed? Fiore states that
'Paul's "opponents" are…specific and *rarely* the typical, negative models of the
Pastorals'.[28] But one of these 'rare' occasions, as Fiore himself acknowledges, is
Phil. 3.18–19. I would argue, against Fiore, that the use of the stereotypical
negative example there does not just serve as a foil to Paul's positive example in
the previous verse, but occurs in a highly polemical context. The negative example
serves Paul's polemic in this chapter; it is not just a hortatory device.[29] Fiore, for
me therefore, does succeed in illuminating the clearly hortatory features of the
Pastorals – in particular, their use of example – but fails to demonstrate that the
opponents only function as negative examples to serve the overall hortatory purpose of the Pastorals.

The attempts surveyed so far to reconstruct the opponents from the polemical
passages in the Pastorals have led, on the one hand, to broad agreement concerning

---

28. Fiore (1986: 223), my italics.
29. See Hawthorne (1983: xliv–xlvii, 162–68).

the Judaizing-Gnosticising position of the opponents (but this definition lacks any specificity) and, on the other hand, to great differences in detailed identification. However, literary approaches either fail to do justice to the urgency of the language in the Pastorals or fail to provide a convincing description of the opponents. In the light of the unsatisfactory conclusions reached to date it is hoped that a fresh approach using social-scientific methods will yield fresh insights. Before I turn to such an approach, however, three other significant contributions will be examined.

4. *The Opponents in the Light of Competing Images of Paul*

a. *The Pastorals and Jewish-Christian Ecstatics*
Goulder (1996) argues, as I shall do in a subsequent chapter, that the Pastorals are thoroughly polemical and that, therefore, paraenesis serves polemic and not the other way round. He recognises that the opponents are Jewish Christians but takes the analysis further by a sustained mirror-reading of the texts. Goulder's major contribution to the debate involves the reconstruction of the opponents' Christology from a mirror-reading of 1 Tim. 3.16. He disputes the consensus that this text is a citation from a pre-existing hymn and argues that it has been carefully constructed to advance the author's polemical purposes. For Goulder there are two signals in the passage that indicate its polemical nature. First, the church is described as στῦλος καὶ ἑδραίωμα τῆς ἀληθείας and, as Goulder rightly notes, ἡ ἀλήθεια is one of the terms used as a shorthand for the author's own theology as against the false teaching of the opponents. Second, he argues that ὅς,[30] which in both *UBSGNT*[4] and *NA*[27] is printed as part of the first line of the rest of the verse which is set out in hymnic form, actually belongs with the preceding τὸ τῆς εὐσεβείας μυστήριον. In this way, according to Goulder, the author proclaims that the mystery of godliness is a person: 'great is the mystery of godliness who...', whereas the opponents too thought they had the answer to the mystery of godliness. 'They thought it was the aeons, he thought it was Christ' (1996: 251). Analysing each phrase of the 'hymn' as being composed with a view to countering the opponents' teaching, Goulder concludes that the opponents held to a docetic Christology which denied both Christ's incarnation and bodily resurrection. Furthermore, the reference to angels in this text is also polemical; the angels, far from being objects of worship, 'are reduced to having been spectators when God raised Jesus' body from death' (1996: 254).

The angelic reference, together with mention of 'deceitful spirits and doctrines of demons' in the very next verse enables Goulder to make links with the worship of angels of Col. 2.18 and the false prophetic utterances of 1 Cor. 12.1–3 and 1 Jn. 4.1–3. In this way Goulder argues that the opponents were Jewish-Christian charismatics who valued ecstatic visionary experiences. He, like Towner, connects the

---

30. As there is no masculine antecedent most scholars assume that what follows is an extract from pre-existing tradition in which there was an antecedent for ὅς, see, for example, Dibelius and Conzelmann (1972: 61). Marshall (1999: 523) however, suggests that this could be an example of a *constructio ad sensum* with the relative pronoun in line with BDF §296 (although this text is not mentioned in BDF).

opponents with those addressed in 1 Corinthians and Colossians. Further evidence, according to Goulder, comes from the insistence of the Pastorals that no one has seen God (1 Tim. 1.17 and particularly 1 Tim. 6.16). Commenting on this verse, Goulder states: 'What I say three times is true; and what I deny three times is said to be true by someone else (1996: 246). In other words, the strength of the denial that anyone has seen God suggests that the opponents were making this very claim.

Goulder is on target, in my view, although he undoubtedly is guilty of over-interpretation, a common danger in mirror-reading.[31] He also too readily equates the mention of aeons and μῦθοι καὶ γενεαλογίαι with Gnosticism. I shall return to Goulder's work in Chapter 6.

b. *The Pastorals and the Acts of Paul*

MacDonald (1983) argues that the Pastorals were written in an environment in which there were competing claims on the Pauline legacy. It is likely, therefore, that the Pastorals were written to combat all these competing claims including those of Gnostics, Jewish Christians, and possibly Marcionites. However, they were especially written, MacDonald argues, to combat the image of Paul conveyed in oral legends circulating at the time which were eventually recorded in the apoc-ryphal *Acts of Paul (AP)*. MacDonald seeks to demonstrate, by an analysis of three stories in *AP* (Paul and Thecla, Paul and the baptised lion, and the martyrdom story) that the author of *AP* utilised existing oral legends. He seeks to show how each of these three stories circulated independently; furthermore, he attempts to demonstrate the orality of these legends by their characteristically folkloric content and by their conformity to the conventions of oral narratives.

Oral narratives, unlike written ones, need both storytellers and sympathetic audiences to survive. The legends display a woman's point of view which strongly suggests that the storytellers were women. MacDonald suggests that further evidence for this is provided by Tertullian's statement that some people told the story of Thecla to legitimate women teaching and baptising. He argues that the storytellers were probably located in south central Asia Minor due to the accurate references to local geography in the Thecla story. From an analysis of the content of the legends MacDonald concludes that the storytellers appear to be primarily celibate women outside the household who were hostile to Rome and alienated from Asia Minor society.

MacDonald notes that 52 out of 242 verses in the Pastoral Epistles are devoted to refuting false teachers.[32] However, only in 1 Tim. 4.1–5 does the author engage his opponents in direct theological discourse. What is most significant is that characteristics of Paul as depicted in the legend tradition are opposed. 2 Tim. 3.6–7 describes precisely the actions attributed to Paul in *AP* in connection with Thecla, Artemilla, and Eubola. Tit. 1.10–15 likewise demonstrates concern for the household. 1 Tim. 4.1–3 contradicts the Paul of *AP* in three ways. First, chastity was a

---

31. See Barclay (1987).
32. 1 Tim. 1.3–11; 4.1–5, 7–8; 6.3–10, 20; 2 Tim. 2.14–19, 23; 3.1–9; 4.3–4.; Tit. 1.10–16; 3.8–9. Schlarb (1990: 14) states that almost one third of the letters is more or less directly concerned with the problem of the false teachers.

requirement for resurrection in *AP*. Second, Paul is a vegetarian and teetotaller in *AP*. Thirdly, in the Pastorals asceticism is inspired by demons whereas in *AP* asceticism is associated with divine revelation. 1 Tim. 2.11–15 provides the greatest contrast between the Pastorals and *AP*.

In addition, MacDonald argues, the many points of similarity between the Pastorals and *AP* make it likely that the author of the Pastorals knew the legends at some stage in their oral transmission. Certain references to Paul's associates and experiences in the Pastorals cannot be accounted for in terms of independent historical reminiscences of events in Paul's life, nor in terms of dependence upon Acts or Paul's letters. Thus they are either products of the author's imagination or taken from oral tradition. As many of these names and episodes also occur in *AP*, and as literary dependence of one of these documents upon the other is highly unlikely,[33] it appears that both authors knew the same oral legends about Paul.

MacDonald concludes that the Pastorals stand in a literary tradition which sought to domesticate the apocalyptic radicalism of the church. They share this orientation with Ignatius and Polycarp. The evidence of second-century Asia Minor, he argues, witnesses to vitality and growth in Christianity as the bishops sought to make the church more socially acceptable. However, some Christian groups found this accommodation unacceptable and the second half of the second century witnessed a resurgence of apocalyptic radicalism. This struggle against Montanism was not simply a struggle over doctrine; it was a struggle between the authority of the bishops and charismatic authority. This struggle was anticipated in the Pastorals.

c. *The Pastorals and Proto-Montanism*

Ford (1971) goes further than MacDonald and suggests that the Pastorals may actually be combating 'Proto-Montanism'. Ford argues that Montanism was a Jewish-Christian heresy as was the heresy combated in the Pastorals (1971: 339–40). She notes, in connection with 1 Tim. 4.1–5, that Montanus and the two prophetesses, Maximilla and Priscilla, 'were accused of paying heed to deceitful spirits and the doctrines of demons,' that they dissolved marriages, and that they abstained from wine, introduced new fasts, and abstained from certain foods (1971: 340–41). She suggests that 'genealogies and myths' might refer to the attempt by Montanists to 'trace their prophetic succession or pedigree through Agabus, Judas, Silas, the daughters of Philip, Quadratus and Ammia of Philadelphia' (1971: 341); and to the various rumours, visions and interpretations propagated by the Montanists (1971: 341).

Ford argues that the emphasis on self-control, the use of the mind, and sound or healthy teaching in the Pastorals needs to be understood against a background of ecstatic prophecy. The stress on sobriety and self-control cannot be because the heresy advocated sexual licence and intoxication – this would contradict the emphasis of 1 Tim. 4.1–5. Consequently:

---

33. But see Bauckham (1993: 105–52). Bauckham argues that the author of *AP* used 2 Tim. and Titus, but not 1 Timothy, as sources.

...these words are directed, not against immorality, but against a 'holy roller' type of spirituality, that is, ecstatic and frenzied prophecy. Recent exegesis has confirmed the view that tongues and prophecy at Corinth were not ecstatic and that the community was fairly controlled. The gifts of tongues and prophecy were placed under the same regulations; both could be commenced or discontinued at will. Quite different was the Montanist view (1971: 342).

She goes on to note the ecstatic, uncontrolled and violent nature of Montanist prophecy (1971: 343). In addition, she suggests that the subordination of women in the Pastorals may be directed against the elevation of women in Montanism (1971: 343–44). Finally, Ford speculates that the emphasis on church order in the Pastorals may be directed against the elevation of charismatic prophets in the community (1971: 344–45). She concludes:

> In conclusion I should say that the Pastorals may present us with the first attempt to quell Proto-Montanism, a prophetical movement within the church before the rise of Montanus and his women. It was not a prohibition of the charismatic element in the church – indeed, it was a long time before Montanists were convicted, precisely because the facet of the community which they represented was a genuine one. The danger in the new charismatic movement was the elevation of prophet or prophetess above the status of presbyters and bishops; the introduction of lack of sobriety or frenzied prophecy; the writing down of prophecies is on the same level as Scripture; the development of an elect or 'spiritual' element in the church as opposed to the *psychichi* and the too progressive emancipation of women.
>
> This theory of Proto-Montanism in the Pastoral Epistles must remain a pure hypothesis but it is perhaps worth some further consideration (1971: 345–46).

In my view Ford's hypothesis is indeed worthy of further consideration. This thesis seeks to investigate her theory by the use of sociological methods together with a fresh socio-historical analysis of Montanism. I now turn to the use of the sociology of deviance to see whether this can throw fresh light on the nature of the opponents in the Pastorals.

Chapter 2

A SOCIAL-SCIENTIFIC APPROACH

1. *Introduction*

The approaches outlined above have produced various solutions to the question of the opponents in the Pastorals. I have demonstrated above the unsatisfactory nature of the conclusions reached by proponents of the view that the opponents came from a Jewish/Gnostic background. Literary approaches have correctly highlighted the stereotypical nature of the polemic employed in the Pastorals but fail to provide a convincing description of the opponents. Karris has stated: 'One of his [the author of the Pastoral Epistles] key weapons against the opponents is name-calling' (1973: 549). The use of names to label those considered deviant in some way has been fruitfully explored in the sociology of deviance.

2. *The Use of Models*

The sociologist Tony Blasi has argued that it is inappropriate to import contemporary sociological models when examining the New Testament data (1988: 1–2). Instead we must proceed inductively from a detailed examination of the data to the most general sociological concepts suggested by the evidence. For Blasi, the sociological concept which can most appropriately be applied to the data is that of a social movement. Blasi is rightly critical of much of the work of biblical scholars seeking to apply contemporary social-science models to the New Testament. For example, Neyrey (1986) is a classic case of making the data fit the model.[1] This propensity to make the data fit the model is a very real problem for those wanting to use social-science models in New Testament studies. This point has been well made recently by Horrell (1996: 9–18) and (2000). Nevertheless, unlike Blasi, I do not think it is necessary to advocate a purely inductive approach. As Elliott (1995: 48) has rightly stated, social-scientific criticism is neither exclusively inductive nor exclusively deductive but rather involves a back-and-forth movement of suggestion checking between evidence and hypothesis. Familiarity with the data being examined is, of course, most essential. However, I would argue, it is then possible to select an appropriate contemporary social-science model to apply to the data heuristically. The use of such models can never fill in gaps in the data, but it can often

---

1. See my critique in *The Use of Sociological Methods in New Testament Studies* (Unpublished MA research paper; University of Sheffield, 1994): 94–98.

lead to fresh questions being asked of the text.[2] As John Barclay has stated, specifically in connection with deviance theory:

> ...deviance theory is no magic wand with which to solve the many intricate problems which confront the historian of early Christianity. It can only be used in conjunction with minute historical analysis of the sources and cannot fill in the gaps which they leave (1995: 125).

And again:

> ...rightly employed this [symbolic interactionist] perspective can enable us to ask new questions of the historical material we study: it can suggest some interesting directions in which to look, though not, of course, what we will find when we look there (1995: 118).

3. *Approaches in the Sociology of Deviance*

As I am concerned with looking at the opponents in the Pastorals from a sociological perspective, the first area to be considered is the sociology of deviance. The author of the Pastorals clearly considers the opponents to be deviants (Tit. 1.16). According to Kelly (1989: 53) there are seven major theoretical perspectives in the sociology of deviance.[3]

- functionalist perspective;
- culture conflict perspective;
- cultural transmission theory (Still's 'differential association theory');
- anomie or opportunity theory;
- radical-conflict theory;
- social control theory; and
- interactionist perspective (labelling theory).[4]

Of these, the following are particularly useful heuristically for an examination of the opponents in the Pastorals:

---

2.   In what follows I use the model of the status degradation ceremony in this way. However, with this important exception, like Still, I am more interested in 'using social-scientific theory to support and supplement exegetical research' (1999: 84 n. 2). I am very sympathetic to Horrell's (2000) critique of the use of models in social-scientific approaches to the New Testament, but remain persuaded that models, with appropriate caution, can be used heuristically. As Esler (2000: 108) states: '[A model] is not a description of empirical reality, but rather an explicit simplification and accentuation of empirical reality used for organizational and heuristic purposes and derived from contemporary social-scientific research'.

3.   Kelly (1989) is an excellent reader with extracts from the leading theorists in the sociology of deviance.

4.   To this list should be added feminist perspectives. However, there is no overarching feminist approach to the sociology of deviance. Rather, as Downes and Rock (1995: 304) point out, feminist approaches form 'a diverse body of work united by the critical view that the understanding of the criminality of women, and the role of gender in theories of deviance in general, have been ill served both by traditional and new criminologies'.

a. *Differential Association*
Still (1999: 90–93) has provided an excellent summary of cultural transmission theory which, when applied to deviance, is known as differential association theory. One of the key insights of this approach is that deviance is learned through symbolic communication with others. This approach is relevant to the Pastorals where those labelled as deviants are invited into households and 'captivate silly women' (2 Tim. 3.6). These women are then considered deviant by the author and they too spread the values of the deviant culture by 'gadding about from house to house' (1 Tim. 5: 13).

b. *Social Control*
Social control theory, as exemplified by Hirschi (1969), argues that deviance occurs when an individual's societal bonds are weakened or broken. This perspective, therefore, focuses on the social bonds which produce conformity. According to Hirschi there are four elements to the societal bond. First, *attachment* to others who socially conform makes deviant behaviour less likely. Second, there is *commitment* to conformity out of fear of the consequences of non-conformity. This element recognises that any potential deviant must consider the cost of deviant behaviour in terms of the risk of losing the investment of time, energy, etc. in pursuing normative activities. This assumes that in any society the interests of most persons would be endangered if they were to engage in deviant acts. Thirdly, *involvement* in conventional pursuits leaves little time and/or energy to engage in deviant ones. Fourthly, an individual's *belief* in terms of internalising societal norms forms a strong control against deviance.

   Social control theory is useful as a means of examining the strategy of the author of the Pastorals in the face of deviance. He emphasises believers' *attachment* to one another as members of the same household (1 Tim. 3.15); he spells out the potential consequences of non-conformity (1 Tim. 1.19–20); he encourages the *involvement* of all sections of the community (Tit. 2: 1–10); and the paraenetic sections serve to reinforce the values the author requires of the community.

c. *Labelling Theory*
As Still (1999: 94) has pointed out, labelling theory was popular among sociologists in the 1960s and 1970s. Since then the predominant perspective has been social control theory. Nevertheless, this perspective on deviance has been particularly favoured by New Testament scholars, with varying degrees of success.[5] As I shall seek to show below, this perspective on deviance is the most heuristically useful in connection with an examination of the opponents in the Pastorals.

   The use of labels in power contests and the acquisition of a master label by those perceived as deviant have been fruitfully explored in this symbolic interactionist perspective on deviance. The use of labelling theory does pose a methodological problem. As a symbolic interactionist perspective, labelling theory focuses on the interaction between deviants and those who label them as deviants. Consequently,

---

5.   See Still (1999: 86–88) for a summary and critique.

attention is paid to actors on both sides of the labelling process. The problem is that, when we come to ancient texts such as the Pastoral Epistles, we do not have any access to the 'deviants'. We only have the point of view of those doing the labelling as embedded in the texts. Nevertheless, the value of labelling theory for the purposes of this paper is precisely due to the fact that it begins with the assumption that no act is intrinsically deviant. Labelling theory thus draws attention to the significance of the labellers in the deviance defining process. This aspect can usefully be employed heuristically to ask fresh questions of the text. As Esler has stated: 'Models are heuristic tools, not ontological statements. Accordingly, they are either useful or not, and it is meaningless to ask whether they are "true" or "false"' (1995: 4).

A central facet of labelling theory is that deviance should not be regarded simply as a set of characteristics possessed by the deviant. It is only behaviour in some contexts and engaged in by certain people that is defined as deviant, whereas in other contexts or involving other actors no such labelling occurs. Consequently, the notion of deviance is best described as a process of interaction between those labelled deviants and those doing the labelling. The interactionist perspective, at least in theory, thus focuses as much on those defining deviance as on those perceived as deviant. In the now famous words of Becker:

> Social groups create deviance by making the rules whose infraction constitutes
> deviance, and by applying those rules to particular people and labeling them as
> outsiders. From this point of view, deviance is not a quality of the act the person
> commits, but rather a consequence of the application by others of rules and sanc-
> tions to an 'offender'. The deviant is one to whom that label has successfully
> been applied; deviant behavior is behavior that people so label (1963: 9).

This does not mean, as some have argued, that labelling theorists such as Becker regard the deviant act itself as irrelevant to the labelling process. Becker himself states: 'It is not my purpose here to argue that only acts which are regarded as deviant by others are "really" deviant' (1963: 19). Lemert helpfully distinguishes primary and secondary deviation. Primary deviation is concerned with how deviant behaviour arises. Lemert rightly recognises that the causes of such behaviour are multi-factorial. Deviance arises 'in a wide variety of social, cultural, and psychological contexts...' (1972: 48). Secondary deviation is concerned with the process by which deviants come to be regarded as outsiders and the consequences of such labelling for the deviant. Labelling theory focuses on this process of secondary deviation. Three key questions concerning this process are.[6]

1. Who applies the label of deviant to whom?
2. What consequences does the application of a label have for the person labelled?
3. Under what circumstances is the label of deviant successfully applied?

6.   Becker (1963: 3).

i. *Deviance as Power Struggle*. If deviance is seen as a process of interaction between those doing the labelling and those labelled then deviance needs to be understood in the context of social conflict. Indeed Lofland goes so far as to define deviance as follows:

> Deviance is the name of the conflict game in which individuals or loosely organized small groups with little power are strongly feared by a well-organized, sizable minority or majority who have a large amount of power (1969: 14).

Schur too notes that deviance is a process of social typing which occurs when certain people feel threatened by others (1980: 4). For Schur deviance is essentially political because it is concerned with the distribution of a certain kind of social power. He notes:

> ...what is most essentially at stake in such situations is the power or resource of moral standing or acceptability. Other appropriate terms for this would include propriety, respectability...and rectitude... Individuals on the receiving end of the deviantizing process face as a result the prospect of a significant lessening of moral standing, and often they vividly experience it (1980: 6).

The deviantising process is thus an example of 'moral stratification' which Schur (1980: 7) regards as an important element in the stratification order of any society. Both Lofland and Schur emphasise that deviance outcomes reflect underlying power struggles. In such power struggles deviance outcomes are profoundly influenced by techniques of persuasion and pressure. Propaganda is thus a key weapon in the deviantising process.

ii. *Master Status*. If the deviance process is successful the deviant acquires a master status derived from the particular area of deviance engaged in. Thus the person who commits acts of theft, for example, is labelled a thief. In this way the offending person is no longer perceived as just another person. Rather, he or she is categorised, stereotyped and thereby depersonalised. Very often people will then engage in a process of retrospective interpretation through which the previous history of the offending person is reread and thus reinterpreted in the light of the newly perceived deviant status.

iii. *Status Degradation Ceremony*. A particular example of this process is the 'status degradation ceremony' which I have described and applied to the Pastoral Epistles in Pietersen (1997). In this article, I draw on the work of Garfinkel (1956) who describes a status degradation ceremony as: 'Any communicative work between persons whereby the public identity of an actor is transformed into something looked on as lower in the local scheme of social types'. For Garfinkel status degradation ceremonies inevitably involve *public* denunciation. Such a denunciation involves a denouncer, a party to be denounced (the perpetrator), something that the perpetrator is accused of doing (the event), and witnesses to the denunciation. Garfinkel (1956: 422–23) analyses the components of public denunciation as follows:

1. Both the perpetrator and the event must be removed from the realm of the ordinary and placed in the extraordinary.

2A.   Both the perpetrator and the event must not be seen as unique but as typi-
      cally symbolic of some negative feature(s) of human existence.

2B.   The typical characteristics of both the perpetrator and the event must be
      appreciated by the witnesses by means of the availability of a 'dialectical
      counterpart'. In this way the witnesses, ideally, cannot conceive of the per-
      petrator or the event without reference to this positive counterconception.

3.   The denouncer must be regarded by the witnesses as a public rather than a
      private figure. As a public figure the denouncer is perceived to draw upon
      communal experience rather than upon unique, personal experiences.

4.   The denouncer must highlight the core values of the witnesses and deliver
      the denunciation in the name of those core values.

5.   The denouncer must be invested with the right to speak in the name of these
      ultimate values.

6.   The denouncer must be seen by the witnesses as a supporter of these values.

7.   The witnesses must be made to experience their distance from the person
      being denounced.

8.   The denounced person must be defined as standing outside the legitimate
      order.

An analysis of the Pastorals demonstrates that at least part of their function is
that of public denunciation as defined by Garfinkel:

1.   The opponents are removed out of the realm of the ordinary. Hymenaeus
      and Alexander are blasphemers and have to be handed over to Satan (1 Tim.
      1.20). The opponents pay attention 'to deceitful spirits and teachings of
      demons' (1 Tim. 4.1); they are like Jannes and Jambres who opposed Moses
      (2 Tim. 3.8).

2A.   The stereotypical nature of the polemic of the Pastorals, in particular the
      vice lists of 1 Tim. 1.9–10; 6.4–5; 2 Tim. 3.2–5; Tit. 3.3, serves to detract
      from specific events and to typify the opponents as evil.

2B.   Paul (1 Tim. 1.13–16; 2 Tim. 3.10–11), Timothy (1 Tim. 4.12–16), and Titus
      (Tit. 2.7–8) function as dialectical counterparts to the opponents. The quali-
      ties of ἐπίσκοποι, πρεσβύτεροι and διάκονοι (1 Tim. 3.1–13; Tit. 1.5–9)
      likewise serve as dialectical counterparts to the deeds of the opponents.

3.   The denouncer is no less than Paul himself whose identity as apostle (1 Tim.
      1.1; 2.7; 2 Tim. 1.1; Tit. 1.1), herald and teacher (1 Tim. 2.7; 2 Tim. 1.11)
      highlights Paul as a public figure.

4.   Paul, as denouncer, underscores the core values of the witnesses (the com-
      munities addressed in the Pastorals). For example, he highlights love, a
      good conscience, and sincere faith in 1 Tim. 1.5; godliness (εὐσέβεια) is a
      major emphasis (1 Tim. 2.2; 3.16; 4.7,8; 6.3,5,6,11; 2 Tim. 3.5; Tit. 1.1).

5.   Throughout the Pastorals Paul's right to speak in the name of these values is
      simply assumed.

6.   Paul's insistent exhortation to Timothy and Titus to 'teach these duties' (e.g.
      1 Tim. 4.11; 6.2; 2 Tim. 4.2; Tit. 2.1) emphasises that Paul is a firm sup-
      porter of these values.

7. Timothy and Titus (and through them the communities addressed) are urged to distance themselves from the opponents and their practices (e.g. 1 Tim. 4.7; 6.11,20; 2 Tim. 3.5; Tit. 3.9–11).
8. Hymenaeus and Alexander, as key opponents, have been ritually separated from a place in the legitimate order; they have been 'turned over to Satan' (1 Tim. 1.20). Although hope is held out that the opponents may return to the fold (2 Tim. 2.24–25), they are currently perceived as in 'the snare of the devil, having been held captive by him to do his will' (2 Tim. 2.25). Titus is exhorted to have nothing more to do with anyone who persists in causing divisions after two warnings (Tit. 3.10).

If the Pastorals are perceived as fulfilling the function of a status degradation ceremony then, according to Garfinkel's definition, they serve to transform the public identity of those opposed. I am convinced that the opponents addressed in the Pastoral Epistles came initially from within the Christian community. They are accused of having suffered shipwreck in the faith (1 Tim. 1.19); having renounced the faith (1 Tim. 4.1); having missed the mark as regards the faith (1 Tim. 6.21); and having swerved from the truth so as to upset the faith of some (2 Tim. 2.18). The Pastorals are, therefore, involved in the transformation of their identity from insiders to outsiders. If the denunciation is successful this transformation is total; even though the opponents were previously members of the community this counts for nothing. They are now regarded as outsiders. Furthermore, they are now perceived as always having been deviants:

> The work of the denunciation effects the recasting of the objective character of the perceived other: The other person becomes in the eyes of his condemners literally a different and *new* person. It is not that the new attributes are added to the old 'nucleus'. He is not changed, he is reconstituted. The former identity, at best, receives the accent of mere appearance... What he is now is what, 'after all', he was all along (1956: 421–22).

The recognition that the Pastorals function as a status degradation ceremony suggests that the prime purpose of the Pastorals is to combat the opponents. The Pastorals, on this view, were not written primarily as a manual of church order. Furthermore, the use of 'name-calling' in the polemic of the Pastorals suggests the stereotyping process of deviance defining highlighted by labelling theory. As we saw above the deviance process reflects an underlying power struggle. We therefore have to ask the question: whose interests are threatened by whom?

Clearly it is the leadership of the Pauline communities addressed by the Pastorals who feel threatened. The letters purport to be written by Paul, the founder of these communities, and are addressed in the first instance to Timothy and Titus – the prime leaders of these communities. I would argue that the need to resort to status degradation suggests not only that the opponents were once insiders, but that they were prominent insiders. This is made explicit in 1 Tim. 1.3 and Tit. 1.11 where the opponents are clearly in a position to teach in the communities. This is significant because the Pastorals themselves emphasise the teaching role of community leaders (1 Tim. 3.2; 5.17; Tit. 1.9). In this context Fee's suggestion (1988: 7–10) that the Pastorals reflect the situation hinted at in Paul's address to the

Ephesian elders in Acts 20.30 needs to be taken seriously. It may well be that some of the opponents were elders in the community.

If the Pastorals are read through the lens of labelling theory then fresh questions can be asked of the list of qualifications for an ἐπίσκοπος (1 Tim. 3.1–7; Tit. 1.7–9), πρεσβύτερος (Tit. 1.5–6), and διάκονος (1 Tim. 3.8–13). Schur has pointed out that the deviantizing process is actually a form of moral stratification. In this light the passages concerning overseers, elders and deacons are not merely descriptive lists of qualifications for community leadership. These passages too serve the overall polemic of the letters. They reinforce the view that true leaders of the community occupy the moral high ground. These passages, the emphasis on virtues such as godliness (εὐσέβεια), dignity (σεμνότης) and particularly moderation/respectability (σώφρων and cognates), and the stereotypical vice lists combine to highlight the moral stratification process at work in the Pastorals. On this view the moral qualities of the community leaders are highlighted in order to contrast the low morality of the opponents. In this way the opponents are disqualified from any leadership role in the community. Through the process of retrospective interpretation the communities addressed will come to see that the opponents all along were never really 'true' leaders.

Paul is presented as a teacher in 1 Tim. 2.7 and 2 Tim. 1.11 – a term that he nowhere else applies to himself. The teaching role of Timothy (1 Tim. 4.11, 13, 16; 6.2; 2 Tim. 4.2) and Titus (Tit. 2.1, 7) as Paul's representatives is also emphasised. This emphasis on Paul, Timothy, Titus, and other church leaders as teachers serves as a foil in order to label the opponents as false teachers. They teach a different doctrine (1 Tim. 1.3), they desire to be teachers of the law but do not understand what they are saying (1 Tim. 1.7), they pay attention to deceitful spirits and teachings of demons (1 Tim. 4.1), they are teachers who serve people who cannot put up with sound doctrine (2 Tim. 4.3), they teach for sordid gain (Tit. 1.11). The emphasis on true teachers, combined with the rhetoric against the opponents, serve to create the master status of 'false teacher' for the opponents. Whereas previously they may have been regarded by the communities as faithful representatives of Paul's teaching they are now to be regarded as heretics. If the status degradation strategy of the Pastorals were successful they would then come to be regarded as having always been false teachers through the process of retrospective interpretation.

4. *Status Degradation and the Authenticity of the Pastorals*

At this point some attention has to be given to the question of the authenticity of the epistles. If the Pastoral Epistles are authentic then they function straightforwardly as a public denunciation by Paul of his opponents. However, if they are pseudepigraphic then the status degradation ceremony is cast in the past – it is opponents who are contemporary with Paul whose identity is transformed. As Bauckham (1988) has persuasively argued, the didactic purpose of New Testament letters means that if there are any pseudepigraphical letters in the New Testament they must find some way of bridging the gap between the supposed addressees and the real readers. The question is, therefore, how can a status degradation ceremony set in the past function as one for the present situation of the author? From a socio-logical perspective, a status degradation ceremony from the past cannot function as such in the present unless, in some sense, the present is seen as being a continuation of that past degradation ceremony. This requires more than an analogous situation. By definition a status degradation ceremony involves real actors – these cannot just be actors from the past. In this connection the role of Timothy and Titus in the Pastorals is crucial. Paul is absent (1 Tim. 3.14; Tit. 3.12) and so Timothy and Titus are exhorted to tackle the opponents. It is not only Hymenaeus and Alexander as contemporaries of Paul who have been ritually separated from a place in the legiti-mate order, so too have opponents contemporary with Timothy (2 Tim. 2.24–26). It is Timothy and Titus in the first instance who are made to experience their distance from the opponents. Consequently, if they are pseudonymous, *the status degrada-tion strategy of the Pastorals can only work if Timothy and Titus are still alive and active in leadership.* Bauckham points out that as well as the references to oppo-nents and false teaching contemporary with Paul there are references to false teach-ing and apostasy in the future (1 Tim. 4.1–3; 2 Tim. 3.1–5; 4.3–4). These suggest that false teachers of the real readers' time are being referred to. This appears to be confirmed by the change in tense from future to present in 2 Tim. 3.6–8 and by the fact that the prophecy concerning false teachers in 1 Tim. 4.1–3 is followed immediately by their refutation.[7] Bauckham argues that this point strongly sug-gests pseudepigraphy.

> So it seems that the material about false teaching in the Pastorals, when taken as a whole, amounts to a careful and deliberate attempt to bridge the gap between the situation at the supposed time of writing and the real contemporary situation of the author and his readers (1988: 493).

In 2 Tim. 3.1–8 the apostates appear in the future from Paul's perspective but in the present from Timothy's. This, the other instructions to Timothy as to how to deal with the opponents, and the expectation that Timothy would survive until the parousia (1 Tim. 6.14), serve to convince Bauckham that the letters were written during Timothy's lifetime. My contention too is that, in light of the roles of Timo-thy and Titus, the Pastorals can only function effectively as status degradation cere-mony if they were written during their lifetime. Of course, this requires at least their active collusion in the fiction of Paul's authorship, or even their actual involve-ment in authorship.[8]

5. Conclusion

I shall argue, in the light of the above analysis, that there was a power struggle taking place in the immediate post-Pauline communities between factions with

---

7.   See too Dibelius and Conzelmann (1972: 64, 120–21).

8.   The dating of the Pastorals to the period immediately after the death of Paul is also argued by Marshall in his recent commentary (1999: 83–92), although Marshall is not persuaded that either Timothy or Titus were the actual authors. In my opinion, Marshall's arguments are thor-oughly convincing.

competing memories of Paul. The Pastorals claim to represent authentic Pauline tradition and claim him as the teacher *par excellence*. The function of Paul in the Pastorals is crucial. The opponents are labelled as false teachers, I suggest, because they were advocating a different view of Paul. As has long been noticed one of the mechanisms employed in the Pastorals for the maintenance of the symbolic universe of the communities is to downplay the dynamic nature of charisma when compared with the undisputed Pauline letters.[9] If, as I shall argue, the Pastorals' emphasis on such core values as self-control, sobriety and sound teaching serves a polemical as well as a hortatory function, then this emphasis, together with the lack of emphasis on charisma, suggest that the opponents advocated a much more ecstatic spirituality as proposed by Ford (1971: 342).

The question concerning this downplaying of charisma leads to the issue of the problematic relationship between charisma and its institutionalisation. I shall investigate this in the following chapter.

9.   See, for example, Dunn (1975: 347–50).

Chapter 3

THAUMATURGICAL PERSISTENCE AND THE INSTITUTIONALISING PROCESS

1. *Introduction and Definition of Terms*

Campbell (1994: 103) notes that there is often confusion over the term 'charisma' in the scholarly literature concerning the nature of Paul's authority. This confusion arises out of failing adequately to distinguish between Paul's theological use of the term and Weber's sociological terminology. Charisma can thus be used in two senses. Weber's analysis is specifically concerned with charisma as a type of *authority*. In this sense charisma is an extraordinary quality possessed by individuals which enables them to exercise authority over their followers. Charisma, in this Weberian sense, is concerned with leadership and structures of authority. The first half of this chapter, which is concerned with institutionalisation, utilises charisma in this Weberian sense. In it I seek to show that charismatic authority must inevitably become institutionalised if any movement based on such authority is to survive beyond the first generation. To do this I follow Weber's analysis on the routinisation of charisma as refined by Holmberg (1978), who utilises Berger and Luckmann's (1967) concept of institutionalisation. This analysis serves to confirm that the scholarly consensus that the Pastoral Epistles reflect the increasing institutionalisation of Pauline Christianity is sociologically well founded.

In the second half of this chapter I utilise charisma in its other sense. Here it is not the concept of charismatic authority that is being analysed; rather it is the concept of charisma as possession of 'spirit' by ordinary members of the community in such a way that extraordinary manifestations of 'spirit' form an integral part of the life of the community. In this sense a charismatic community is not just a community subject to charismatic authority (in the Weberian sense); rather it is a community in which charismatic phenomena are manifest among the ordinary members of the community. Dunn articulates this concept of charisma well in the case of the Pauline communities:

> If it is the (experienced) Spirit who creates community in the first place, so it is the Spirit experienced in charismata who sustains community. This comes out with greatest force in Paul's exposition of the church as body in 1 Cor. 12.14–27. Whatever other influences shaped Paul's concept of the church as the body of Christ, it is clear that in this passage the dominant influence is the typical Stoic use of the metaphor of the body to describe the relationship between individual and society. In Paul's development of the metaphor, however, it becomes an expression not simply of community but specifically of *charismatic community*.

...The many members who make up the one body (1 Cor. 12.14) are not simply individual believers, but individual believers *as charismatics* (vv. 4–11, 27–30) – that is, believers through whom the Spirit of grace may manifest himself in diverse ways at any time... At no time does Paul conceive of two kinds of Christians – those who minister to others and those who are ministered to, those who manifest charismata and those who do not. *To be a Christian is to be charismatic; one cannot be a member of the body without sharing the charismatic Spirit* (1975: 264–65, his italics).

It is a commonplace to assume that the undoubted institutionalisation of the Pauline communities was inevitably accompanied by the attenuation or even extinction of charisma in this second sense. Dunn, as we shall see below, certainly believes this to be the case. In the second half of this chapter I shall argue that far from dying out, charisma can persist, or even intensify, over time. In order to prepare the ground for subsequent chapters on the Pastorals, I focus on one form of charisma – that of thaumaturgy. This is defined as the demand for miracles and oracles. I argue below that it is legitimate to focus on thaumaturgy as there were undoubtedly thaumaturgical aspects to the Pauline communities. MacMullen (1984) argues persuasively that the persistence of thaumaturgy was a major factor in the growth of Christianity in the second and third centuries CE. I also utilise the anthropological work of Lewis (1989) and the sociological work of Wilson (1973) in order to highlight the conditions under which thaumaturgy can persist.

This chapter, therefore, seeks to question the scholarly consensus that the institutionalisation of the Pauline communities was inevitably accompanied by the loss of charismatic phenomena – in Dunn's view a fading of the vision of charismatic community (1975: 347–50). The Pastoral Epistles may well have been written in an environment which reflects both the process of institutionalisation and the persistence of charismatic enthusiasm, at least in the form of thaumaturgy. A case study of a Christian new religious movement (NRM) in the following chapter demonstrates that institutionalisation and the intensification of thaumaturgical demand can, in fact, happen simultaneously. I shall argue that this was also the case for the Pastorals.

2. Institutionalisation

a. Introduction

Margaret MacDonald, in common with many scholars, sees the Pastoral Epistles as reflecting the increasing institutionalisation which took place in the Pauline communities. She seeks to investigate 'the transformation of the church from its charismatic beginnings, evident in the authentic Pauline writings, to its more tightly organized form, evident in the Pastoral Epistles' (1988: 6–7). In doing so she draws on Berger and Luckmann's work on institutionalisation (1967: 70–85) and Weber's work on the routinisation of charisma.[1] She argues that Pauline communities developed through three stages. The first, reflected in the authentic Pauline letters, is one of 'community-building institutionalisation'. The second, reflected

---

1.   See below, page 41.

in Colossians and Ephesians, is that of 'community-stabilizing institutionalisation'. The third stage, reflected in the Pastorals, is one of 'community-protecting institutionalisation'.

In connection with the Pastorals, MacDonald utilises the church-sect typology of Troeltsch (1931: 331–43). After considering the Pastorals' concern to have the approval of outsiders, the universal vision of salvation expressed in them (1 Tim. 2.3–4), the relationship of women to the false teaching condemned in the Pastorals, the role of widows, and attitudes to wealth, MacDonald concludes that the Pastorals represent a community which can be characterised as a sect, but which is moving towards the church-type (1988: 163–202). She also draws on Verner's work (1983) to suggest that the prevailing domestic ideal acted as an important means of stabilising community life as the church, and its leadership patterns, became increasingly modelled on the household. MacDonald's short chapter on ritual in the Pastorals leads to the conclusion that the main emphasis in passages dealing with ritual is one of the need for control. This is particularly evident in connection with the activity of women during worship (1 Tim. 2.9–15).

In her final chapter MacDonald utilises the sociology of knowledge to examine the issue of orthodoxy and heresy from a fresh angle. False teaching threatened the symbolic universe of the community. In such a situation fresh mechanisms for the maintenance of the symbolic universe are required. These mechanisms require legitimation – they need to be explained and justified. These legitimations lead to the growth and transformation of the symbolic universe, which in turn legitimates the transformed social reality. A further process of institutionalisation thus takes place – that of community-protecting. In this process firmer boundaries are created to protect the symbolic universe from unwanted intrusion. In this context, if the author sees the household as the fundamental structural unit of the church, then any threat to the household becomes a serious threat to the symbolic universe.

b. *Max Weber*

As MacDonald has rightly suggested, Weber's work on the routinisation of charisma[2] remains the essential starting point for any investigation into the development of the structures of the Pauline communities in the decades immediately following Paul's death. Due to the piecemeal translation of Weber's writings into English, prior to the publication of *Economy and Society*, he has often been misunderstood as advocating a simple dichotomy between charismatic and bureaucratic authority. In fact, Weber developed his analysis of charisma within a *threefold* typology of legitimate authority. Legal authority (bureaucracy) is based on 'belief in the legality of enacted rules and the right of those elevated to authority under

2.   The following analysis is drawn from both Weber's early work on charisma contained in Part Two of *Economy and Society* (1968: 1111–157), written in 1913 (1968: 1133), and his later conceptual exposition (1968: 212–16, 241–54), written at some time between 1918 and 1920 (1968: XCIV). *Economy and Society* is a translation of M. Weber, *Wirtschaft und Gesellschaft. Grundriss der verstehenden Soziologie*, based on the fourth German edition (ed. J. Winckelmann; Tübingen: J.C.B. Mohr [Paul Siebeck], 1956): 1–550, 559–822, as revised in the 1964 paperback edition (Köln-Berlin: Kiepenheuer & Witsch).

such rules to issue commands'. Traditional authority is based on 'belief in the sanctity of immemorial traditions and the legitimacy of those exercising authority under them'. Charismatic authority rests on 'devotion to the exceptional sanctity, heroism or exemplary character of an individual person, and of the normative patterns or order revealed or ordained by him' (1968: 215). Furthermore, as is characteristic of Weber, these are *ideal* types; no actual authority structure corresponds in detail to any of these types. In addition, Weber clearly points out that these types should not be treated in isolation; he notes the complexity of actual authority structures and acknowledges that any specific authority displays characteristics of more than one of his ideal types. He explicitly states that his typology is not meant to be exhaustive and that its usefulness lies, in any given case, in being able to distinguish what aspects of an organisation can legitimately be identified as falling under or approximating one or another of his three categories (1968: 262–64).

i. *Charismatic Authority*. For Weber charismatic authority, unlike bureaucratic (legal) and patriarchal (traditional) authority, meets extraordinary needs. The other two types are structures of everyday life. Pure charisma is essentially personal and needs to be continually proved to the followers of the bearer of charisma.

> The term 'charisma' will be applied to a certain quality of an individual personality by virtue of which he is considered extraordinary and treated as endowed with supernatural, superhuman, or at least specifically exceptional powers or qualities. These are such as are not accessible to the ordinary person, but are regarded as of divine origin or as exemplary, and on the basis of them the individual concerned is treated as a 'leader' (1968: 241).

Such bearers of charisma have a sense of mission and demand that others obey and follow them by virtue of this mission. Consequently, if those to whom charismatics feel sent do not recognise them their claims collapse. In addition, if it appears that bearers have lost their charisma – either by failing to produce proofs of their powers, or, most importantly, if they fail to benefit their followers – their charismatic authority usually disappears.

In charismatic communities subject to charismatic authority the leader appoints an administrative staff which is chosen in terms of the charismatic qualities of its members. The staff and apparatus of the charismatic social structure are adapted to the demands of the mission of the charismatic leader. In a pure charismatic structure the staff do not receive any salary or any other kind of orderly compensation. Instead they share in the goods that the leader has received which the leader distributes among them without any accounting or contractual mechanism. Weber insists that pure charisma rejects any methodical rational economic conduct. This does not mean that charisma necessarily demands the renunciation of property or acquisition – the charismatic warrior, for example, actively seeks bounty. What is despised is the seeking of a regular income by means of continuous economic activity devoted to this end. Support is either voluntary or gained by force, depending on the type of charismatic authority (prophet or military leader).

The charismatic leader typically preaches, creates, or demands new obligations. By its rejection of the old order and its demand for a fundamental change in the attitude of its followers, charisma can be seen to be a revolutionary force. Charisma demands internal change of its followers which, in turn, can lead to fundamental changes in the material and social conditions of society.

ii. *The Routinisation of Charisma*. Due to its essentially personal nature charismatic authority is inherently unstable. It depends upon charismatic qualities being demonstrated time and time again.

> The charismatic hero derives his authority not from an established order and enactments, as if it were an official competence, and not from custom or feudal fealty, as under patrimonialism. He gains and retains it solely by proving his powers in practice. He must work miracles, if he wants to be a prophet. He must perform heroic deeds, if he wants to be a warlord (1968: 1114).

Charisma arises out of the collective excitement produced by extraordinary events. As such pure charisma can only exist in the early stages. The demands of everyday life inevitably result in charismatic authority becoming institutionalised and transformed in the process. This process arises from the 'desire to transform charisma and charismatic blessing from a unique, transitory gift of grace of extraordinary times and persons into a permanent possession of everyday life' (1968: 1121). This arises out of the genuine desire of followers to ensure the continuation of the movement together with the staff wanting to put their own position on a much more stable everyday basis. Typically this happens with the disappearance of the charismatic leader and with the consequent problem of succession. The way in which the problem of succession is met has crucial implications for the subsequent development of the charismatic organisation. Weber suggests the following possible solutions:

1. The search for a new charismatic leader on the basis of certain distinguishing characteristics. This results in a process of traditionalisation in which traditional rules for the selection of successors reduce the purely personal character of leadership.

2. The selection of a new leader by revelatory techniques such as oracles, lots, divine judgments, etc. In this process the focus switches to the legitimacy of the technique of selection being used. The result is a form of legalisation.

3. The designation of a successor by the original charismatic leader.

4. The designation of a successor by the charismatic staff. This should not be construed as election – it is a question of arriving at the correct designation of the person who is truly endowed with charisma. Typically unanimity is required. Nevertheless, this solution often results in legitimacy being based on the correctness of the process by which leadership was acquired as in (2) above (e.g. the process of coronation).

5. The conception that charisma is transferred by heredity. In this case some of the other methods may still have to be used to select the proper heir from within the kinship group. In other situations the principle of primogeniture resolves the problem. Hereditary charisma depends only upon belonging to the correct kinship group. Personal charisma may be totally absent.

6. The conception that charisma may be transferred from the bearer to another. This dissociation of charisma from a particular individual makes it an objective, transferable entity. This often leads to the development of the charisma of office.

Charismatic authority resides in the office rather than in the personal qualities of the individual occupying the position.

In addition to the problems of succession, administrative staff play an important role in the routinisation of charisma. In order for the movement not to disintegrate there must be a procedure for recruiting new staff and a transition from the voluntary support of the staff to their regular remuneration. Recruitment may well involve requirements for training or tests of eligibility – these are important steps away from the original basis of recruitment involving personal charisma alone. However, the decisive step for Weber comes in the alteration of charisma's anti-economic character. This is an inevitable step arising naturally out of the desire for security. Positions of authority and social prestige are legitimised as a result, and the income of staff is regularised. In addition, the organisation has to adapt administratively to the needs of everyday life. This often involves traditions of administrative practice and judicial procedure being adopted. It also involves some definite order being adopted in the organisation of the administrative staff itself. Finally, the costs of routine administration have to be funded. Nevertheless, vestiges of the original hallmarks of the charismatic organisation are still retained in the transformed structure through the status which is acquired either by hereditary charisma or by the charisma of office.

c. *The Routinisation of Charisma in the Pauline Communities*
Holmberg (1978: 149–50) summarises Weber's concept of pure charismatic authority in the religious sense in the following way:

The leader is considered to have a personal calling direct from God accompanied by magical or other extraordinary powers. The leader is considered to be the community's personal 'saviour' and lives an extraordinary life involving no paid or routine work, no family life, and no property, and which does not conform to traditional custom and belief. The leader's God-given mission is radical and revolutionary. A new message of salvation is proclaimed, the old order is attacked, and rules for a new way of living are formulated. The mission's ultimate aim is the renewing of the entire social order. The leader's followers regard the charismatic as a hero or superhuman who participates in divine reality through superior insight, strength, or goodness. Their relationship to the leader is one of devotion, awe, and absolute trust resulting in obedience and support. The charismatic community founded by the charismatic thus all believe, obey and support the leader; they all have experienced an internal revolution which leads to a new way of living manifested in various concrete ways; they all are aware of belonging to an élite who possess salvation. Within the charismatic community there is an outer group of followers who continue their ordinary way of life, and an inner group of 'disciples' or 'staff' who share in the extraordinary life of the leader. The people in this inner group are personally called by the leader on the basis of their charismatic qualification; they abandon family, occupation, property, and tradition to live in a communistic relationship with the leader; they are designated their tasks directly by the leader and have no independent authority, rank, or sphere of competence. As a result the staff function as the élite of the élite closely related to the leader.

I will now use Holmberg's summary to examine Paul's authority. He has a definite sense of mission (e.g. Rom. 15.15–20) and the conviction that he had received
'grace [χάρις] and apostleship to bring about the obedience of faith among all the
Gentiles' (Rom. 1.5). He is conscious of a divine call to be an apostle (Rom. 1.1; 1
Cor. 1.1; 2 Cor. 1.1; Gal. 1.1). He does display extraordinary powers (Rom. 15.19;
2 Cor. 12.12); however, he does not appear to dwell on these powers. He does not
regard himself as the 'saviour' of the communities he founded – Jesus Christ fulfils
this role as far as Paul is concerned; nevertheless, Paul does use terminology such
as 'father' in relation to them (1 Cor. 4.15; 1 Thess. 2.11). He lives as a celibate,
travelling preacher and to this extent his life can be viewed as extraordinary. However, as will be discussed further below, his own method of support does not conform to Weber's charismatic typology. Paul's message is clearly one of salvation
resulting in a transformed way of living. His eschatological hope is for the transformation of the entire creation (Rom. 8.18–25). However, Paul's message cannot be
construed as revolutionary in any political sense (Rom. 13.1–7). With regard to the
relationship of the communities founded by Paul to him, we see that there is clear
respect and the expectation that they should follow his example (1 Cor. 11.1); there
is certainly devotion and trust, possibly awe as well, which results in obedience and
some forms of support (e.g. hospitality). However, this falls far short of emotional
intensity or hero-worship; indeed the latter is specifically discouraged by Paul
(1 Cor. 1.10–17). Furthermore, Paul's letters demonstrate that his leadership does
not go unquestioned in the communities he founded. From Paul's letters we see
that he does have a group of workers (staff); however, only some are personally
chosen by him,[3] others appear to have worked to some extent independently of
him.[4] Those involved in itinerant work with Paul would have had to have left their
homes and families to share in the 'extraordinary' life of Paul. Junior members of
the 'staff' receive their tasks directly from Paul and do not appear to have any
independent authority, rank, or sphere of influence.

The above analysis demonstrates that Paul's authority can be classified as charismatic according to Holmberg's summary. However, this classification is not
unproblematic. The points at which Paul's charismatic authority differs from
Weber's model, some of which were noted above, may only serve to highlight
Weber's insistence that no actual example will conform to his ideal types in every
detail. However, Weber's model of pure charisma, particularly his insistence on
charisma's anti-economic character,[5] really only directly applies to Jesus and the
group around him as recorded in the gospels. Consequently, the primitive church
which arose after the death of Jesus must be characterised as a charismatic
movement one step removed from its original state. Although the movement still
regards itself as in relationship with its 'leader', who is considered to have risen

---

3.   E.g. Timothy and Titus.

4.   E.g. Barnabas, Apollos, Silvanus, Priscilla and Aquila.

5.   The concept that pure charisma rejects any form of rational economic conduct is central to
Weber's definition of charismatic authority. Indeed, as highlighted above, Weber considers the
dilution of the anti-economic stance as a decisive factor indicating the process of the routinisation
of charisma.

from the dead and to be actively present in their groups through his Spirit, sociologically speaking the leaders of the early Jerusalem church function as the charismatic 'staff' of Jesus. Paul too is considered to be one of the staff (1 Cor. 1–4;
15.8–10; Gal. 2.7–9).[6] Consequently, Paul fulfils a dual role. In Weberian terms
he is both a member of staff and a charismatic leader in his own right. Thus the
movement, from its inception, has already encountered Weber's problem of charismatic succession. Furthermore, as Holmberg rightly points out (1978: 160–61),
certain persistent features of Paul's conduct suggest that Pauline authority cannot
be characterised as purely charismatic. This is particularly true of Paul's attitude
to money which cannot be described as anti-economic. He is prepared to work to
support himself (1 Cor. 9.3–18; 1 Thess. 2.9), and adopts a distinctly pragmatic
and rational approach to the organisation of the collection for the church in
Jerusalem (1 Cor. 16.1–4).[7] Holmberg concludes his discussion on the nature of
Paul's charismatic authority by warning against an over-simplified developmental
model of the primitive church moving from a pure 'chaotic' charismatic state to
an ordered non-charismatic one. He rightly argues that what we encounter in the
Pauline mission itself is an authority which cannot be characterised as pure charisma but which is a mixture of charismatic, traditional, and rational elements. In
other words, we already encounter, in Paul's mission itself, what Weber termed
'routinised charisma' (1978: 161).

d. *Criticisms of Weber's Concept of 'Routinised Charisma'*
It is important to note that Weber has been criticised for two fundamental reasons.[8]
First, in combining routine and charisma in one concept, Weber is both confusing
and self-contradictory as he clearly regards them as opposing concepts. By persisting with the term he appears to regard routinised charisma as, in some ways, fundamentally different from traditional or rational-legal authority but it is not at all

6.   Holmberg (1978: 151–53) demonstrates how the apostles, including Paul, fit Weber's
understanding of charismatic staff. They are considered to have been personally called by Christ.
They have charismatic qualifications of their own manifested in miracles, prophecy, and wisdom.
They have left occupation, property, and, in some cases, family to devote themselves to their
leader's mission. There is an awareness that they have been appointed to their task directly by the
risen Christ. This awareness resulted in an élite-consciousness manifested in their special title 'the
apostles of Jesus Christ' and in their own self-awareness.

7.   Theissen (1982: 27–67) persuasively argues that two types of Christian itinerant preachers
came into conflict in Corinth over the question of their subsistence. The first, 'itinerant charismatics', modelled themselves on the Jesus movement in Palestine. Weber's anti-economic emphasis
continues to apply to these charismatic preachers. However, Paul belonged to the second group –
'community organisers'. Theissen argues that there were a number of socio-political, socio-
economic, socio-ecological, and socio-cultural factors which account for the different emphases. In
particular, Paul's mission was an urban one. 'Anyone like Paul who wished to travel from city to
city in order to missionize the world as it was then known could not put into practice that radical
renunciation of planning and foresight required by the commissioning speeches [of Jesus as
recorded in the gospels]: ship's passage must be paid for; stuck in a city without money, one could
hardly proceed to "help oneself" ' (1982: 38).

8.   See Friedrich (1961: 22), Blau (1963: 305–16), Tucker (1968: 753) and Holmberg (1978:
164–66).

clear as to how this is the case. It would have been better to have talked about the transformation of charismatic authority into one of the other two types of authority.

Second, Weber is unclear as to how the process of routinisation commences. Sometimes Weber suggests that leaders themselves may be involved in the routinising process:

> Primarily, a religious community arises in connection with a prophetic movement as a result of routinization (*Veralltäglichung*), i.e., as a result of the process whereby either *the prophet himself* or his disciples secure the permanence of his preaching and the congregation's distribution of grace, hence insuring also the economic existence of the enterprise and those who man it, and thereby monopolizing as well the privileges reserved for those charged with religious functions (1968: 452, my emphasis).

However, as noted above, Weber generally appears to emphasise the problem of succession following the death of the charismatic leader as the point at which routinisation begins to set in. Thus routinisation appears primarily as an afterthought – an unintentional consequence of the longing for the continuation of the charismatic community. Holmberg rightly notes that Weber emphasises the economic interests of the staff and their desire for a more permanent form of security as the decisive factors in the routinisation process. At this point, as Holmberg notes, Weber passes over the systemic needs of the organisation and moves away from sociological analysis to a 'crude psychologizing about personal motives' (1978: 165). What Weber fails adequately to recognise is that routinisation, far from being a 'suffocation' of charisma,[9] is inherent in the charismatic impulse as such, as I seek to show below.

Weber refuses to discuss the content of charisma; instead he emphasises a charismatic movement's 'highly personal experience of divine grace and god-like heroic strength' (1968: 1115). However, this does not adequately explain the effects of charismatics on their followers. It is not merely the medium that gives rise to a charismatic movement, but the message as well. Wonder workers may attract a crowd wherever they perform, but it takes content to transform a crowd attracted by wonders into a movement of social change. Charismatic movements have characteristically been movements of change. Weber himself hints at this when he states: 'Charismatic belief revolutionizes men "from within" and shapes material and social conditions according to its revolutionary will' (1968: 1116). However, if charisma is concerned not only with personal transformation but also with the transformation of the social order, then it must from its conception seek institutional manifestation. Charisma is thus not only destructive and revolutionary in relation to the old order, as Weber emphasised so well (1968: 1115–117), it also has a constructive impulse. As Holmberg rightly notes:

9.   Weber's own terminology: 'Every charisma is on the road from a turbulently emotional life that knows no economic rationality to a slow death by suffocation under the weight of material interests: every hour of its existence brings it nearer to this end' (1968: 1120). Thus, for Weber, economic interest is the arch-enemy of charisma: working against it from its very beginning and eventually bringing about its downfall. Weber is not saying here that charisma itself has inherent routinising tendencies.

> A charismatic movement should not be interpreted as a kind of rapture or as
> enthusiastic flight from society to a predominantly emotional, freakish way of
> communal life. It is an attempt to build the society (church, party) anew, from the
> 'roots', in principle nothing less than the founding anew of society (1978: 146).

In conclusion, Weber's typology of legitimate authority structures does have
rich analytical power. However, in the way he defined charismatic authority, he
failed adequately to recognise that by 'routinisation of charisma' he meant the
transformation of charisma into either traditional or rational-legal authority. This
leaves charisma, for Weber, as an inherently unstable and ultimately short-lived
phenomenon. I would argue rather that the concept of charisma can be made much
more analytically useful by recognising that charisma itself (as opposed to other
factors external to charisma) has institution-building motives inherent within it. It
is to this process of institutionalisation that I now turn.

e. *Institutionalisation*

As noted at the beginning of this chapter, MacDonald's work on the Pastoral Epistles draws on both Weber (routinisation) and Berger and Luckmann (institutionalisation). Holmberg (1978: 167–75) too draws on Berger and Luckmann. For Berger
and Luckmann (1967: 70–72) institutionalisation begins with a process of 'habitualisation'. This involves the frequent repetition of an action until a pattern emerges.
Once this pattern is recognised the action in question can be performed in the same
manner with the same economical effort. Habitualisation makes it unnecessary for
each situation to be defined from scratch. This results in the freeing of the individual
from the burden of much everyday decision making to concentrate on such deci-
sions as are required for new situations. The 'background of habitualized activity
opens up a foreground for deliberation and innovation' (1967: 71). Habitualisation
can apply to a solitary individual detached from any social interaction, but when
such interaction does occur, and there is a corresponding observation and sharing of
patterns, a process of 'reciprocal typification' occurs. This process is the prerequisite for institutionalisation. 'Institutionalization occurs whenever there is a reciprocal typification of habitualized actions by types of actors. Put differently, any such
typification is an institution' (1967: 72). Berger and Luckmann explain what they
mean by offering an example of a hypothetical situation in which two persons, *A*
and *B*, from entirely different social worlds begin to interact:

> As *A* and *B* interact, in whatever manner, typifications will be produced quite
> quickly. *A* watches *B* perform. He attributes motives to *B*'s actions and, seeing the
> actions recur, typifies the motives as recurrent. As *B* goes on performing, *A* is
> soon able to say to himself, 'Aha, there he goes again'. At the same time, *A* may
> assume that *B* is doing the same thing with regard to him. From the beginning,
> both *A* and *B* assume this reciprocity of typification. In the course of their
> interaction these typifications will be expressed in specific patterns of conduct.
> That is, *A* and *B* will begin to play roles *vis-à-vis* each other. This will occur even
> if each continues to perform actions different from those of the other. The pos-
> sibility of taking the role of the other will appear with regard to the same actions
> performed by both. That is, *A* will inwardly appropriate *B*'s reiterated roles and
> make them the models for his own role-playing... Thus a collection of recipro-

cally typified actions will emerge, habitualized for each in roles, some of which will be performed separately and some in common. While this reciprocal typification is not yet institutionalization (since, there only being two individuals, there is no possibility of a typology of actors), it is clear that institutionalization is already present *in nucleo* (1967: 74).

As long as there are only two individuals the routinised activities, although tending to persist, still remain accessible to deliberate intervention by either individual. However, once a third party is introduced the character of the social interaction is decisively changed. The routinised world of *A* and *B* is now made available to another. This world has a history and, as such, confronts the third party as external to it. Now, in the process of mutual interaction, the routinised actions become historical institutions – there is a process of crystallisation in which 'the institutions are now experienced as possessing a reality of their own, a reality which confronts the individual as an external and coercive fact' (1967: 76). At this point, ' "There we go again" now becomes "This is how these things are done" ' (1967: 77).

Berger and Luckmann's analysis demonstrates that the process of institutionalisation finds its origins in *any* social situation which persists over time.[10] This provides an important correction to Weber's understanding of the routinisation of charisma. This cannot now be understood as arising out of the desire for the continuation of the charismatic community following the death of the charismatic leader. Instead, the very creation of such a charismatic community implies the process of institutionalisation. We have seen above that Paul's mission, in Weberian terms, can best be classified in terms of routinised charisma. The concept of institutionalisation further refines this classification. The Pauline churches are thus to be understood as both charismatic and institutionalised.

This combination gives rise to what O'Dea has termed the 'five dilemmas in the institutionalization of religion' (1961). He notes that what he calls the 'charismatic moment' – a period of intense religious experience accompanied by vitality and enthusiasm – would be ephemeral unless embodied 'in institutional structures to render it continuously present and available' (1961: 32). However, this tension between the charismatic moment and its institutionalisation results in five dilemmas. First, there is the dilemma of mixed motivation in which the original wholehearted devotion to the mission of the charismatic founder is replaced by more self-interested motivations, typically in subsequent generations. The second dilemma concerns the need to objectify ritual which can lead to its alienation from personal religious response. Thirdly, there is the dilemma of administrative order which corresponds closely to Weber's concept of the routinisation of charisma. Fourthly, there is the dilemma of delimitation in which the need to give concrete definition to the goals and ideals of the organisation can result in a set of rules which stifles the original charismatic moment. The final dilemma concerns that of power. As an

---

10. Berger and Luckmann, in seeking to do justice to the human construction of social reality, do overplay the objective 'givenness' of such 'reality' and are in danger of the error of reification. For a critique of their theory see Horrell (1993), (1996) and (2000). Nevertheless, their account of institutionalisation, suitably modified for the transformational effects of social actors, remains persuasive.

organisation founded in a 'charismatic moment' becomes more successful there is a temptation for its leaders 'to avail themselves of the close relation between religion and cultural values in order to reinforce the position of religion itself' (1961: 37). For O'Dea these processes are inevitable and represent facets of the fundamental dilemma which concerns the transformation of the charismatic moment so as to render it continuously available. O'Dea's model has been criticised by Mathisen (1987) who finds little evidence of the second and fourth dilemmas in his case study on the development of the Moody Bible Institute in Chicago. Nevertheless, as Mathisen admits, O'Dea's model has met 'nearly uniform acceptance' (1987: 302). I shall demonstrate in the next chapter that his model, with some refinement of the fifth dilemma, is relevant to the case studied there. The question remains, therefore, whether the tension between the charismatic moment and its ongoing institutionalisation eventually stifles the original vitality and enthusiasm or whether the memory of the charismatic moment can serve to subvert or transform the institutionalising process. At this point it is useful to consider Holmberg's notion of 'open' and 'controlled' institutionalisation.

Holmberg (1978: 198–204) persuasively argues that, if the basis of charismatic authority, as Weber suggests, is proximity to the sacred, the really crucial form of proximity to the sacred in the early church was that of being in close contact with the divine word. Thus apostles, prophets, and teachers have primary authority in the Pauline churches (1 Cor. 12.28), and their authority is charismatic. However, within the Pauline charismatic communities there is inevitably a continuing process of institutionalisation. Holmberg correctly discerns that this process is in principle, at least in the early stages, 'open'. In other words, it may proceed in many different directions. This helps partly to explain the variety of institutional solutions to the needs of churches in different locations as exemplified in the Pauline letters. Given the developing and 'open' nature of institutionalisation the latest stages in the process are always the most insecure until they have become fully part of the stabilised background of the social world in question. At this point it is important to recognise that potential innovations do not inevitably become institutionalised. As charismatic authority is based on proximity to the sacred, and once some temporal distance has been achieved so that proximity is conceived in spatio-temporal terms, sacred tradition becomes of great importance. Consequently, any innovation has to be fundamentally in accordance with existing sacred tradition.[11] This means that as time passes institutionalisation becomes less 'open' and becomes what Holmberg calls 'controlled institutionalisation'.

> The result is that as time passes the institutionalization of Church life and of authority becomes increasingly less free to develop in any possible direction. Cult, doctrine and organization do not simply develop out of free interaction between members of small independent local groups of Christians. On the contrary, what we see is a controlled process of development although it is not controlled by one person or central institution but by a corporate tradition which guides the emerging functional differentiation and its institutionalization (1978: 201).

---

11. Holmberg gives as examples local custom, prophecy, and gnosis, which must conform to what the apostle considers to be true and upbuilding, citing Gal. 1.8; 1 Cor. 5.1–5; 8.1–2; 10.23; 14.37–38 (1978: 200).

What we encounter, therefore, in the Pauline churches is 'open' institutionalisation becoming increasingly 'controlled' as time passes. MacDonald expresses this process well in her use of three stages of institutionalisation in the Pauline churches: 'community-building', 'community-stabilising' and 'community-protecting' institutionalisation. The Pastoral Epistles clearly reflect the latest stage in this institutionalisation process with their emphasis on the received tradition.[12] In addition, they reflect the move towards the charisma of office noted by Weber with the increasing institutionalisation of the requirements of the office holder.[13]

The analyses above combine to support the view that the Pastorals reflect the institutionalisation of the Pauline communities. This, of course, has been the predominant view of scholarship on the Pastoral Epistles. The sociological analysis thus far suggests that the scholarly consensus is well founded. However, this position is usually accompanied by the view that the vitality of the charismatic moment inevitably declined with increasing institutionalisation. I suggest on the contrary that, alongside the undoubted process of institutionalisation, account needs to be taken of the persistence of the charismatic moment, and it is to this matter that I now turn.

3. *Thaumaturgical Persistence*

a. *Introduction*
There is no dispute that the Pauline congregations began as charismatic communities. Dunn, after a careful discussion of the nature of authority in the Pauline communities, sums this up well:

> Paul thinks of each of his churches as a charismatic community... Charismata are not some optional extra which a church may lack and yet remain the body of Christ. On the contrary, *charismata are the living actions of the body of Christ. The body of Christ only comes to realization in any place through the manifestations of grace.* 'Body of Christ' and 'charismatic community' are synonymous expressions of Paul's ecclesiology. Without community, charisma is both rootless and fruitless; but without charisma, community is both graceless and lifeless (1975: 297, his italics).

Dunn also subscribes to the view that the Pastorals represent evidence of the institutionalisation of the Pauline communities. He points in particular to the fading of the parousia hope, the emergence of a concept of charisma of office rather than charisma as the free manifestation of the Spirit through any member of the community, and the crystallization of faith into a coherent body of tradition (1977: 344–62). He concludes:

> Early Catholicism is the typical second generation solidifying and standardizing of forms and patterns which were much more spontaneously diverse in the enthusiasm of the first generation, so that, for example, the institutionalization of the Pastorals is the post-Pauline reaction to the failure of the Pauline vision of char-

---

12. For example, 1 Tim. 1.10b–11; 6.3, 20; 2 Tim. 1.13–14; 2.2; Tit. 1.9.
13. 1 Tim. 3.1–13; Tit. 1.5–9.

ismatic community to provide an enduring structure of internal and inter-church relationships (1977: 364).

Dunn thus concurs with the analysis of the Pastorals presented so far in this chapter. In addition, he subscribes to the view that the Pastorals represent the fading of Paul's vision of charismatic community (in the second sense defined in the introduction to this chapter):

> Clearly then [in the Pastorals] the vision of charismatic community has faded, ministry and authority have become the prerogative of the few, *the experience of the Christ-Spirit has lost its vitality*, the preservation of the past has become more important than openness to the present and future (1975: 349, my emphasis).

Dunn articulates the scholarly consensus well: institutionalisation is accompanied by the loss of vitality of charismatic experience. Nevertheless, the question remains as to whether this must inevitably be the case. Does charisma necessarily become attenuated or even die out with the passage of time, or can it persist or even intensify over time? This question does not appear to have been adequately addressed. The Pastorals can clearly be shown to demonstrate the process of institutionalisation described above and the analysis usually stops at this point. However, I shall seek to show below that, in certain situations, charisma continues to persist and may even intensify. If this is the case, the question then becomes: do the Pastorals simply represent the (inevitable) institutionalisation of Pauline charismatic communities or are they themselves, at least in part, a response to *increasing* charismatic enthusiasm in those communities? Weber's definition of charisma is deliberately broad in order to encompass charisma arising in different spheres. In order to focus the discussion I want to concentrate specifically on that form of religious charisma known as thaumaturgy.[14] So as to avoid confusion I shall be working with Wilson's definition of thaumaturgy as the highly individualistic demand for supernatural help in the form of miracles and oracles[15] (1973: 24–25).

---

14. Weber himself employs charisma in this sense in connection with the sociology of religion. He notes that it is not every person that has 'the capacity to achieve the ecstatic states which are viewed, in accordance with primitive experience, as the pre-conditions for producing certain effects in meteorology, healing, divination, and telepathy. It is primarily, though not exclusively, these extraordinary powers that have been designated by such special terms as 'mana', 'orenda', and the Iranian 'maga' (the term from which our word 'magic' is derived). We shall henceforth employ the term 'charisma' for such extraordinary powers' (1968: 400). It is not surprising, therefore, that there is confusion in the scholarly literature. From now on the terms charisma and thaumaturgy are utilised interchangeably unless otherwise indicated. Charisma, in the classic Weberian sense (concerning a form of leadership and structure of authority), will be referred to as 'charismatic authority'.

15. Charismatic phenomena in the Pauline communities were, of course, wider than this definition of thaumaturgy; nevertheless, miraculous and oracular phenomena are recorded in Paul's listing of the charismata in 1 Cor. 12.8–11 (e.g. gifts of healing, the working of miracles, prophecy, speaking in tongues, etc.). Paul speaks of signs, wonders and mighty works accompanying his apostolic ministry (Rom. 16.19; 2 Cor. 12.12; cf. Gal. 3.5). There can be no doubt, therefore, that there were thaumaturgical aspects to the Pauline communities.

b. *Christianizing the Roman Empire*

MacMullen sets out to answer the question as to how, by 400 CE, Christianity had succeeded in successfully displacing or suppressing the other religions of the Roman empire's population. He begins at the close of the New Testament period in 100 CE. At that point in time he notes:

> Had the church been wiped off the face of the earth at the end of the first century, its disappearance would have caused no dislocation in the empire, just as its presence was hardly noticed at the time. I think no one would dispute that – or expect any more exact measurement of Christianity's weight. Simply, it did not count (1984: viii).

MacMullen, in common with other historians, recognises the crucial significance of the conversion of Constantine in 312 CE and the subsequent Edict of Milan the following year. Nevertheless, prior to 312 CE, the church already predominated in at least one area at the beginning of the second century,[16] and by the beginning of the fourth century had about five million members.[17] Consequently, MacMullen analyses the growth of the church in three periods: prior to 312 CE; 312 – around 380 CE when the church was gaining ascendancy and material benefits began to accrue to those belonging to the church; and the last decades of the fourth century when the church had grown confident enough to produce conversion by coercion. It is the first of these periods which is of particular interest to this study.

MacMullen notes that the rate of growth in the period prior to 312 CE is puzzling. Such growth cannot be accounted for in terms of the influence of the intellectual elite. Even if the elite included many Christians, non-Christians did not tend to read Christian writings. In any case the majority of Christian literature was intended for internal consumption. Scholars are generally agreed that even the Apologetic literature served mainly for internal use.[18] Furthermore, at least three-quarters of the population were illiterate. Consequently, the only real explanation of growth has to be found in the context of face-to-face encounters. Once again, at this point, we must discount the influence of Christian intellectuals. Encounters between Christians and non-Christians at this level were rare.

> The reason was social. The church before Constantine had only a tiny share in what was at all times a tiny segment of the population, the elite; and the setting

16. The success of Christianity in and around one of the small coastal towns of Pontus, according to Pliny the Younger writing around 112 CE, was such that pagan temples had been deserted, religious ceremonies had fallen into disuse, and there was little demand for meat from sacrificial victims. Pliny, *Ep.* 10.96.9–10.

17. MacMullen arrives at this estimate for 300 CE 'by supposing an empire of 60 millions and Christians close to a tenth within the eastern provinces (which were more populous)' (1984: 135 n. 26). He goes on to note that an estimate either twice as large, or only half as large, would be 'almost demonstrably wrong'. Stark (1996: 4–13) has refined this estimate by projecting growth at 40 per cent per decade through to the middle of the fourth century CE. This gives a figure of just over six million Christians for 300 CE. Stark notes that the average growth rate experienced by the Mormon church over the last century has been 43 per cent per decade and is happy to conclude that 'the actual number of Christians in the year 300 lay within the range of 5–7.5 million' (1996: 6).

18. According to MacMullen (1984: 21, 131 n. 14).

usually assigned to its leaders is the catechetical schools, to which were admitted
only persons already converted (1984: 33).[19]

This leaves contact with the broad ranks of ordinary people as the prime means of
growth. However, the question remains as to how they were reached. It was often
dangerous to give evangelising speeches in public. Celsus, writing at some point
in the second half of the second century CE, notes, concerning the Christians, 'if
anyone does still wander about in secret, yet he is sought out and condemned to
death'.[20] Nevertheless, there certainly were Christian wanderers who evangelised.[21]
Furthermore, in at least some instances, wonder-working formed an integral part of
their message.[22] Miracles, MacMullen argues, and, in particular, exorcisms were
likely to lead to mass conversions when they occurred in the public arena. Speaking of miracles which demonstrated the superior power of the Christians' god over
other gods, MacMullen states:

> Driving all competition from the field head-on was crucial. The world, after all,
> held many dozens and hundreds of gods. Choice was open to everybody. It could
> thus be only a most exceptional force that would actually displace alternatives and
> compel allegiance; it could be only the most probative demonstrations that would
> work. We should therefore assign as much weight to this, the chief instrument of
> conversion, as the best, earliest reporters do (1984: 27).[23]

In other words, thaumaturgy was at the heart of public conversion to Christianity.
MacMullen regards thaumaturgy, rather than potential social and psychological
rewards, as the prime factor in such conversions.

Apart from the success of itinerant Christian wonder-workers the growth of
Christianity must be accounted for in terms of steady evangelising in private
settings. Such evangelism can be seen to be highly significant when it is noted,
despite the effects of individual wonder-workers, 'that, after Saint Paul, the church
had no mission, it made no organized or official approach to unbelievers; rather, it
left everything to the individual' (1984: 34). Celsus himself demonstrates this to
be the case. He not only refers to those who 'display their secret lore in the market
places', but also to the 'wool-workers, cobblers, laundry-workers, and the most

19. Although the point is valid, MacMullen overstates his case. Schools, catechetical or
otherwise, were not necessarily as closed as MacMullen implies. Alexander (1995) argues that
there were both public and private school settings.

20. Origen, *C. Celsum* 8.69.

21. MacMullen insists that these wanderers should be largely discounted as they directed their
attention primarily to existing believers. However, the evidence which he cites (3 Jn 5–8; *Didache*
11–13; Origen, *C. Celsum* 3.9) does not seem to me to point conclusively in this direction.

22. Eusebius, *H.E.* 3.37. Celsus' reference to those Christians who 'display their secret lore (τὰ
ἐπιρρητότα) in the market-places' (Origen, *C. Celsum* 3.50) probably refers to thaumaturgical
practice. See MacMullen (1984: 137 n. 32). Cf. especially Gregory the Wonder-worker operating
in Pontus around the middle of the third century CE, (1984: 59–61).

23. MacMullen cites Justin, Irenaeus, Tertullian, Cyprian, the Acts of Peter, and the example of
Gregory the Wonder-worker. He notes that: 'On occasion, exorcisms are specified as the cause of
conversion – in Ephesus…in Palestine, Italy, Africa, or Gaul' (1984: 28, 134 n. 9).

illiterate and bucolic yokels' who expound their beliefs in private houses.[24] The normal points of contact for ordinary Christians with non-Christians 'lay quite inevitably at street-corners or at places of employment, or in the working quarters of dwellings, just as Celsus says…' (1984: 40). MacMullen goes on to argue that in such private settings any conversation about religion would most likely concentrate on the relief of sickness or deformity. To demonstrate this point MacMullen constructs a hypothetical scenario:

> Testing to see if I can imagine in some detail a scene that conflicts with no point of the little that is known about conversion in the second and third centuries, I would choose the room of some sick person: there, a servant talking to a mistress, or one spouse to another, saying, perhaps, 'Unquestionably they can help, if you believe. And I know, I have seen, I have heard, they have related to me, they have books, they have a special person, a sort of officer. It is true. Besides and anyway, if you don't believe, then you are doomed when a certain time comes, so say the prophecies; whereas, if you do, then they can help even in great sickness. I know people who have seen or who have spoken with others who have seen. And healing is even the least that they tell. Theirs is truly a God all-powerful. He has worked a hundred wonders'. So a priest is sent for, or an exorcist; illness is healed; the household after that counts as Christian; it is baptized; and through instruction it comes to accept the first consequences: that all other cults are false and wicked, all seeming gods, the same (1984: 40–41).

MacMullen thus argues that the working of miracles, both in public and private settings, was crucial to the growth of Christianity prior to Constantine. He recognises that non-Christian wonders were equally reported and believed. However, in the latter case such believers were not lost to paganism – they simply added one more god to those they venerated. In the case of Christianity the difference lay in its exclusivity – to believe in the Christian god was to deny all other gods (1984: 108–109).

Although MacMullen is convinced of the importance of thaumaturgy for the growth of Christianity he recognises that the evidence is sparse. Nevertheless, he is prepared to state: 'If the evidence for steady evangelizing in private settings…is combined with the evidence for successes en masse, the two in combination do seem to me adequate to explain what we know happened' (1984: 29). If MacMullen is right then it is clear that, *far from disappearing, thaumaturgy persisted and, in some cases, intensified throughout the second and third centuries CE*. In view of the importance of this observation I will examine two other works analysing contemporary phenomena which add weight to MacMullen's convictions concerning the importance of thaumaturgy.[25]

24. Origen, *C. Celsum* 3.55.
25. MacMullen's conclusions that the growth of Christianity must be accounted for by a combination of conversions in private settings and conversions en masse by thaumaturgical means have been called into question by Stark (1996) who demonstrates, for example, the effectiveness of social networks and survival rates of Christians in epidemics as prime factors which adequately account for the growth rate. Nevertheless, in connection with epidemics, Stark is prepared to concede that 'a much superior Christian survival rate hardly could seem other than miraculous' (1996: 90). It seems to me that MacMullen, using evidence based on his extensive acquaintance

c. *Ecstatic Religion*

Lewis (1989) examines a wide variety of ecstatic forms of religion. By this he means those forms of religion which regard highly the seizure of human beings by divinity. Such transcendental experiences are typically understood as states of 'possession' and generally involve trance-like states of mental dissociation. As those who are thus possessed are typically sought out to cure illnesses, control the weather, or pronounce oracles, the phenomenon of ecstasy falls within the ambit of thaumaturgy as defined above. It is beyond the scope of this study to interact in any detail with Lewis' work. What is of significance are Lewis' conclusions concerning the factors which enable ecstatic phenomena to persist over time.

Lewis distinguishes between what he calls central and peripheral possession cults. The latter tend to involve women and those from the lower strata of society. Lewis argues that this form of possession functions as an oblique strategy of protest against discrimination in highly stratified societies.

> In addition to explaining illness, peripheral possession can thus be seen to serve an oblique aggressive strategy. The possessed person is ill through no fault of his own. The illness requires treatment which his (or her) master has to provide. In his state of possession the patient is a highly privileged person: he is allowed many liberties with those whom in other circumstances he is required to treat with respect. Moreover, however costly and inconvenient for those to whom his normal status renders him subservient, his cure is often incomplete. Lapses are likely to occur whenever difficulties develop with his superiors. Clearly, in this context, possession works to help the interests of the weak and downtrodden who have otherwise few effective means to press their claims for attention and respect (1989: 27–28).

Consequently, in societies which recognise ecstatic religion, ecstatic phenomena continually recur amongst the marginalised and oppressed. Lewis further argues convincingly that in such societies these forms of protest are controlled and contained by the use of witchcraft allegations. Those subordinate men or women who have become leading shamans tend to be singled out for denunciation as witches. Such accusations of witchcraft on the part of those of higher social status serve to discredit the subordinate shamans and diminish their status. 'Thus, if possession is the means by which the underdog bids for attention, witchcraft accusations provide the countervailing strategy by which such demands are kept within bounds' (1989: 109). On the other hand, should such peripheral cults succeed in gaining such popularity that they succeed in supplanting the old established order and become new establishment religions, ecstatic phenomena tend to become themselves marginalised and treated as potentially subversive. At this point we are on the familiar ground of the institutionalisation of charisma. Lewis illustrates this in a Western context with reference to the Quakers but then notes:

with ancient sources, has succeeded in drawing attention to the persistence of thaumaturgy into the second and third centuries CE, even if thaumaturgical demonstrations did not lead to the mass conversions he postulates.

> Where, however, such cults do not attain a comparable degree of acceptance, or are passively opposed or even actively persecuted, as long as they retain the support of oppressed sections of the community, possessional inspiration is likely to continue with unabated vigour. This is the situation with most Pentecostal movements, and in the independent or separatist churches in Africa and America and elsewhere... (1989: 118).

Central possession cults, on the other hand, are not cults of the oppressed or marginalised. In these cults those who are possessed by spirits are at the centre of the religious life of the community, and play a crucial and direct role in the establishing and monitoring of customary morality.

> Far from simply expressing obliquely the tolerated protests of the underprivileged against the dominion of their earthly masters, possession is now the idiom in which those who contend for the leadership in the central religious life of the community press their claims for recognition as the chosen agents of the gods. Shamanism is now no longer a special form of particularist protest, but, on the contrary, a central religious institution fulfilling...a host of functions which vary with the social structure in which it is embedded (1989: 119).

In the case of these central possession cults, Lewis recognises the potential for the attenuation or extinction of enthusiasm through the process of institutionalisation. However, the fact remains that central possession cults do 'not always develop established priesthoods which would render enthusiasm redundant' (1989: 157). Lewis argues that, for ecstasy to continue in these cults, there have to be overwhelming physical and/or social pressures creating a situation of general instability for small and fluctuating social groups. Consequently, according to Lewis, both peripheral and central possession cults imply the existence of acute pressures. In the case of peripheral cults these pressures arise from the oppression of marginalised members of society. In the case of central cults these pressures are external to the society as a whole and are felt by everyone.

Lewis' analysis is highly suggestive for the Pastorals. For, although Pauline Christianity cannot be classed as a whole as 'ecstatic' due to Paul's concern for order in congregational meetings and his stress on the cognitive content of the gospel, there were undoubtedly ecstatic elements to it (at least at Corinth).[26] Given this ecstatic element, according to Lewis this is likely to persist as a form of 'peripheral possession cult' amongst the marginalised within the community. In this connection it is interesting to note that, according to the author of the Pastorals, women are particularly prone to falling prey to the opposition. As Pauline Christianity cannot be classified *in toto* as 'ecstatic', Lewis' analysis of central possession cults is not relevant. The highlighting of the possibility of the persistence of ecstatic phenomena amongst marginalized groups within a community by Lewis forms an important corrective to the view that Pauline Christianity simply institutionalised

---

26. Paul's concern to impose order and to stress cognitive content in his discussion of the charismata in 1 Cor. 12–14 strongly suggests that the situation there was out of control and that ecstatic, dissociative states were prevalent in the Corinthian community.

over time. At this point it is necessary to move from the focus on ecstatic religion to thaumaturgy generally in order to extend Lewis' conclusions.

d. *The Thaumaturgical Response to the World*

In his 1973 work, Wilson extended and refined his earlier typology of sects which had previously been based specifically on Christian sects. In this later monograph, Wilson deliberately seeks to construct a set of ideal types which serve to categorise new religious movements (NRMs) generally, and not just those arising in a Christian context. He therefore seeks to move away from the church-sect typology utilised by both Troeltsch (1931) and Niebuhr (1929). In focusing on NRMs Wilson's work is both more general and more specific than Lewis'. It is more general in that it is concerned with all types of religious response, not just ecstatic ones. It is more specific in that it is concerned with new movements, rather than established religious movements which are the focus of Lewis' analysis. Wilson begins by recognising that every sectarian movement manifests some degree of tension with the world. Any NRM must, therefore, have some soteriological element to it. Any religious response involves the seeking of salvation in a world in which human beings feel the need for some form of supernatural help. NRMs seek such salvation in some other way than through the orthodox or dominant religious tradition. Wilson proceeds from this fundamental insight to construct a sevenfold typology of NRMs in terms of their response to the world. Each response to the world involves a different conception of the nature of evil and, consequently, of the ways in which it can be overcome.

i. *Wilson's Typology of NRMs*. 1. The *conversionist* response sees the world as corrupt due to the corruption of human beings. Salvation, therefore, involves a supernatural transformation of the self. This does not change the nature of the objective world, but fundamentally changes one's subjective orientation to it. Salvation involves a conversion experience, and the conversionist response 'is not concerned simply with recruitment to a movement, but with the acquisition of a change of heart' (1973: 22–23).

2. The *revolutionist* response sees the world as so corrupt that only its supernaturally wrought destruction will save humanity. This destruction results in the creation of a transformed new order in which salvation is experienced. This salvation is conceived of as imminent.

3. The *introversionist* response sees the world as irredeemably evil and so salvation can only be attained by the fullest possible withdrawal from the world. Such a response may be an individual one, but in terms of a movement it results in separated communities preoccupied with their own holiness and means of isolation from the wider society. Salvation is achieved only by belonging to such a community.

4. The *manipulationist* response conceives of salvation in distinctly this-worldly terms. What is required is not the transformation of the self, nor the destruction of the world, nor withdrawal from the world; rather, salvation involves supernaturally acquired new techniques to overcome the problems of the world. 'It is the scarce goods of this world – health, wealth, longevity, happiness, success, and high status

– which constitute the saved condition. Illness, incapacity, pain, poverty, and death are the things from which one seeks to be saved' (1973: 24).

5. The *thaumaturgical* response has a narrower conception of salvation than that of the manipulationist response, and is essentially particularistic. As this is the specific response with which this section is concerned, I will give Wilson's definition in full:

> The individual's concern is relief from present and specific ills by special dispensations. The demand for supernatural help is personal and local: its operation is magical. Salvation is immediate but has no general application beyond the given case and others like it. There is little likelihood of generalizing this response or producing elaborate ideological formulations for it: where doctrine is developed it is often of little importance in the attainment of salvation. Healing, assuagement of grief, restoration after loss, reassurance, the foresight and avoidance of calamity, and the guarantee of external [*sic*] (or at least continuing) life after death are the elements of the salvation which is sought. The evils feared are all highly specific, and it is from their particular incidence (not from their universal operation) that salvation is sought. *Miracles and oracles, rather than the comprehension of new principles about life, are the instruments of salvation in this case* (1973: 24–25, my emphasis).

6. The *reformist* response seeks to reform the world by means of supernaturally given insights as to the ways in which social organization should be amended. This response seeks salvation in the present world through its gradual transformation. This orientation results in a much larger element of accommodation to the wider society than in the previous responses.

7. The *utopian* response seeks the entire reconstruction of the present world according to divinely given principles. It is much more radical than the reformist response in that it insists on the complete replacement of social organization.

Wilson goes on to note that the revolutionist, thaumaturgical, and conversionist responses 'place far greater emphasis on the autonomous operation of the supernatural than do the others' (1973: 28). Wilson's work specifically concentrates on tribal and third-world peoples; in this context manipulationist, reformist, and utopian types are unlikely. He also notes that in the early stages of culture contact '*indigenous* and *spontaneous* conversionist and introversionist sects are equally unlikely' (1973: 48, his italics). His work consequently focuses on thaumaturgical and revolutionist sects in the context of tribal and third-world peoples.

ii. *The Cultural Conditions Necessary for a Thaumaturgical Response.* Wilson notes that thaumaturgical practice in less developed societies tends to form part of the traditional religion itself. New thaumaturgical movements arising in this context do not, therefore, offer a distinctive type of response. They tend to arise for one or both of two reasons: the perception that traditional religious procedures are inadequate (particularly following the impact of a superior culture), and/or out of reaction to attempts to prohibit traditional practices on the part of the new authorities. Wilson notes that these thaumaturgical movements display remarkable similarities even though they may come from widely differing cultural contexts. A constant factor appears to be that they occur in situations of prolonged instability caused by the impact of a foreign culture on the traditional culture. For example,

Wilson compares 'Zionist' churches of South Africa with the movements known collectively as *Pocomania* in Jamaica. Despite the different cultural contexts, thaumaturgical practice in these two groups is broadly similar. Wilson notes that both societies 'have been characterized by unstable patterns of social and familial relationships…racial antagonisms; the strong sense of persistent exploitation; populations that are largely illiterate and that lack, and often seek, authoritative interpretations of their social circumstances and expectations' (1973: 60). Wilson's conclusion that new thaumaturgical movements emerge in conditions of prolonged instability corresponds closely to Lewis' description of the conditions necessary for the persistence of ecstasy in ecstatic religions – namely, a situation of general instability arising either out of the oppression or marginalisation of a minority group, or the sense of threat to the community as a whole.[27] It would appear, therefore, that questions arising out of Lewis' analysis concerning the persistence of ecstatic movements may be cautiously applied to thaumaturgical movements generally. However, Wilson's analysis of the conditions necessary for *thaumaturgical* persistence are of even greater value for this study.

iii. *Thaumaturgical Persistence.* Wilson points out that most thaumaturgical movements, by their very nature, tend to be transient and local in character. Movements typically evolve around the magical powers of a thaumaturge and, consequently, quickly die out following the death of the leader. Alternatively, movements may fulfil a cleansing and purifying function such as the purging of an area of witches; once again, such movements either move on or wither once the specific mission is accomplished. Nevertheless, the demands for thaumaturgy, in terms of healing, reassurance, and protection, are persistent and endemic in less advanced societies. This persistent demand for thaumaturgy means that new thaumaturgical movements may continually arise in quick succession around new thaumaturges. On the other hand, some thaumaturgical movements do persist as recognisable movements over a considerable period of time. Wilson notes the following possibilities for such thaumaturgical persistence:

First, the thaumaturge may train a number of apprentices who eventually establish themselves as thaumaturges in their own right. This pattern does not really effectively result in a single widespread thaumaturgical movement. For, what tends to happen is that there is just a diffusion of a set of practices through local operators. Usually there is no effective central control and so there is a strong tendency for localism and the emergence of rivalries between practitioners.

Second, various thaumaturges may come together to form some sort of league or association. This pattern has evolved in Brazil. Nevertheless, such associations

---

27. Both scholars, of course, recognise that there may be other responses to such conditions of instability than thaumaturgy or ecstasy – for example, political revolution. They are simply pointing out that these factors seem to be necessary for the emergence of thaumaturgy or the persistence of ecstatic religion, not that they are sufficient. Wilson is very clear that each thaumaturgical movement has to be examined in detail to arrive at causal explanations specific to that movement. He also notes: 'There are cases of societies in which economic exploitation, relative deprivation, cultural shock, and anomie are identifiable but in which…we have no reports of new cults of popular thaumaturgy' (1973: 498–99).

have proved to be extremely fragile and, in any case, tend to be much more suited to urban contexts than rural ones.

Thirdly, thaumaturgy may itself become institutionalised by assimilating itself to older patterns of religious practice within a society. In this case thaumaturgical practice 'may, rather like a secret society, acquire a certain stability and persistence as an integrated part of the social system. In such cases it is assimilated to, or becomes a facet of, traditional religious preoccupations' (1973: 150). This category appears to resemble Lewis' 'central possession cult'.

Fourthly, thaumaturgical movements may succeed in institutionalising the oracular and the miraculous in such a way that they become integral to the life of the community without losing their immediacy and spontaneity. This typically happens in movements which adopt patterns of organisation from the conversionist model exported from western societies. In this case the movement typically consists of a number of congregations all of whose members seek personal blessings. Spiritual power is no longer concentrated in the hands of a single thaumaturge but is diffused throughout the congregation. Everyone, therefore, in the context of the congregation, is a potential thaumaturge. Individual thaumaturges may still arise within such movements, but they are either integrated into the institutionalised leadership, or they inevitably leave and found their own movements. Wilson argues that it is the diffusion of charisma which appears to be decisive in creating such relatively permanent thaumaturgical movements.

It is this fourth case which is highly relevant to this study. Wilson argues that thaumaturgy can be institutionalised and thus persist *without losing its immediacy and spontaneity* precisely in situations where thaumaturgical practice is combined with a conversionist orientation and model.

> The thaumaturgical response…is a recurrent, and as yet inextinguishable, characteristic of religion… It stands in tension, often, with the revolutionist response; but it is much more readily accommodated in conversionist movements. The conversionist model, exported from more advanced societies, has perhaps provided the best organizational base for the thaumaturgical response; it provides, in the emotional freedom on which conversionism relies, a context suitable for wonder-working and the distribution of special, particularized benisons. Local discretion is often sufficient to allow considerable latitude in the interpretation of basic teachings, and doctrine is never a supreme concern of conversionist movements. The emphasis on a heart-experience can readily accommodate the direct operation of the deity in offering miracles, even if these contravene the specific expectations which a conversionist movement – at its most doctrinally pure – would acknowledge as legitimate. The amalgamation of conversionist orientations and the demand for wonders, healings, and reassurance, is perhaps the most effective pattern of regulation for thaumaturgy (1973: 131).

4. *Conclusion*

Weber's analysis of charismatic authority does have rich analytical power. Nevertheless, his own analysis resulted in a concept of charismatic authority as inherently unstable and transient. He failed to see adequately that charismatic authority itself has built into it institutionalising tendencies; for any charismatic movement, to earn the right to be classified as a movement, must seek for a degree of permanence. Holmberg has persuasively argued that the Pauline churches themselves display the characteristics of the institutionalisation of charismatic authority. Although the process of institutionalisation is initially 'open', and can consequently proceed in many directions, institutionalisation becomes less free to develop in any direction as time passes and a body of sacred tradition is built up. Increasingly any innovation in the church has to be seen as fundamentally in accordance with existing sacred tradition. The Pastorals clearly reflect this stage of the institutionalisation process which MacDonald has aptly named 'community-protecting institutionalisation'. Nevertheless, despite this scholarly consensus that the Pastorals reflect the institutionalisation of charismatic authority in the Pauline communities, I have sought to show in this chapter that such a position does not represent the whole picture. MacMullen argues for thaumaturgical persistence as a key factor in the growth of the church prior to Constantine. Nevertheless, he admits that we simply do not have sufficient evidence to demonstrate this conclusively. Consequently, I have sought to supplement his work with two contemporary studies in the fields of anthropology and the sociology of religion. Lewis' study suggests that ecstatic religion persists either within one segment of society which has been marginalised, or within a society as a whole when that society is inherently unstable due to the threat of external pressures. I have suggested that Lewis' conclusions are relevant, particularly in connection with women in the Pastorals. For women seem to have played a prominent role in promoting ecstatic religion in Corinth.[28] Furthermore, Wilson has demonstrated that similar conditions to those elucidated by Lewis are necessary for the emergence of new thaumaturgical movements generally. As there were clearly thaumaturgical elements to Pauline Christianity, this at least leads to the conclusion that questions arising out of Lewis' analysis can be legitimately posed to the Pastorals.

In addition, Wilson has demonstrated that the thaumaturgical response persists most effectively when it is combined with a conversionist movement. This is highly suggestive for the Pauline communities can best be classified as conversionist in orientation.[29] Given the thaumaturgical element to Pauline Christianity, we have precisely the appropriate mix for thaumaturgical persistence according to

28. See Wire (1990).

29. Paul's letters continually reflect his concern to proclaim the gospel. The successful result of this proclamation includes Gentiles turning to God from idols (1 Thess. 1.9). He can rejoice that Christ is proclaimed whatever the motive behind such proclamation (Phil. 1.15–18). Paul's concern is to proclaim the gospel in areas which have not yet been evangelised (Rom. 15.18–24). Paul's communitarian emphasis is not combined with a desire to withdraw from the world; his communities cannot be classified, therefore, as introversionist. Furthermore, although Paul believed in the imminent parousia of Christ (1 Cor. 15.51; 1 Thess. 4.17), and there was a millenarian element to his teaching (e.g. Rom. 8.18–25), his letters do not focus on the coming overturn of the present world order; thus Pauline Christianity cannot be properly classified as revolutionist either. In addition, as 1 Corinthians especially exemplifies, Pauline Christianity was not gnostic or manipulationist (e.g. 1 Cor. 8.1–3). As Johnson states, remarking on 1 Cor. 2.6–7: 'This wisdom is not the revelation of esoteric cosmic realities but a profound, even connatural, learning of the ways of the Spirit's working among the people (1 Cor. 2.12)' (1986: 277). Finally, the millenarian element in Paul's teaching precludes Pauline Christianity being classified as either reformist or utopian.

Wilson. However, Wilson's analysis concerns tribal and third-world contexts. He is not at all convinced that thaumaturgical persistence can be sustained in a western context, and that, therefore, his conclusions can be more widely applied. He believes that the thaumaturgical response is highly attenuated and marginalised in western society. Instead contemporary demand for magic in a western context is found within the new manipulationist sects of the modern world. Wilson's caution concerning our own contemporary context suggests that we cannot easily switch from his analysis of contemporary third-world thaumaturgy to the Pauline communities in the final quarter of the first century CE. However, in the following chapter I shall seek to show that Wilson, writing as he did in 1973, inevitably underestimated the impact of the charismatic movement on western Christianity. The charismatic movement, I shall argue by examining one particular Christian NRM, demonstrates that Wilson's argument that thaumaturgical persistence is sustained in a conversionist context applies equally well to our contemporary western society. This analysis, as we shall see, demonstrates that the institutionalisation of charismatic authority and the intensification of the thaumaturgical response can occur simultaneously within a conversionist sect. Armed with the results of this analysis I shall then argue in a subsequent chapter that the Pastoral Epistles reflect both the institutionalisation of charismatic authority and the intensification of charisma, in the form of thaumaturgy, in the Pauline communities addressed.

Chapter 4

A CASE STUDY

1. *Introduction*

The history of the 'House Church Movement' or 'Restorationism' has been well documented by Walker (1998). In this chapter I shall be examining one particular Restorationist church and tracing its development over a twenty-five year period from the mid-1970s to the late 1990s. The church in question is Bristol Christian Fellowship (BCF) as I have detailed first-hand knowledge of this church. I was a member between 1974 and 1999; from 1984 to 1992 I was an elder in the church and between 1986 and 1992 I was a member of the salaried staff.

I shall begin by outlining the history of BCF from its beginning through to the end of 1999. I shall then give my own analysis of the tension between the ongoing institutionalisation of the church and the potential subversion of the institutionalising process by thaumaturgical demand. I am in a good position to give such an analysis as I have been an 'insider' from the outset through to the summer of 1992 and again from 1997 to 1999. I also observed a handful of meetings in 1994 and 1995 following the outbreak of what has come to be known as the 'Toronto Blessing' in mid-1994. However, I have also supplemented my observations with comments arising out of a questionnaire, which was sent out to every member of BCF in July 1999 who had also been a member in October 1991, and from detailed interviews with three members of BCF, two of whom are elders and have been involved from, or near, the beginning of the church.

2. *Beginnings*

BCF began with the merger of two groups in the summer of 1974. One group had been meeting in Patchway, a suburb in North Bristol, since the late 1960s. This group was led by Hugh Thompson. The second group met in Olveston, a village some ten miles north of Bristol, under the leadership of Peter Lyne. The latter group began meeting in Spring 1974 in Peter Lyne's home. I joined the Olveston group a few weeks after it began and before its merger with Patchway. At that time the Olveston group consisted mainly of students from Bristol University. Significantly, two original members of the group of seven (identified by Walker as at the heart of the emergence of Restorationism)[1] led the groups.

---

1.   Walker (1998: 75–82) identifies these seven as: Arthur Wallis, Peter Lyne, Bryn Jones, David Mansell, Graham Perrins, Hugh Thompson and John Noble.

Prior to the merger Hugh Thompson moved away from Bristol and Tony Pullin succeeded him as leader of the Patchway group. Shortly after this joint meetings were arranged between the two groups and, after a short period of time, the two groups merged under the overall leadership of Peter Lyne. The new fellowship (which eventually became known as BCF) began to grow slowly and a significant point was reached when a number of students, who at this time formed a sizeable proportion of BCF, graduated. Most of these students decided that their membership of BCF took priority over jobs and so only looked for work within Bristol in order to remain part of the fellowship. Nearly everyone did find work within Bristol and thus the potential decimation of what, at that time, was still a very small group was avoided.

In 1977 Peter Lyne and his family moved to New Zealand in order to plant a new church along Restorationist lines. Tony Pullin took over the leadership but after a short period handed over to Dave Day who had also been involved with the Patchway group from its formation. Some time later Dave Day too left for a period to work with Peter Lyne in New Zealand, but not before a leadership team had been formed around him. Dave Day was succeeded by Steve Hepden, who was one of the key members of the leadership team at that time. This quick succession of leadership in its formative years meant that BCF had to face Weber's problem of the succession of charismatic authority very early on. In each case the existing leader appointed the new leader with general approval from the membership. Another consequence of the rapid succession of leadership was that no one person was in a position of leadership long enough to dominate the overall life of the fellowship. What could have been a period of great instability as one leader succeeded another was not experienced that way by the members of the fellowship due to the necessary emergence of strong team leadership which served to alleviate the inevitable problems when one leader is succeeded by another. Under Steve Hepden's leadership, for example, a team of four elders emerged with Hepden functioning as *primus inter pares*. This team leadership, functioning as Weber's 'charismatic staff', provided a sense of continuity. From its inception, therefore, BCF experienced both charismatic authority and its routinisation in the way suggested by Holmberg's refinement of Weber discussed in Chapter 3 above.

3. *Distinctives*

a. *Christianity as an Everyday, Lived Reality*
From the beginning BCF wanted to get away from what was perceived as the religious formalism of the mainline Protestant denominations. The fellowship fostered a strong sense of friendship and community among its members. Although not subscribing to a commune mentality, members regularly exchanged possessions, shared cars and generally sought to give one another practical aid. Acts 2.43–47 and 4.32–37 were favourite texts. The emphasis was on the lived reality of day-to-day Christian experience. Members were suspicious of any form of piety that engendered an 'other-worldly' mentality, labelling such as 'super-spirituality'. For example, an

early issue of *Fulness* magazine[2] was devoted to healthy living.[3] In the editorial to this issue, Graham Perrins, another of Walker's original seven, writes:

> When Jesus said 'I have come in order that you might have life – life in all its fulness [sic]', some have limited his meaning to include only spiritual life. Life then becomes synonymous with conventions, ministry, prayer meetings, the baptism in the Holy Spirit or some such experience.
>
> Nothing could be further from the truth. Life for Jesus could mean nothing less than a full-orbed experience of God's provision for the whole man. God intended that man should enjoy creation, that the whole of life should vibrate with his love, the common and mundane throb with his glory, the small and insignificant fulfil his purpose.
>
> Some Christians are so intense in their spirituality that they cannot relax and enjoy God or his creation. They have an aura of religiosity that casts a shadow on the simple things of life…
>
> The division between sacred and secular is so often artificial and cloaks much unreality. This issue stresses the need to bring food, exercise, and the home, as much as ourselves, into the realm of God's kingdom.[4]

b. *Conversionist*

BCF is an evangelical fellowship and, as such, is best classified as 'conversionist' according to Bryan Wilson's sevenfold typology of new religious movements.[5] The world is viewed as corrupt because of the corruption of human beings. Consequently, the world can only be transformed by the transformation of human beings. However, human beings are incapable of bringing about their own transformation; divine intervention is the only way of achieving transformation. As Wilson (1973: 22–23) rightly highlights, conversionist movements are 'not concerned simply with recruitment to a movement, but with the acquisition of a change of heart'.

c. *The Charismatic Dimension*

BCF, like other Restorationist churches, grew out of the Charismatic Movement which began to affect the mainline Christian denominations in the 1960s. As such there was an emphasis on the restoration of the χαρίσματα of 1 Cor. 12–14. A doctrine of baptism in the Spirit as a second experience, in line with Pentecostal teaching, was espoused. Members were encouraged to seek spiritual gifts and use them in congregational meetings. Glossolalia, together with corresponding interpretation and prophecy, were particularly encouraged. Whilst not insisting, in Assemblies of God fashion, on glossolalia as *the* sign of baptism in the Holy

---

2.   This was a magazine published by that stream of Restorationism labelled by Walker as 'R2'. Many members of BCF had a subscription to this publication. No issues of the magazine were dated. Volume 30 was the last issue of *Fulness* published. It was succeeded in March 1982 by the short-lived *Dovetail* magazine.

3.   *Fulness* 12; this particular issue includes articles on being honest, enjoying life, wholefoods (including a recipe for 100 per cent wholemeal bread), playing squash, coping with pressure, and interior design.

4.   *Fulness* 12: 3.

5.   Wilson (1973: 18–30).

Spirit, nevertheless standard teaching was that all who were baptised in the Spirit had the potential to exercise glossolalia. There was thus a very real tension between the emphasis on being real in everyday Christian living and the corresponding suspicion of a 'super-spiritual' piety on the one hand, and the desire for spiritual gifts on the other.

d. *Eschatology*

As well as the conversionist and charismatic strands BCF also contained a powerful millenarian element in its early teaching. There was a sense of eschatological imminence. Much of the rhetoric concerned the possibility of the church at large reaching maturity within one generation and thus heralding Christ's *parousia*. There was much teaching on the 'Ephesians 4 ministries' of apostle, prophet, evangelist, pastor and teacher which emphasised their eschatological role in bringing the church 'to the measure of the full stature of Christ' (Eph. 4.13).

In addition, teaching that emerged from the Latter Rain Movement[6] in Canada in the late 1940s concerning the 'manifest sons of God'[7] heavily influenced BCF. This teaching identified the 'overcomers' of Rev. 2–3, the 144,000 of Rev. 7 and 14, and the male child of Revelation 12 with a group of end-time Christians who would be perfected and enter into bodily resurrection in advance of Christ's *parousia*. The emergence of this company would signal the final events leading to Christ's *parousia* and the beginning of his millennial reign. It was fervently believed that the possibility existed that the current generation of Christians would see the emergence of these 'manifest sons of God' and members were encouraged to aspire to being one of this elite company.[8]

Charles Schmitt typifies such teaching:

> In yet a further vision of this final divine purpose, John sees the 'first fruits' brought forth upon the earth – first fruits of the plenteous harvest that is just about to be reaped. In Revelation chapter 14, John describes this spearhead of men and women as 'first fruits to God and to the Lamb', peculiarly set apart for the Lord himself. First fruits are an interesting happening. *Somehow first fruits heed the call to perfection first. And as such they are the prophetic forerunners, the spearhead of the harvest that is to follow. There is within first fruits an early response to God's call to maturity...*
>
> The Lord Jesus is presently pleased to call forth, just for himself, the prophetic first fruits of that great harvest, a prophetic herald of the *victory about to be born. And these are shaping up to be those among us who are passionately dogging his steps, in sensitive tune with him, following him with clean hands and a pure heart. O Lord Jesus, I want to be in that number.*[9]

---

6. This movement began in 1948 in Saskatchewan and is named after Joel 2.23 which predicts blessing from God in terms of 'former' and 'latter' rains (KJV). The 'former rain' was identified with Pentecost and the 'latter rain' with a final, great outpouring of the Spirit before the *parousia* of Christ which began with the Saskatchewan revival.

7. The phrase is taken from Rom. 8.19 in the KJV.

8. For further details see Oropeza (1995: 58–65).

9. Charles Schmitt, 'First Fruits', *Fulness* 19, p. 20, my emphasis.

As I shall seek to show below, the combination of conversionist, charismatic and millenarian elements in the formative years is crucial to BCF's subsequent development.

4. *Development*

Dave Day returned after two years in New Zealand working with Peter Lyne and took over the leadership of the fellowship again from Steve Hepden. Peter Lyne also returned to Bristol for a period in the mid-1980s. Peter, Dave and Steve, together with their wives Linda, Rhi and Chris, formed the Bridge Ministries Apostolic Team in 1984 with Raewyn Fraser, a New-Zealander who had worked with the Lynes and the Days in Auckland, arriving as team administrator in January 1985. The team began to work with a number of churches in Wales and the West Country and also functioned with a team of BCF leaders (myself included) as elders of BCF. In May 1985 Bridge Ministries and BCF ran a Spring Bank Holiday Celebration just north of Bristol – an event which attracted many Christians from the surrounding area. The event was so successful that it ran annually for several years. The following year saw the start of the 'Apostolic School' – an annual twelve week course for international church leaders with participants from Ghana, Zambia, India, New Zealand, USA, Norway, Switzerland, France and the UK.

The high profile which BCF enjoyed as a result of these and similar events meant that the 1980s was a period of rapid growth for BCF. The growth in numbers led to the purchase of BCF's first building, the Ark, to host regular meetings. A second building, Severn Ridge, was subsequently purchased to host training activities such as the Apostolic School. As the church grew the focus shifted from the small meetings in homes of the early days to much larger, centralised gatherings. Small home groups continued as a means of providing a pastoral base for every member but there was a significant shift of emphasis to larger meetings. The increase in numbers, together with the corresponding increasing focus on meetings, meant that the early emphasis on the church being a community of friends sharing everything in common, whilst always remaining a core value in the thinking of the leadership, was inevitably eroded. I can remember several periods in the early years when services were abandoned altogether in order to concentrate on building relationships between members of the church. This no longer happened once the church grew to a significant size. The very success of the church contributed to its increasing institutionalisation.

In addition, as large meetings multiplied, there was increasing scope for the exercise of spiritual gifts associated with the mainstream Charismatic Movement. John Wimber, from California, held a major 'Third Wave' conference in Britain in 1984.[10] Although at this time Wimber did not have a direct influence on BCF

10. Wimber was associated in the early 1980s with the missiological work of Peter Wagner at Fuller Theological Seminary in California. Wimber, and the Vineyard Fellowships which arose out of his ministry, associated the 'third wave' (the first wave being identified with classical Pentecostalism and the second wave with the Charismatic Renewal) with a grand scale religious awakening characterised by 'signs and wonders' as the primary means of evangelism. Walker (1998:

(few people from the church attended his conferences), nevertheless his profile within mainstream Renewal inevitably meant that his teachings and style of ministry percolated into the life of the church. Consequently, people with recognised charismatic healing and prophetic ministries were regularly welcomed. Words of knowledge[11] and personal prophecies to individuals proliferated. Indeed, Steve Hepden was recognised as being particularly gifted in these areas.

Thus the 1980s were a peculiar mix for BCF. On the one hand, the emphasis on meetings, training courses, the purchase of buildings, etc. were signs of increasing institutionalisation. On the other hand, the meetings themselves provided a vehicle for classic thaumaturgical elements to emerge.[12]

Another significant development which occurred in the 1980s was an increasing emphasis on the church being involved in all areas of society. A major element of Restorationist eschatology concerned the church coming to full stature prior to Christ's *parousia*. Dispensationalist eschatology and its fondness for 'the Rapture,'[13] popular in some parts of the Evangelical constituency (particularly the Brethren from whom a number of Restorationist leaders came), was caricatured as 'Christ whisking a tired, defeated church off the scene before things get too bad for the church to cope with'. In contrast, Restorationist eschatology was concerned with the church, as the bride of Christ, 'making herself ready' for his *parousia* (Rev. 19.7). It was believed, therefore, that an eschatological sign of the imminence of Christ's return would be the rise of the church as a force to be reckoned with by society.[14] As far as BCF was concerned, its increasing success in terms of growth and profile resulted in the more extreme elements of Restorationist eschatology (associated with the Latter Rain Movement as explained above), being dropped.[15] Nevertheless, the Restorationist emphasis on the significance of the church was an ideal platform from which teaching from a quite different tradition could begin to influence BCF. A number of people within BCF, who had significant roles within the church, either visited or had friends who had visited the Institute for Christian Studies in Toronto. A major concern of the Institute, which has close

310) goes as far as to state: 'I do not think that it is exaggerating too much to say that Wimber, and the style and methodology of the Vineyard Fellowships, has been the greatest influence in mainstream Renewal since the ministry of the late Canon David Watson and the hey-day of the Fountain Trust in the 1970s'.

11. The practice of specifically identifying various needs within the congregation publicly, without previously being told what those needs are, has been widely identified in charismatic circles with the 'word of knowledge' of 1 Cor. 12.8.

12. Wilson (1973: 25) identifies the thaumaturgical response in terms of the desire for miracles and oracles. The emphasis on 'signs and wonders' together with words of knowledge and personal prophecy fit precisely Wilson's 'miracles and oracles'.

13. The terminology comes from a particular interpretation of 1 Thess. 4.17.

14. A. Pullin, 'The Sleeping Beauty', *Fulness* 14, p. 9 sums this up well: 'Within weeks God began to write on my heart something of the true hope of the Church; the glorious hope of a bride made ready to meet her bridegroom... I saw that this age was not going to fade out, closed by the removal of the Church as an embarrassing failure, but that it was going to conclude in a blaze of glory...'

15. There was never any official repudiation of this teaching. It simply disappeared over a period of time from BCF's vocabulary.

links with the Vrije Universiteit, Amsterdam and is consequently shaped by the philosophy of Herman Dooyeweerd[16] and the political thinking of Abraham Kuyper, is the social and cultural embodiment of Christianity. This is well expressed by Nicholas Wolterstorff in his Foreword to *The Transforming Vision*, a book which was read by many members of BCF:

> A deep disappointment and a profound longing motivate this book. The authors, themselves Christians, observe that vast numbers of their fellow North Americans count themselves as Christians. Yet Christianity is ineffective in shaping our public life. What effectively shapes our public life and our society generally is our adulation of science and technology and economic growth. Christianity for the most part stands in the wings and watches. That is their disappointment. Their longing is that things may be changed – that Christianity may receive social and cultural embodiment. For in this they see the life and guidance and hope that our society so badly needs.[17]

Walsh and Middleton argue for a comprehensive, Christian cultural vision and call for Christians to develop specifically Christian responses to every area of societal life. As far as BCF was concerned, this resulted in a number of members being encouraged to form Christian businesses, and one or two began to think of more direct involvement in politics. The most significant development, however, was the establishing of a Christian school called Oakhill in September 1984.[18] Many BCF members with primary school aged children put them into Oakhill and the school also attracted some children from families not involved with the church. All the teachers and ancillary staff were members of BCF. The success of the school depended upon enormous resources from BCF in terms of time, personnel and finance.

After the initial success of the school tensions began to develop within BCF. Some of the elders were concerned at the significant amount of BCF resources being poured into the school which left insufficient resources for other projects. Some of the leaders felt more time, energy and finances should be devoted to evangelistic outreach. At the end of the 1980s, therefore, the church began to experience considerable, competing demands on its resources between those concerned primarily with:

- the internal development of BCF, especially pastoral care and healing and prophetic ministry;
- the external links of BCF with other churches both in the UK and in the rest of the world fostered through the work of Bridge Ministries;
- evangelistic outreach; and
- the church affecting every area of society focused on Oakhill school.

---

16. Especially his *A New Critique of Theoretical Thought* (Amsterdam/Philadelphia: H.J. Paris/Presbyterian and Reformed, 1955 and 1957).

17. Walsh and Middleton (1984: 9).

18. The vision for a Christian school emerged some time before BCF had any direct influence from teaching from the Institute for Christian Studies (ICS). Nevertheless, the ICS link proved a stimulus to providing an environment within BCF where a Christian school could flourish.

After several years of holding the above in tension the competing demands became too great. One of the elders, I shall call him Bob, who had championed concentration on evangelistic outreach, left to found a new church in Liverpool. Several members of BCF joined him in the move to Liverpool. The decision was also made by both the elders and the governors of Oakhill school to separate the school from BCF (the school had previously functioned under the auspices of the BCF Charitable Trust) and a separate trust was set up for the school. One of the results of this separation was that BCF parents with children about to start school increasingly did not view Oakhill school as the natural first choice. The decreasing intake, together with a decision to move into secondary education which proved financially untenable, led to the school's eventual closure in the early 1990s. The fallout from these two events was considerable. Bob had been involved with the church since Patchway days and many church members could not understand the reasons for him leaving. The school had involved many BCF people – parents, teachers and helpers; its demise left numerous people confused and disillusioned, particularly as it promised so much. A number blamed the leadership of BCF for abandoning the school and, as a result, left the church. Others left because they did not feel that the eldership was embracing the vision for the cultural and social embodiment of Christianity. This was the first time in its history that BCF experienced significant numbers leaving.

Then, in 1994, the phenomenon known as the 'Toronto Blessing'[19] hit BCF. This provided a fresh impetus for many who had been worn out and somewhat disillusioned following the sustained period of internal tension in the late 1980s and early 1990s. It also provided a renewed focus for meetings and revitalised the desire for 'signs and wonders' which characterised John Wimber's ministry.

However, BCF did not embrace the 'Toronto Blessing' wholeheartedly. I moved to Sheffield in 1992 to pursue further study at the Department of Biblical Studies at the University there. I was concerned by a number of elements of the 'Toronto Blessing' and shared my concerns with the BCF elders in a series of correspondence and meetings with them. My own disquiet culminated in the book, *The Mark of the Spirit?*, which was edited by me and published in 1998. Although the elders did not share my views, I know I was taken seriously by them as I had been a fellow-elder until my departure in 1992. In my view a combination of elements, including the early Restorationist dislike of anything resembling 'super-spiritual' piety, my expressed concerns and the perceived excesses arising out of the 'Toronto Blessing', resulted in the elders adopting an ambivalent stance towards the phenomenon.

---

19. This phenomenon began in a Wimber Vineyard Church in Toronto, Canada – Toronto Airport Vineyard, which subsequently became Toronto Airport Christian Fellowship (TACF) – on 20 January 1994. In the early days it was characterised by outbreaks of laughter, weeping, groaning, shaking, falling and strange, animal-like sounds. In the UK it is reckoned that the phenomenon began in the Anglican church, Holy Trinity Brompton, in April 1994 when Eleanor Mumford, from the Southwest London Vineyard, shared her experience in Toronto with the congregation. For further details see Beverley (1995), Oropeza (1995) and the official publication of TACF, *Spread the Fire.*

Since the outbreak of the 'Toronto Blessing' there has been a marked desire in the elders to return to the foundational, core values of BCF which include commitment, relationship and friendship. These core values, combined with a renewed sense of mission, are particularly embraced in the 'cell church'[20] model espoused by Ralph Neighbour.[21] The leadership are currently seeking to remodel BCF as a 'cell church'.[22]

5. *Analysis*

The above history highlights the complex nature of BCF's development. It began as a small group of people determined to be non-institutional and to prize relationship between members very highly. Built into BCF's core values was a suspicion of religiosity and unreal spirituality. The following statement neatly sums up the attitude to such spirituality:

> In certain circles there is a hidden law. All problems have to be resolved with a word from God, a tongue, a prophecy or a word of knowledge. If you have a sin problem you have got a demon. If you are insecure you were probably dropped out of your cot when you were 13½ days old and you need the healing of memories and so on. I am not belittling the manifestation of the spirit, *but I am coming to see that many Christians need some sane common-sense, not special 'spiritual' answers.*[23]

As such, BCF was far from thaumaturgical in nature. Nevertheless, it has always been a charismatic church and so embraced spiritual gifts such as glossolalia and

---

20. 'A cell based structure allows each member to become a disciple and to disciple others. While senior leadership is imperative, the ministry is not performed by a precious few paid staff members, but by everyone in the church.
'While the church may number into the hundreds of thousands of members, the membership does not feel lost in a sea of people. These 'gigachurches' are made up of thousands of small groups of 10–15 people who meet weekly for worship, ministry, outreach and fellowship. The difference between a church with small groups and a cell based church is that the entire structure is based on these small communities. They are not tacked on as a program, and no other programs compete with them.
'Cell members around the world live in basic Christian community. These small groups of people share their daily lives. They exercise, shop, babysit, and eat together as often as possible. They invite unbelievers to be a part of their lives as well. This daily interaction brings many to Christ because of lifestyle evangelism and a strong witness that reaches far beyond door knocking or crusades.'
The final paragraph could easily have been taken from an issue of Fulness magazine. The above is actually taken from the web site of Ralph Neighbour's organisation, Touch Outreach Ministries: http://www.touchusa.org/store/content/introcell.asp
21. See especially, R.W. Neighbour Jr, *Where Do We Go From Here? A Guidebook for Cell Group Churches* (Touch Publications, 1990).
22. This was as reported in 1999, since then the emphasis has changed somewhat with some elements of the church embracing the 'cell church' concept and others remaining ambivalent. However, as I have not been involved in the church since 1999, I do not feel qualified to provide additional analysis without conducting further research.
23. G. Coates, 'Being Yourself', *Fulness* 12, pp. 4–6 (6); my emphasis.

prophecy. From my own involvement in the church since 1974, I would say that as Restorationist teaching increased (emphasising the eschatological role of the 'Ephesian 4 ministries' of apostle, prophet, evangelist, pastor and teacher in bringing the church to maturity) so the emphasis on glossolalia decreased and directional or exhortational prophecy for the church as a whole came to the fore. However, as specifically Restorationist emphases declined in the 1980s, prophecy to individuals and words of knowledge became more pronounced. I can remember many meetings in this period in which people were called forward and prophesied over in a very specific manner. There was a significant shift in this period, in my view, from the apostolic and prophetic emphases of the 1970s and early 1980s to a pastoral emphasis which, combined with the charismatic dimension, led to a focus on the supernatural relief of individuals' present and specific ills. In other words, a shift to what Bryan R. Wilson defines as the thaumaturgical response to the world.[24]

The tensions in the late 1980s and early 1990s, particularly in connection with Oakhill school, left a large number of people in the church (who had invested enormous amounts) with their hopes dashed. Some, as a result, left the church; many of the others experienced profound cognitive dissonance. In addition, others who had been in the church since the early days also experienced cognitive dissonance as a result of the failure of the House Church at large to meet expectations. Many of the original members, myself included, expected far more to have happened within twenty years than actually did. The original millennial fervour has, to a large extent, dissipated. The 'manifest sons of God' had failed to appear. The collapse of the outward, societal focus epitomised by Oakhill school together with the cognitive dissonance arising out of dashed eschatological expectations created, in my view, an environment in which the already existing thaumaturgical element could come increasingly to the fore within BCF.

The change of outlook frequently produced as a result of cognitive dissonance often leads previously millenarian movements to adopt an introversionist response to the world by means of voluntary social, or even geographical, withdrawal.[25] However, BCF's conversionist orientation, together with the thaumaturgical elements already in place, meant that it did not transform itself into such an introversionist movement. Rather, the way was open for its transformation into a thaumaturgical movement as suggested by Wilson (1973: 348–83).[26] It was into this context that the 'Toronto Blessing' arrived in 1994.

The 'Toronto Blessing' is intensely thaumaturgical as can be seen from these few quotes taken from the TACF magazine, *Spread the Fire* (STF).[27]

> Where do I see it going? Lois Gott had a wonderful prophetic word about how we are now in an introductory and preparatory phase of the Blessing.

24. See Wilson (1973: 24–25).

25. See, for example, Esler (1994: 110–30).

26. For further discussion concerning the attraction of thaumaturgy see Pietersen (1998a: 17–27).

27. A considerable amount of the material relating to the 'Toronto Blessing' contained in this chapter is also to be found in my chapter in Klutz (2003: 157–67). I have reproduced it here as I consider it essential to the flow of the argument.

There are much greater blessings yet to come. Her prophecy indicated that we are currently in a time similar to the ministry of John the Baptist and will soon be coming into a time resembling the ministry of Jesus where powerful signs, wonders and miracles will take place.

We're tremendously excited. We're starting to see spontaneous healings occur during the meetings with no one actually praying for people. It seems as though the Lord is taking us to even higher heights and an even greater anointing.

Particularly in England, the power of the Spirit is beyond anything I've ever seen. It's a further call for all of us not to seek after manifestations, but to look beyond the manifestations enjoying the bountiful and biblical root that is being produced in hundreds and thousands of lives both in meetings and people alike.[28]

Pastor Greasley tells not only of dramatic conversions, but also of some miraculous healings of people in his church. 'One woman who was admitted to hospital to have a cancerous tumour removed was given a special release to attend a Sunday morning meeting at the All Nations Centre. After sensing a powerful touch from God, she returned to the hospital only to find that the tumor had completely vanished'.

Greasley reports that another woman, Lynda Reilly, had been suffering from a deteriorating eye disease and required thick-lensed glasses. However, the morning after attending a meeting at the Centre, she couldn't see with her glasses. On removing them she found she had perfect 20/20 eyesight. Both cases have been medically documented.[29]

We have seen the manifestation of God's power in this renewal, but it does not compare to what is on the way. One of the characteristics of an apostle is the working of signs, wonders and miracles (Rom. 15.19; 2 Cor. 12.12). When apostolic anointing is released, we will see the greatest miracles since the book of Acts and they will draw crowds. We read in Acts that people brought their sick to the apostle Peter just so that his shadow could pass over them and heal them.

We are already beginning to see miracles at Harvest Rock Church in Pasadena, California. We have been hosting renewal meetings every night since March 1995, and we have seen God touch, heal and save many.

In February 1995 a young woman in her 20s came to a renewal meeting and was healed of severe scoliosis. She had been scheduled for an operation the following week.

As a member of our ministry team prayed, she fell on the carpet speaking in tongues. While she lay there for two hours, her back was completely straightened. Amazed, her doctor ordered X-rays which showed a perfectly aligned spine. The girl asked for a copy of the X-rays to show to her pastor. He was so delighted with what God had done, that as an expression of gratitude, his church, Oikos Community Church, donated $4,000 to support renewal services in Pasadena.

In another instance, while I was preaching in Sunderland, England, I felt God say that He was healing someone's ear. A little girl came forward. When I had given the word, her hearing aid exploded. She took it off and found she could hear

---

28.   John Arnott, 'Moving into Increasing Anointing', *STF* 1.3 (1995).
29.   Gary Pritchard, 'British Church: Laughing in the Rain', *STF* 1.4 (1995).

perfectly. Not only that, but she had also been wearing thick glasses. Her eyes were healed as well. Ken and Lois Gott, pastors at Sunderland, report that she continues to do well a year later.[30]

I have observed that in renewal God has provided accelerated emotional healing for Christians to prepare them for the next level of anointing which will include signs, miracles and wonders. Those of us who remain bound by self-hatred and lack of self-acceptance, will be vulnerable to demonic attack when the next wave comes, and will be unreliable vessels for God's anointing. If we minister out of our woundedness, our emotional pain will distort the anointing.[31]

Whenever God moves in revival, there is always an increase in signs and wonders. Since 1994 we have seen a dramatic increase in them as the River of God's Spirit keeps flowing throughout the world. The Bible clearly teaches that we should expect miracles from God today. Hebrews 13.8 says, 'Jesus Christ is the same yesterday, today, and forever'. If it is reasonable to expect the miracle of the new birth, which is clearly the greatest miracle, then it is also reasonable to expect God to do lesser miracles and signs that will glorify His great name and draw an unbelieving generation back to Christ. Not a single verse in scripture teaches that God will ever cease to do miracles. The Bible is full of miracles, in every book and practically on every page.[32]

The 'Toronto Blessing' also heightened expectations of revival and encouraged prayer for widespread revival.

David Yonngi Cho describes prayer as the key to every revival in the history of christianity. Many believe the renewal at airport vineyard began as a result of thousands praying for revival internationally. Airport's renewal is sustained by prayer. Prayers include repentance, thankfulness, forgiveness and intercession for leaders.[33]

Stibbe (1995: 10) believes that the Toronto phenomenon is the first sign of what he calls 'a fourth wave'. He identifies this fourth wave with global revival (1995: 21–29).

The latest evidence concerning the thaumaturgical nature of the 'Toronto Blessing' emerged from Toronto in March 1999. Reports of people receiving gold fillings in their teeth were published on the Internet. The following is an extract from one of these reports:

On Wednesday evening March 3rd, 1999 miracles began happening in people's teeth. By Thursday evening, over 50 people were on the platform at Toronto Airport Christian Fellowship testifying to having received what appeared to be gold or bright silver fillings or crowns, which they believed had supernaturally appeared in their mouths after receiving prayer during the Intercession Conference. Many received one, two, three or more, and in some cases up to ten changed fillings! On the Saturday night of the conference, there were 198 on the platform saying that God had given them a dental miracle. By Sunday night, well over 300

---

30. Che Ahn, 'Introducing Signs, Miracles & Wonders', *STF* 2.6 (1996).
31. Grant Mullen, 'Would the Real You Please Own Up?', *STF* 3.4 (1997).
32. John Arnott, 'How to Discern Signs and Wonders', *STF* 5.3 (1999).
33. 'Connecting with God', *STF* 1.1 (1995).'

people were testifying to this unusual sign. Testimonies, even now, are continuing to pour in.

Our leadership have encouraged people to verify these miracles with their dentists, who in some cases, have been understandably hesitant to explain why their patients' fillings have become so shiny and have changed in colour from dark amalgam to bright silver or gold. In a few cases, dentists were able to show from their records that the gold was put in their mouths previously by the dentist and not by God. These people had apparently forgotten that this work had been done. The majority of these incidents however, seem to be beyond explaining, other than that God has given these wonderful gifts.

After the conference, delegates returned home and dental miracles surprisingly began to happen to some of their friends and family members. Some are testifying that these miracles happened while watching conference sessions on video tape. Reports of people's fillings turning a bright silver or gold color are coming in from South Africa, Australia, England, Mexico and across Canada and the USA. The excitement here at TACF is electric with the news of how these dental miracles are so rapidly spreading.

TACF is encouraging people to obtain dental confirmations. We will do a follow-up report in the near future and publish our findings. Meanwhile dental miracles, along with many other healings, continue to take place at the nightly meetings. Things that we have seen happening in Argentina and Brazil for fifteen years are starting to happen here now. Conversions to Christ have also increased! While we are thankful for the miracles and healings that are taking place, our eyes are on Jesus and it is Him alone we look to and worship.[34]

For many people within BCF, disillusioned with either the failure of the church to impact society or to have reached full stature within twenty years, the 'Toronto Blessing' arrived in a timely manner to alleviate the cognitive dissonance. If Restorationism and the societal emphasis have not produced results maybe the 'Toronto Blessing' would. Furthermore, both Restorationism and the societal emphasis were more concerned with a corporate response – they emphasised the role of the church as a whole. The 'Toronto Blessing', on the other hand, certainly in the initial stages, has been far more about an individual response. This, of course, is a highly postmodern shift, but it is not my intention to analyse the phenomenon further along these lines in this study.

However, the response of the church is more complex than this. As can be seen below from the interviews, BCF has not wholly embraced the Toronto phenomenon. Thaumaturgy is proving intensely attractive but it has by no means won the day. The interviewees speak of the polarising effects of the 'Toronto Blessing'. Although there are undoubtedly a number of reasons for this, I think the crucial factor has been the leadership's own ambivalence. In addition, much of the teaching in the early years of the church concerned Christianity being to do with the whole of life and not just church services. One of the results of the 'Toronto Blessing' has been a proliferation of services. This is encouraged by the very ethos of the 'Toronto Blessing' which is to hold regular services in order for people to 'soak' in the presence of God. TACF itself has been holding services every night,

---

34. Official Press Release dated 17 March 1999 from Toronto Airport Christian Fellowship (TACF) published on the Internet at: www.tacf.org/confs/archives/intercession99/pressrelease.html

apart from Mondays, since 1994. It seems to me that the leadership strongly desire to return to what they describe as the 'core values' of BCF – or, in my terms, its 'tradition'. Indeed the structural change to cell church represents a return to the small group ethos that characterised the early years of the church. In the case of BCF, therefore, it would appear that teaching and tradition are in tension with thaumaturgy and it looks at this point in time that one of the results of the failure to embrace the thaumaturgical response is to return to BCF's foundational teaching (albeit with the more eschatological Restorationist emphases removed) and to its tradition.

6. *Validation*

In order to check my analysis above I sent a questionnaire out to every person selected as outlined in the next section. Second, arising out of the responses to the questionnaire, I conducted a number of in-depth interviews utilising a standard series of questions as prompts. The results of these are set out in the following sections.

a. *Questionnaire*
After obtaining permission from the BCF elders I sent out a questionnaire, including a stamped, addressed envelope for its return, to every person, resident within the Bristol area, listed on the BCF address list for July 1999 who was also listed on the address list for October 1991. This gave a population of everyone who had been a member of the church for at least seven years. Out of this population I eliminated three people who, from my own knowledge, I decided would find a questionnaire too intimidating. In addition I was asked by the BCF leadership not to send a questionnaire to one member of the church for pastoral reasons. This left a total of 249 people. The actual questionnaire used is reproduced in Appendix 2.

The purpose of the questionnaire was twofold. First, I wanted to obtain qualitative feedback on the perceived key changes in the development of the church together with both the perceived response of the church as a whole to those changes and the respondent's personal response. Second, I wanted quantitative data to trace the way various characteristic elements of a charismatic, Restorationist church have been emphasised over time. The results would thus serve to check my own analysis of BCF's development and provide key indicators of the degree to which BCF is perceived to have become institutionalised.

i. *Results*. 98 questionnaires were returned – a response rate of 39.4 per cent. Although the response rate was not high I did not consider, from my knowledge of BCF, that further attempts to obtain additional responses would be productive. I was not hopeful, at the start of the exercise, of obtaining more than about 25 per cent response rate so the actual response rate was much better than expected. For the purpose of quantitative analysis I listed each of the key changes mentioned in the questionnaires and ranked the key changes according to the number of responses mentioning each change. Tied scores by this ranking were then further ranked according to the level of significance attached to the change by each respondent mentioning that change. The results of this ranking are recorded in Appendix 3.

The various emphases mentioned on the questionnaire required a score from 1 to 5 at three points in time. The data was fed into a spreadsheet by year taking 1999 as the current year; the joining year was ascertained from the answer to question two and the mid-point was taken as:

$$Joining\ Year\ +\ \frac{(1999 - Joining\ Year)}{2}$$

If the result was not an integer then the above equation was rounded up. This resulted in the following data set.

ii. *Data Set.*

Year	Number of Respondents	Year	Number of Respondents
1973	2	1986	3
1974	1	1987	10
1975	4	1988	9
1976	4	1989	38
1978	1	1990	10
1979	7	1991	14
1980	3	1992	13
1981	2	1993	6
1982	2	1994	35
1983	3	1995	15
1984	7	1999	98
1985	6		

In view of the low numbers for all years up to and including 1988 I decided that there was insufficient data to carry out any meaningful quantitative analysis. I therefore restricted my analysis to qualitative responses. In addition, due to the paucity of data for the earliest years, I chose to skew my in-depth interviews towards elders who have been in the church from, or very near to, the beginning.

iii. *Significant Changes.* The top five changes all concerned relatively recent structural changes or changes in personnel. 71 per cent mentioned the recent change to a cell church organised on lines suggested by Ralph Neighbour. 58 per cent mentioned the related change from meeting as relatively small, geographical communities to meeting in much larger regional units.[35] 23 per cent regarded BCF joining the Pioneer[36] network of churches as a significant event. 33 per cent listed changes

35. As BCF grew it developed a 'cell, congregation, celebration' structure. Members met regularly in relatively small, geographical, congregations comprised of several smaller home groups or cells; the whole church met once a month. The focus tended to be on the congregations. Under the new 'cell church' structure the old home groups have given way to new style cells and the congregations have been combined to form three regional units; the whole church still meets once a month. The focus is now on the cells and the regional meetings.

36. In the mid-1990s BCF joined Pioneer which is a network of churches led by Gerald Coates, many of them Restorationist in origin, and identifying themselves as 'new churches'. Walker

in the eldership or wider leadership as significant and 12 per cent noted the number of people leaving the church.

Ten respondents listed the 'Toronto Blessing' as a significant change and an equal number listed diminishing supernatural expectations, making these sixth and seventh respectively. The 9 per cent who mentioned growth, in contrast to people leaving, making growth the eighth most noteworthy change, had significantly all been members of the church for at least twelve years and the mean length of membership of these respondents was 19.8 years. Most of those who listed growth, therefore, had joined BCF when it was relatively small and had witnessed the period of greatest growth during the 1980s. The ninth and tenth most significant changes concerned a greater emphasis on mission and on youth.

Interestingly, equal numbers mention 'Toronto' with its emphasis on supernatural manifestations and its opposite – decreasing supernatural expectations, and both of these score very highly on the scale of perceived changes. This seems to support the tension between institutionalisation and its potential thaumaturgical subversion highlighted in my analysis above.

iv. *Comments From Respondents Concerning Changes*. The move to cell church has had a very mixed response as can be seen from the following comments from respondents:

> 'The way cell church was brought in was a bit ham-fisted. It seemed to be that many of the people were not in agreement to its implementation.'
> 'I'm not in favour of cell church or the concept. We seem to have lost all leadership. Seems as if we have to throw out "baby & bath water"'.
> 'I fully support cell church'.
> 'The principles are excellent but there is a group which find it hard to change.'
> 'For goodness sake – can't we stick to something!! I feel the emphasis on "cells" and growth alienates some (i.e. me!)'
> 'Having been to a number of cell church/cell leader training events and read a reasonable amount of literature I feel very positive about the cell church theory but frustrated that it doesn't seem to be working very well. Cells seemed to be formed and closed down and not everyone is involved. I think it's a hard thing to change to, it probably has to grow up from grass roots.'

Although the leadership clearly want the church to move in this direction it appears that much more work will have to be done in order for the rank and file membership to own it.

A number of comments highlighted the issue of institutionalisation:

> 'It is generally less friendly. More distance between leadership and those on extremities.'
> 'It has become more of an "established" church. BCF is dynamic but no longer so 'alternative' as it was.'

(1998: 360) explains the concept as follows: 'In fact, the idea of "new church" is more sociological than theological. These are independent networks, or one-off fellowships, that are outside the established denominational structures. But other than being evangelical and charismatic, there is little which binds them together'.

'Institutionalisation – loss of radical spirituality, conservative approach, cerebral replaces passion. Probably the result of loss of values, average age, inertia, boredom, settling, etc. There is little to separate BCF from a dozen other churches in Bristol.'

'The move from houses to buildings was part of the initial institutionalisation of BCF.'

'I would like to go to a younger, more "radical" church, but stay with BCF out of a sense of faithfulness and wanting to please God, not 'shop around' for churches.'

'We are now settlers rather than pioneers. Inevitable in many respects, due to age changes, growth of families and spread of many of our original pioneering concepts into the mainstream churches.'

'All these [the changes listed by this respondent] have caused a loss of radical Christian living – body expression – and created a more institutional feel.'

'My basic belief is that BCF's days are numbered primarily because the people who started the church have been unable to hand over leadership to dynamic people. The main reason for this is that the original leaders were dynamic but they feel threatened by the next generation.'

Comments on the emphasis on social and cultural engagement, and particularly Oakhill school, appear to reinforce my own remarks. For example, one respondent expresses 'delight' when Oakhill school started and 'disappointment and sadness' when it closed. The opening and closing of the school were the only significant changes listed by this respondent. The following observations were also made:

'After flirting with interacting with the world (education/social action), BCF retreated into religious shell.'

'I think what happened over Oakhill was highly significant in the development of the church and changed the focus of teaching/belief/action. Although the personnel of the church are today different, and the proportion of those involved in Oakhill still in the church is very small, I believe it still has an effect on what we do both for spiritual and other reasons.'

'As new parents when we joined BCF the education of our children in a Godly way was our primary concern. It was very much a community at Oakhill and many of the people who were involved formed much of the energy in pioneering. The way things simply fell apart remains with us even now. These areas now seem to be a wasteland and are not discussed.'

'Not personally much affected [by the Oakhill school experience] but it seems to have left us without courage to pursue an agenda of social transformation.'

'[In connection with Oakhill school] I feel that the church overextended itself and should have concentrated on the infant and primary sector, not go into secondary level.'

There were mixed comments concerning the 'Toronto Blessing' which also were not surprising in the light of my own analysis:

'Disappointment by BCF that its primary vision was unrealised. It adopted Toronto for a new *raison d'être*.'

'Very welcome. Apart from the benefits to individuals affected directly, it induces the awe and fear of God we need in our materialistic and scientific society. But we need more.'

'I am uncomfortable with a lot of the emphasis of 'Toronto' whilst recognising that I can't fit God into my boxes. My suspicion is that the changes are transient and probably not important in the long run. [The emphasis on mission and out-reach] perhaps faded a bit with the introverted 'shaking' and blessing/revival of the past 2–3 years. Now seems far more prominent again.'

'Have seen lives changed in ways I've not seen before (including my own). Much deeper relationship with God. Long term fruit emerging.'

'Brought a significant measure of renewing/refreshing but has not led to expected revival. Leadership seems unsure where this should go next and has not coped well with disillusionment on many.'

'I worry about the radically different model of church implied by Toronto, i.e. focus on big meetings.'

'Overall, the vision of the church remains the same and profound movements of the Holy Spirit (the 'Toronto Blessing' etc.) have, on the whole, enriched the church and some fruit has been long lasting.'

'I always felt a spectator, a second rate Christian, because nothing ever seemed to 'happen' to me. However, I felt the church tried to embrace it sensibly.'

'For some people the 'Toronto Blessing' has been life-changing. Personally I would prefer to outwork my faith in less self-centred ways. I find some manifesta-tions something I would prefer not to happen to me.'

The fifth comment above reflects my own remarks concerning the ambivalence of the leadership over the phenomenon. The final comment demonstrates that this ambivalence was not just restricted to the leadership!

b. *Interviews*
I carried out taped, in-depth interviews lasting an hour each with four members of BCF – three of whom are elders in the church and have been part of the key leadership for many years. One of the elders interviewed has not given permission for his statements to be used in this publication, although he was happy for his comments to be used in my original thesis. For the sake of anonymity I shall call the remaining two elders Richard and Paul. I deliberately chose a number of elders who had been involved from, or near, the beginning of BCF due to the paucity of quantitative data for the early years and also as a check on my own perspective as an erstwhile elder of the church. The fourth was with an ordinary member of the church who has been a member for fourteen years; I shall call him James.[37] The interview was semi-structured in that I asked each interviewee an initial question, based on the specific reasons each of them had joined BCF as disclosed on their responses to the questionnaire, followed by the following questions:

1. The church has gone through a number of structural changes over the years. The latest change to a cell church structure was the key change listed by more respondents than any other by a large margin. What are your own feelings about cell church?

37. The fact that all the interviewees are male is purely circumstantial. A further two interviews were planned with females. However, one of these did not take place because of unforeseen time constraints and the other interviewee went into hospital on the scheduled date of the interview!

2. There have been a number of changes in the eldership and main leadership over the last few years. How do you feel about these?
3. BCF is very much into its second generation with many children of long-standing members now grown up. What effects do you think this has had on the church?
4. How do you feel about BCF becoming a part of the Pioneer network?
5. In ranking the key changes mentioned in the returned questionnaires by the number of respondents listing them, people leaving BCF came fifth. Why do you think a number of people are leaving the church?
6. Sixth highest was the effects of the 'Toronto Blessing'. How significant do you feel this has been in the life of the church?
7. Seventh highest was the perception that the church has diminishing super-natural expectations. This is certainly borne out by the trend lines[38] over time arising out of the responses concerning the degree of emphasis given to areas such as deliverance, miracles, healing, etc. This seems surprising given the emphasis on supernatural manifestations arising out of the 'Toronto Blessing'. How do you account for this?
8. The trend lines which emerge out of the responses concerning emphases of BCF are very interesting. Nearly all the trends show diminishing emphasis over time; the only exceptions are prayer, revival and social justice.
    a. What are your reactions to these findings?
    b. How do you account for the three exceptions?
9. Please comment on the degree to which you feel BCF has become institutionalised.

I asked additional questions as they arose from responses to the above questions.

I have detailed transcripts of each of the three interviews; however, in what follows, for the sake of conciseness and readability, I present only a few stretches of edited transcript[39] relying mainly on short quotes and summaries to convey the interaction process.

i. *Cell Church*. Richard, who was the most positive of all the elders interviewed about the 'Toronto Blessing', is ambivalent about cell church:

> I think in principle it is a very dynamic model of church growth and I do think it is a model which, in theory at least, can sustain a rapid growth of numbers probably better than any other model that I know of. I have been quite slow personally in the uptake into cell church, but from what I can see I think it is good, I am happy with it. I feel it is quite a brave step, but I also feel in our own church we still have yet to make it really work, and there's a sense I feel in which we have absorbed the theory but are still working out the practice and haven't adequately really got it into our own experience as a church. I think the youth in the church are absorbing it quicker and making it work faster. I do think there is a certain element of fatigue that comes into people who have been in the church for a long time and have been

---

38. Trend lines, based on taking the mean score for degree of emphasis on a scale of one to five for each year from the questionnaire, were shown to each of the interviewees. They were included in my original thesis but have not been reproduced here.

39. I edit out all 'um's', similar interjections, pauses and false starts.

through a lot of structural changes some of which haven't produced the hoped for results – you begin to feel 'Oh dear!' You feel that about any change after a certain period of time without really putting yourself into it.

Richard also feels uncertain whether cell church is the best way to facilitate growth. Speaking of the effects of the 'Toronto Blessing' on BCF, he states:

There was a time when there was a sense of excitement and expectancy in our corporate gatherings which I don't feel is there now. I can see that now moving into cell church is a positive, practical step that we could take if we were expecting to see large numbers of people coming into the kingdom in the days ahead – that's the kind of structure that would cope with those and disciple them a lot better and can facilitate growth, growing more rapidly, but there is a part of me that says if we're really going to see the Kingdom of God increased like that with large numbers of people impacted by the gospel then we have to be in tune with what God is actually doing in the present and I don't feel we do that as much now as we did in the past.

Paul is positive about cell church but does not want the concept to become all-embracing:

My feeling is that cells can well express the core values of the church and what I have always wanted is that our structures are servants of the core values and I see cell, ideally, as being a servant of the core values. There is a danger with cells, as I've seen in different places, that it becomes the be all and end all. So you get phrases like 'nothing competes with cells' which I personally think is a limitation because if cells take you away from the core values, or takes people away from their own responsibility and their walk with God then I think things need to compete with cells.

James, after admitting to being cynical about the concept and wondering whether cell church was any different to the home groups of the past, believes that it is a very different way of doing things which can lead to effective mission:

So the cell thing? I was initially a little bit cynical: 'well really is it any different?' But actually the whole idea is completely different and then, as we were taught about it and how churches around the world who are getting somewhere really have that kind of cell structure, so eventually I got quite into it and in many ways have been frustrated that we're not moving fast enough…and I do feel there are people who have seen it all before – this is just rehashing an old sort of thing – but I've been around nearly fifteen years (long enough to have seen a reasonable number of changes) and to me this really is a different emphasis and I think there's no question that BCF wasn't growing by people coming to know God afresh and joining the church which has got to be the way to change, to grow… But I want to see real growth not moving people around kind of growth.

ii. *Leadership Changes*. Leadership changes were clearly perceived by a number of respondents as highly significant. I mentioned in my brief history of BCF's development that one elder, Bob (not his real name), left due to what he felt was a lack of evangelistic emphasis. I also left Bristol in 1992 to pursue further study and Steve Hepden left shortly afterwards to develop his national and international heal-

ing and prophetic ministry. In the 1990s Dave Day handed over the leadership of
BCF to Neil Edbrooke, in order to develop his national and international links.
However, Neil developed a chronic illness which meant that Dave had to take back
the leadership for a period. Neil has subsequently recovered sufficiently to take
overall leadership again and Dave is now a member of the Pioneer network's national core team. Dave still remains an elder of BCF.[40]

Richard does not feel that there has been sufficient change in the leadership:

> I actually feel the changes have not been as significant as I would have liked or as
> many as I'd like. Key people have left although there have been also a lot who
> have stayed in eldership all the way through. I think it has given some sense of
> stability to the church in that they have known some consistency in the elders all
> the way through. If anything I would probably have pushed for more radical
> change than what we have actually had. I would have said more young people.

Paul feels leadership changes have been both positive and negative. He recognises
that the reasons for Steve Hepden and myself moving on were very beneficial for
us but that those moves left gaps in the church which have been difficult to fill. He
does feel that there were painful, relational issues with Bob:

> I think too I would see changes in leadership operating at a couple of levels. At
> one level, if the going has a damaging effect because there are some relational
> issues… So I think with Bob going there were relational issues that were painful,
> and so over and above any gap left by Bob there were the ripples. And I think
> some people not really understanding what was going on and again, very subjec-
> tively, never knowing how much you can tell the church because you don't want it
> to create a problem for someone when there isn't one but then you are accused of
> not informing people. So at one level there is the actual gap because those people
> have gone, but at the other level if the going has caused an undermining then there
> are difficulties. I think for Steve, I think it was right for Steve to go because his
> heart and his ministry was being expressed more and more outside. I think he left
> a gap because Steve has the ability to make people feel wanted and loved… So
> that can leave a gap which I don't think we've adequately filled. And I think with
> you going…there is something of the personality and the history and team
> dynamic that we probably haven't adequately filled.

James, after also speaking about the gaps left by various elders leaving and about
the pain of the Liverpool incident, goes on to speak positively about the changes
because he sees them as an opportunity for others in the church with gifts to
develop:

> So I felt that the change of elders leaving, and not necessarily the vacuum being
> filled, is not a huge problem in that I think there's *loads* of gift out there in the
> church – there's loads of really talented people that God's got his hands on and
> somehow we've got to encourage them into those roles…and I think, I hope, cell
> church and the greater emphasis on the small groups and gaining experience and
> using spiritual gifts and all those sorts of things…[will] develop those sorts of
> things. So I feel that was difficult for the church but I think it's unhealthy for us to

---

40. This has changed very recently with Neil stepping back from overall leadership and Dave,
once again, taking this responsibility. Neil, however, remains an elder in the church.

focus on: 'Oh my goodness! such and such has gone, we'll never be able to do that again!' because actually I see it as an opportunity.

iii. *Second Generation*. BCF, having been around for some twenty-five years, is having to face issues raised by the second generation. A number of long-standing members, including all three elders interviewed, now have older teenagers and/or adult children some of whom have chosen to be part of BCF. It is a pressing question as to how the church caters for, and handles the emergence of new leaders from, its second generation.

Richard feels that Neil Edbrooke's family have modelled a successful intergenerational approach to the church:

> I think the church has become more intergenerational recently than I have ever seen before, which I feel is very largely down to Neil and [his wife] and their kids themselves.

Paul states 'there are healthy signs of us becoming an intergenerational church'. However, he is concerned that older people in the church take the initiative in addressing any potential generation gap. Otherwise, he believes there is a real danger that the young people will leave to form a new church:

> I do see a lot of spark and a lot of impetus and motivation from the second generation, which says at one level something hopefully healthy has been laid when the foundations have been laid. But certainly the challenge is there for the older people to embrace the younger people or they could end up doing what we did 30 years ago which is to go and start something fresh because it's limited where they are. That's a real danger I think.

James is concerned about the lack of young people ready to take leadership roles within the church, but wonders whether the cell church structure will provide a vehicle for leadership to emerge among the young people:

> In connection with younger people taking on the baton there's not a huge number of them it seems – I think there's a big mass out there and the key new people who are perhaps moving eldership way doesn't seem like a big number. But then in the cell church structure there's much more going on in the wider scene, and certainly within my cell there is a sense of people grabbing the vision and the second generation being into…perhaps the cell church is the second generation ethos and potentially can go with the baton and run another good distance and so in many ways perhaps we will be able to achieve some of the dreams, I hope, of people initially in the church.

iv. *Pioneer*. Richard is ambivalent about the link with Pioneer:

> A bit mixed to be honest. I can see strengths in it. It has been helpful at times to have input from the larger network that has got a wider perspective. In practice though I'm not really sure what they contribute and I'm starting to get the feeling that we might be contributing more into Pioneer, which is a good thing. For me personally the issue is much more local. I think it's a lot easier to relate to churches who are like you but from another part of the country. It is harder to relate to churches that are not like you but are on your doorstep and that's where

my heart is. I don't feel negative about it but I don't think it's been quite the positive thing that I would have hoped.

Paul believes that it has been important for BCF to be involved in something bigger:

> I think at the time the thinking behind it was very much where did we as a church
> fit in to what is happening in the city and the nation? And although we did have
> several churches relating to us, at the end of the day there wasn't anyone there for
> us and we wanted to be part of something bigger that would give us a bit more of
> a voice and clout and a resource.

James too believes that the positive benefits of joining Pioneer are the additional resources and support for the elders that the network provides.

v. *People leaving.* All the interviewees recognise that the reasons for people leaving are varied and complex. Because of the multifaceted nature of the issue I have reproduced the responses in full.

Richard states:

> Basically dissatisfaction that expectations have not been met. I think the move
> into cell church has hit hardest those who enjoyed and valued the communities
> they used to have, both in terms of the leaders of the communities and members of
> the communities, and many people have missed the opportunity of social interac-
> tion and other things that they had in the community meetings and organisational
> life and haven't found that it's worked for them in cells, or haven't stayed long
> enough to make it work and have been attracted by other churches in the locality
> which would be more traditional in structure. I think that's a key reason. But in
> the move of the Holy Spirit in the last four or five years I think BCF has steered
> quite a middle course and I think there are some people who have left the church
> because we haven't been more in phase with that and there are others who have
> left because we've embraced it at all. I think there are some who feel that the elders
> are a bit stuck, continuing to debate past issues or really haven't resolved past
> issues adequately.
>
>   Oakhill would be quite a big one and I think that Bob leaving and some of the
> questions which are still lingering – questions among those who have been
> involved with BCF a long time – have made them think 'well I've got better
> things to do with my life than to sit sweating this out'. I think the biggest reason
> would be though the transition to cell – the loss of the communities has been quite
> devastating and the relationships, or whatever else it was that could have held
> them to the church, have not been there as the communities have gone they felt,
> and BCF has lost them. There are other churches in the area which have been
> quite successful and I think that's attracted a number of people from a church that
> is not sure where it is going. I think for the majority of people that I know who
> have left it has been a painful decision; it's not been something they have done
> lightly and by and large they have respect for the members of the leadership of the
> church. They just struggled to cope with the direction that we are going in. A
> number of individual people would have left – it usually comes down to some
> issue or concern that they have that they don't feel has been adequately handled
> and they don't see is going to be adequately handled in the future of the church as
> presented.

Paul's response:

I think there are various reasons so I will ramble a bit. I think once a few start leaving it brings a sense of demoralisation to others. So you then have a domino effect. And I think because a lot of people joined us because we were the church to join at one stage, it doesn't surprise me when there's another church to join they move on. That may be cynical but I don't think so. I think some people have left because we do tend to be middle of the road in quite a lot of our perspectives. So for some people we would be too Torontoised, for others we just aren't Torontoised enough! So many have left because we are not into Toronto enough whereas some have struggled because they thought we were too into Toronto.

I think because we are a fairly moderate group of leaders in terms of personality, style etc. – not in passion and devotion I hope, but certainly in temperament – we aren't enough of something for some people and we're too much of other things for others! And that is one of the ironies of life. I think people are also leaving because change isn't always an easy thing to cope with and for some people there has been a lot of change. So with one of the communities in particular, who have lost a few I think, these are the sort of dynamics that I can see there: Tom [not his real name] stepped back from leadership to retire and he had brought a lot of stability there. There were a lot of older people who had related to Tom as a father figure. He stepped back and a leadership team emerged so, even though Tom led the team, he was very much the father figure. The leadership team which was younger came in – they weren't Tom, they didn't have his experience, operated differently because they were younger, so some people did not cope with the change.

At the same time there were other changes like cell church, like refocusing the meetings elsewhere, so that was a lot of change for some people to cope with. And some people, certainly in an area like that, which can tend to be fairly parochial, because a lot of people have lived there all their lives, could not always relate to what we were doing abroad, they didn't have a vision for that. So a new local church came along and they joined that. I think some people have left because they couldn't see the reason for changes, they couldn't see the reason for cells etc. I think the people who were involved in another community, in the space of three or four years they had a number of major changes. So the couple who were leading stepped back, there was a painful time there when several people left and that disappointed and hurt and upset some people. Then another small church joined which again was a very different dynamic and they changed their meetings to that church and now it's being merged into a region. So there have been a lot of changes and some people handle change much better than others so I think that would be a reason.

I think another reason is that many of the house churches, new churches, have plateaued and things that we tried to bring in which were free and new to the church scene have now been very much accepted by many. So things like small groups, styles of worship, etc., which I think to some extent we helped pioneer in Bristol – those would be commonplace now. So people have so many more options now and I think new churches generally, and that would be true of us, have plateaued. I think the excitement of the early days has gone and that's coupled with disappointment – partly through the passage of time, partly because some of the things we advocated have not happened so just coping with the disappointment etc. So I think there's a lot of other factors like that which have caused people to leave and I think too for a lot of people it's probably the right time for them to move on. I think we have, for many people, taken away some identification points and so, in struggling to find their identity, they would rather go somewhere else where there's less struggle over that rather than being part of the solution.

James states:

I feel it's almost as though they're not having their own personal needs met. That sounds a bit judgmental but the church ethos is actually a God ethos – I think that God is behind this cell thing and this outward looking thing and I think a lot of people have got their agendas about what they think is important and great if…in fact somebody left our cell group recently and moved church and I didn't have a problem with that at all, in fact we blessed him in our cell group because I felt he has got a ministry. God's got his hand on him and in order to continue that ministry he needs to move to another church which has got more people involved in that, because he's very much involved with street work and the like and we just don't have a ministry in that and prison work particularly. And I thought, 'no it's right for him to move to a group where…' and in our cell group he didn't fit in…or rather, not because he was an oddball or anything, but just because we didn't have that and I think he needed that in order to move on in that ministry. And so I think for many people who've gone there is a sense of 'they haven't got my agenda,' and people aren't willing to say 'perhaps I need to put my agenda aside for a bit and run with what is a church wide thing'.

And I think BCF has been full of a lot of very gifted people who have got a lot of enthusiasm and I think, perhaps, if BCF hasn't been very good at developing these apprentices and that can be a fault perhaps to be laid at the door of BCF widely – not the elders – then perhaps people have taken those talents elsewhere because they haven't found an outlet for them. But I think a number of people have also left because they found their power going. I think that was some of the people who left earlier on who suddenly didn't have a role any more, or had a demoted role or something, and felt put out by that and lots of feelings of noses disjointed and this, that and the other which I find very petty reasons for going, but there you are.

But there are lots of good churches there and I was naïve after about two years in BCF and thought every church has got to be like ours because this is the way to go and then I grew up a bit and realised that it was great for me and hopefully for some people but not the right thing for everyone. And so I have been in a number of churches as I've grown up – all sorts of denominations as well – I'm very much an ecumenical and I'm part of the greater church rather than thinking that BCF has to be all and the like. Personal crises, not feeling supported, not what they think is important, and seeing only what they see as important I think have been a lot of issues and I'm sure there's been breakdown in relationships which has meant people have left. But I'm sure one of the main things is a feeling of lack of support and so people have thought 'oh I'll get support elsewhere' but there's a whole lot of new problems in any other church so my feeling is let's work through this. Relationship doesn't grow unless you go through difficult times and work it out. So I feel they've gone and they're gonna miss out because they're going to run into the same problems five years down the line. I know a lot of girls who've gone because there aren't any blokes! There's a social thing as well and that's a tragedy really. I don't quite know how we attract blokes into the church as potential husbands!

vi. *'Toronto Blessing'*. The interviewees all recognise that the 'Toronto Bless-ing' has had mixed response from the church. As I stated above, there was general acknowledgement that the leadership's own ambivalence has been a key factor in this. Richard states: 'there's certainly been a consensus among the people I have asked that [the leaders] only embraced it with one arm and not with both so to speak…'

Significantly, they reflect this ambivalence in their own responses. Richard feels that the 'Toronto Blessing' has been a direct challenge to the institutionalising proc-ess in the church:

> I think that where Toronto is impacting people and churches, mixed in with it somewhere is the sense that we have to get out of our four walls and take the good news out so that our lives really count in the work place and the streets. Although I haven't got first hand evidence of these I suspect that in those sort of situations we will be starting to see supernatural manifestations more and more, if we as a church and we as individuals can take the gospel out into the streets. So I suppose, having been in the charismatic movement in the Seventies, and lived with that for twenty years, I think God is doing something new now, and the Seventies church, which to some degree has become institutionalised and almost traditional, is being challenged by God doing something new and something different.

Paul, on the other hand, recognises that Toronto has been beneficial but is con-cerned that it has led in some instances to self-indulgence:

> And I fear, if I'm honest, that some of the people who are leaving us because we are not Toronto enough have crossed over the line to being self-indulgent… I struggle with people whose life is to go to conferences just to get blessed because we always end up as a local church feeling inferior in comparison to some of those bigger meetings and conferences. I would say that there was something divine about Toronto but as with anything that's divine there is always a mixture and I think if you don't understand what it's all about you end up either with a self-indulgent thing or the disappointed, disillusioned thing and I've seen many churches who have either just got into the self-indulgent or they have got into the disappointed bit because there was no real channel for that, so I think there is an anti-climax to Toronto in a lot of places.

James echoes Paul's concerns over self-indulgence and comments on the polarising effects of the phenomenon:

> I think it's quite a polarising thing actually – I really do. I felt there were those who felt that this was the way to go and you've got to bang sticks and do weird things or you're not in on it. And, as I said, for me I felt I don't actually need that. Those who lots of wonderful things happened to felt chosen by God and those who didn't felt not chosen by God, do you know what I mean? …One of my worries at the time were the kind of 'tonight you can have all your problems you've ever had sorted out' and there was this quick fix mentality and I think that's a bad thing and that permeated a bit of the church and I think actually most of those people have probably left because of what the church has been through of late.

vii. *Diminishing Supernatural Expectations*. Richard points out that the apparent contradiction in the responses probably reflects the fact that the 'Toronto Blessing' has not been about revitalising traditional charismatic spiritual gifts. In this sense supernatural expectations have diminished, but paradoxically this is directly related to the Toronto phenomenon!

> When people talk about supernatural manifestations, I don't know what they're thinking of but to me I am thinking more of the gifts of the spirit-prophecy, word of knowledge, word of faith, healing, things like that. None of those were particularly emphasised out of the 'Toronto Blessing'. What the 'Toronto Blessing' was I believe, or part of the essence of it, was people coming away feeling they've had an encounter with God in a powerful way, and that featured very highly in the testimony of people who have been touched by the 'Toronto Blessing'. Often, although by no means always, that was accompanied by a physical manifestation... I'm not aware that it has led to an increased number of prophecies or what I would call traditional 1970s charismatic spiritual manifestations.

Paul sees this as a sign of institutionalisation. In the case of BCF he also cites Neil Edbrooke's chronic illness as an example of how expectation of the supernatural can be undermined:

> I think that many charismatic churches are more charismatic in name than in nature now and so even with some of the things like speaking in tongues there is not the emphasis that there once was, and I think that influences how faith is generated and how things happen for good or bad. So I think at one level it hasn't been highest on our agenda. I think at another level we have wrestled with and had to hold on to healing and believing in healing and yet at the same time have wrestled with the suffering that people have been in. So Neil's illness would probably typify a lot – you confess the positive but the reality is that it isn't always happening or there's a failure to understand that the purposes of God are bigger than healing. So I would think that probably in areas like healing that would have affected our attitude to the supernatural because with Neil there was lots of prayer and I found that a difficult time...you want to give a clear trumpet call and you want to hold on in faith, but you have got to be real when things aren't working out, you have got to find God whether they are working out or not.

James sees this as a direct reaction to the excesses of the 'Toronto Blessing':

> One of my comments is that this is the classical pendulum swing. I mean to me it's like the pendulum swung probably a bit far in the 'Toronto Blessing' and now it's gone too far the other way but with all these things one hopes the pendulum slows down and finds the right happy medium. So to me I'm sure that is the case now, but I have a heart that actually we're gonna get it right somewhere in the middle when the pendulum comes back but I'm not surprised that's where people are at the moment because there was such a big swing that way – there's gonna be a swing the other way and that's what we're in at the moment. I don't struggle with that. I think we'll see the more spiritual type things develop again and hopefully not to too much of an extreme.

viii. *Trends*. Richard believes the downward trends reflect a period of uncertainty and discouragement:

> I think it reflects that we are in a period of uncertainty. I would say that many churches like us, and certainly partly because of the 'Toronto Blessing,' have been

left with questions but also other changes and structural changes have left us with question marks. Generally when people are in a time of change like that it's easy to feel discouraged about a lot of things.

Paul is not convinced by the trend lines:

I would accept some of the trends more than others. I feel it's easy to be nostalgic and say it used to be like this and I think there would be a lot of areas where we can say it used to be like this and we feel we wish it was like it was back then. So with pastoral care that we referred to earlier, I'm sure that ten years back there were a lot of people that didn't feel pastorally cared for. So I feel there could be a bit of that involved.

James believes the trends reflect the current state of the church which he describes as 'hard graft':

I think we feel our backs against the wall and therefore it's no great surprise that the majority of people say all the magic has gone, it's all hard graft at the moment and so I'm not surprised those trends are going down. I think a lot of the spiritual type things are how confident do people feel to say this is what God's saying. I think God speaks to us just as much but I think there's a sense of 'I feel I've got no energy, I've got no right to say this'.

Richard echoes my own analysis when he states that the upward trend in the emphasis on prayer is related to the effects of the 'Toronto Blessing':

So those in BCF who were affected let's say by Toronto and who have as a consequence got an increased appreciation and love for God because something has happened within them to make them more aware of God's love for them, and in response they want to worship him more and give him more time and attention – the opportunity to create that space in a week to reflect on that and give themselves to it has been one of the factors I think which has been shown here in the response that there has been an increased emphasis on prayer.

He also agrees that the emphasis on revival is related to Toronto. Speaking of the 'Toronto Blessing' he states:

I don't know of any time, certainly in my life, probably in church history ever, where you have that heightened sense of expectation on such a scale, which to me is more than any individual or group could have managed to organise.

On the other hand, Richard has mixed feelings about the social justice trend. He suspects that this is largely related to the high profile given to certain social justice issues recently in the church. However, he believes that there is an underlying sense of disappointment resulting from the failure of earlier attempts at cultural engagement:

I think actually there is quite a lot of discouragement, there's some legacy of disappointment left over from the mid-term BCF era when we did actually I think sense a call to, and make some response in engaging with... (Oakhill being an example, education, politics and business)...to see the gospel affecting those areas of our lives. I think we did throw ourselves into that and in many cases we've got wounded as a result and not really understood why and I think that's left quite big questions in some of the long-standing members of BCF. So I think we've probably withdrawn from that to a degree but I can't deny the genuineness of the call and the concern. So now we're not quite sure how to go forward. The gospel has got to affect these areas of our lives but did we go about it prematurely or lacking something that we needed to really make a difference? In our innocence we did the best we could at the time but we have to say it hasn't had the effects we were hoping for, so in some sense discouragement crept in. And it's still there.

Paul likewise agrees that one of the positive fruits of Toronto has been an increasing emphasis on prayer. He also sees the emphasis on revival as a post-Toronto phenomenon. He is not surprised by the increasing emphasis on social justice because that has been given a high profile in the church of late:

> I do think with prayer, social justice and revival those have been things that have been highlighted currently and I do think you get faith for what you emphasise, and we have released resources into social care... So we have put in resources and I think where you put resources then a profile and things get stirred up. I think there is a growing sense in which people have been touched by the social gospel which is very positive. I think with the prayer there has been nationally and internationally the call to prayer and I think that that's one of the most positive fruits from Toronto – it has made people more aware of prayer... As for a revival, it isn't something we have proactively talked about in the church but we have had a significant grouping who have been affected or impacted by 'Catch the Fire'[41] type things, or by renewal centres, and Gerald from Pioneer has talked a lot about revival so I don't think it's something that we have proactively pushed but there is an environment where it has been talked about... I feel revival would be a post Toronto thing...

James is very excited about the increased emphasis on prayer and social justice. He is unsure about revival but believes that if supernatural manifestations are added to the desire for social justice then the church will once again be an exciting place to be in:

> My impression has been that we've gone through perhaps with the 'Toronto Blessing' a bit of a charismatically wobbly 'let's go for the experience' rather than 'let's get down and stuck into society' and if on the up now is this social action, if that surge of the Holy Spirit stuff comes in and joins that as well, wow what a stonking church we're gonna be!

ix. *Institutionalisation*. Richard's comments on institutionalisation are highly relevant to this study and I will quote him in full:

> It has [institutionalised]. I think everything does inevitably but also we are making noises in the opposite direction. I think we have tried our hardest not to become institutionalised but we don't really understand the dynamics which we have. We don't really understand the dynamics of institutionalisation and so we embrace it unwittingly and then we wake up two years later and find what was really fresh has now become routine. So it's a tricky one; I think we have become institutionalised inevitably which saddens me. I believe the church is called to be non-institutional, is called to leave those things behind and to be fresh in terms of its

---

41. Conferences spawned out of the 'Toronto Blessing'.

response. For example, when we joined the church it was no big deal not to have meetings on a Sunday and it was certainly no big deal not to have a meeting place! Now we do both and spend a lot of time talking about how we meet, where we meet; if we take away the Sunday meetings a lot of people feel threatened. So it must mean that some of the underlying values that were present in the foundation of BCF are no longer held strongly by people who make up a lot of the current membership.

I would love to consider getting rid of our buildings. As you grow larger you get people who you are paying full-time which means a payroll, which means regular income, which means tithing by standing order – that's especially a form of institutionalisation! So in all these ways I can see that we have; and the challenge is knowing how not to. So if you do non-institutionalising things now you can actually be challenging the very structure of what has become BCF. And that raises all sorts of issues.

So I suppose we need to go back to what we feel that our roots were, or what we now feel are our real core values and express those and be willing to dispense with some of the institutional things which grew out of a move of the Holy Spirit but have since become living entities in their own right. Also people get older and become not quite so radical and have more commitments so it is not easy to respond – those would be other factors. Youth coming in will be a help, a help because they challenge the status quo and again they don't have some of the hang ups that older people would have. It's hard as the ship gets bigger to steer it as rapidly as you could in the past. You've got those who are hankering for the old days when things were smaller and you knew everyone, it's quite a conundrum.

Personally I would like BCF to be, and I would like to be, more radical in my response again, and to challenge some of the things which are now accepted and just take a risk. I've found that if you do that you take probably a minority of people with you, you will upset some and have some in between who are not quite sure. But what hope is there for the future? Well the hope I think that there is for the future is if we really have a sense that God is alive and God is real and involved with us – it's hearing what he's saying and doing and responding. Again that means different things to different people and holding it all together is a tricky one. I feel quite challenged because with the rise of the number of young people and the evident sense of commitment and passion that they have, which I whole-heartedly embrace, often people talk about handing on the baton but I'm not ready to give it up yet! I'm embracing them and wanting them to come on, but I'm not ready to let go of something yet because I don't feel I have run it all and there's a sense I feel that if I hand on the baton what is there left for me other than retire-ment and sitting on the sidelines watching? So I resist that aspect of it, but I want to embrace the coming alongside of the youth and I fully support all that that entails but don't feel that my generation – I don't feel that our race is over yet; obviously we've got things to do like passing on experience for those who are new and younger but I don't think that's all. I think there's still new ground to take and I want to be part of the taking of it! So that's quite a challenge.

Paul's response too is worth quoting in full:

I find that the heart of the core leadership is not to become institutionalised. Many people find greater security in what they can put in a box and understand. I do though think we have drifted towards institutionalisation because we have got a body of people that would pull us that way. And I feel also because of size and

structures, you end up having to have structures and the minute you have structures you end up with an institution. I don't think it is wrong to have an institution,
it's when you serve that institution and nothing can change that I think it is wrong.
I think that in organic life the body needs a skeleton, you need structures, it's that
invisible point at which the structures become an institution and when the institution dominates. I think the heart of the leadership is to be flexible; I certainly
would not want change for change's sake but I think the church is going to grow
and develop, and change is inevitable because God is changing us. I feel that if
you lose the flexibility to change then I think you become institutionalised.

I think more recently we have identified some sacred cows and we are trying to
touch the…perhaps I can explain it another way. I think in the early days of the
church people joined because partly of a sense of God doing something new, but
partly because of the core values. Then as the church grew, and I do think over the
years generally the quality of the meetings has been good, and people have joined
because of the meetings and the activities and the projects, so when we revisit the
core values people say 'but we didn't join for these'. And I think we are at that
stage where, because some of the core values have been a bit dormant, as we have
tried to revisit them we have realised people did not join because of them, they
joined because they liked the institution. I think the challenge is how can we make
sure we can stay flexible and how can we make sure that we could identify those
who want to change but find it difficult and how to make sure that we are not just
changing for change's sake because things have not been working like we want?
But I think the shape of the church has got to change for the next century and with
people leaving at times it would have been easier to revert back to what people are
comfortable with and kept everyone, but I think we would have become more
institutional had we done that.

Interestingly, James, the only non-elder interviewed, does not sense that the church
has become institutionalised. He bases his comparison on other established churches.
He acknowledges though that he might feel differently if he had been involved from
the start:

I'm sure if I was one of the people who was there originally and is still here I
might have an impression that it's more institutionalised than I've got from where
I'm looking at it… I've seen it as a church that has continued to – it's never stood
still and I think if anyone says 'gosh we've become institutionalised' go to any…
(I won't mention any particular churches but there's a hundred you could go to
and that's institution for you). To say that our church is becoming institutionalised
compared to other churches is barking mad because it hasn't at all.

7. Conclusion

The above responses clearly highlight the fact that BCF is in a state of transition.
The move to becoming a cell church was the key change listed by more respondents than any other, yet it is clear that the church as a whole has not yet embraced
this change. Cell church is the direction the leadership as a whole wish to go but
even among the leadership there is some tension here. Richard, for example, can
see the advantages of the cell church structure to facilitate rapid growth but wonders whether structural change is sufficient to produce such growth. He believes
that to see rapid growth the church needs 'to be in tune with what God is actually

doing in the present'. That, for him, appears to include being more in tune with the 'Toronto Blessing'. He specifically states that the effects on the life of the church of the 'Toronto Blessing' have not been as significant as he would have liked.

BCF appears to have coped with the various leadership changes despite the recognised gaps left by the departure of some key leaders. Bob's departure particularly had a very negative effect on the church at the time. James, however, recalls that Bob returned on one occasion to speak and sees that as an important healing process:

> ...and because Bob was very...he was a real evangelist...and hearing in retrospect the things he says on coming back from Liverpool and the things that are happening there and thinking, 'gosh that could have been happening here!' We really missed out on that and I think when he came and spoke, I remember not long after he had gone, or maybe it was a couple of years whatever, and he could hardly speak he was in real tears about it and really thinking, 'gosh that was really, really difficult because this has been his real spiritual home'.

There were certainly concerns expressed about the lack of emerging leadership from the second generation. Paul, in particular, is concerned that the BCF young people will move elsewhere or start a new church due to the older people failing to 'embrace' them. James too does not feel there are sufficient numbers of youth 'taking on the baton'. This is a critical area for the church at the present time it seems.

The interviewees on the whole agree that the 'Toronto Blessing' has had a polarising effect on the church and has been one major factor in people leaving BCF. Interestingly, James characterises those who have left the church over the 'Toronto Blessing' as being 'quick fix' people as opposed to those who have stayed who demonstrate 'depth of character'. Paul describes them as 'self-indulgent'. Richard, on the other hand, is not surprised that some have left due to other churches emphasising the 'Toronto Blessing' more. He is disappointed that there is no longer 'a sense of excitement and expectancy in our corporate gatherings'.

The two interviewees who were critical of some of the effects of the 'Toronto Blessing' certainly did not condemn the phenomenon outright. Their attitude is far more ambiguous. James, citing the experience of a cynical friend, states as a result: 'I thought there really is something in the 'Toronto Blessing' because this guy was a no-hoper and he's been absolutely transformed...' Paul begins by stating that one result of the 'Toronto Blessing' for many people was that it restored or rekindled their passion for Jesus. This very ambiguity over the 'Toronto Blessing' has been a factor in people leaving as both Richard and Paul acknowledge.

James and Richard both agree that the general downward trend in most emphases reflects a church struggling with transition; James adds that the prolonged nature of this struggle has left many people tired and lacking in confidence. Paul is more cautious about the results and wonders whether the responses to the questionnaire reflect more of a sense of nostalgia for the past than an actual downward trend. None of the interviewees were surprised by the three exceptions to the general trend as all agreed that prayer and social justice have been particularly emphasised of late and that the emphasis on revival has followed the 'Toronto Blessing'.

The responses to the degree to which BCF has become institutionalised were mixed. Richard feels more strongly than the others that the church has institutional-ised, although he acknowledges that 'we are making noises in the opposite direc-tion'. Paul recognises the institutionalising process but argues that it is not the desire of the core leadership to become institutionalised. Interestingly, it is the two leaders who recognise the degree of institutionalisation. Richard's response, in particular, picks up the argument of this whole thesis. He recognises that institutionalisation is inevitable but also argues that counter-institutionalising forces are often present to challenge that institutionalising process:

> Any corporate thing which involves people inevitably institutionalises over time. I would also add in that God sends new things, or picks the church up by its boot straps, or does something which challenges that institutionalising process.

Furthermore, whatever their specific views on the 'Toronto Blessing', the respon-dents all positively embrace the desire for more of the miraculous. James believes that 'miracles will start happening that really change the world...' Richard suggests that if the church takes the gospel out into the streets 'we will be starting to see supernatural manifestations more and more...sooner or later we are going to see people getting healed as they are prayed for in the shops and in the street and things like that...' Paul acknowledges the need to hold onto the belief in healing in the midst of lack of evidence for healings.

The current stage in BCF's development can be usefully analysed by means of O'Dea's model (1961). BCF was certainly founded in what O'Dea terms a 'charis-matic moment'. Since then the church has undoubtedly experienced the dilemma of mixed motivation. Paul's comments concerning people subsequently joining the church because of the meetings, activities and projects and the recognition that there has to be a return to the 'core values' highlight this. In addition, there has been an objectification of ritual as can be demonstrated by the high ranking of 'professionalisation of worship' in Appendix 3. The response to this has been mixed – there is a recognition that worship has to be much more 'professional' given the large numbers, but this is accompanied by a sense of alienation as people feel less personally involved in acts of worship. The 'Toronto Blessing' can be seen as a reaction to this as its emphasis on personal response does lead to more 'democ-ratisation' of worship. O'Dea's third dilemma, that of administrative order, has clearly affected churches such as BCF as argued by me in Pietersen (1998a: 19–21). As the church grew the initial charismatic authority was inevitably trans-formed into bureaucratic authority and this change, together with the influence of growth and business management strategies, resulted in exhaustion and burnout in some cases. The 'Toronto Blessing' has been a way in which this dilemma has been countered with its demand for a return to the charismatic moment as well articulated by Richard. O'Dea's fourth dilemma concerning delimitation has been paraphrased by Mathisen (1987: 304) as 'the dangers of watering down the original versus a rigidly literal adherence to it'. In the case of BCF, it is the former which has proved problematic and there is a general recognition by the leadership that there has been a diminution in core values. Finally, O'Dea's fifth dilemma, con-cerning power, is too closely modelled on Troeltsch's church-sect typology. O'Dea speaks of the use of power to reinforce the position of a religious organisation within society and cites both Catholic and Protestant confessional states with their 'union of throne and altar' (1961: 37). However, this is unlikely to be a problem in a sectarian response to the world and certainly has not been a dilemma as far as BCF is concerned. Nevertheless, O'Dea's fifth dilemma can be modified to encapsulate the concept of success. Certainly, during the period in which BCF grew rapidly and as such became 'successful' there was an inevitable tendency to seek to maintain the strategies that led to such growth. Numerical growth led, for example, to the demand for buildings and the purchase of buildings, as rightly acknowledged by Richard, was a clear sign of the institutionalising process. Subsequent events, with a number of people leaving and the church diminishing in size, means that this is not at present a major factor in the institutionalising process.

O'Dea's model highlights the factors involved in the ongoing tension between the memory of, and demand for, the charismatic moment on the one hand, and the institutionalising process on the other. The responses of the interviewees confirm that there is an ongoing process of institutionalisation in tension with counter-institutionalising developments. Given the comments concerning the 'quick fix' mentality or the 'self indulgence' of those who have left the church to pursue the 'Toronto Blessing' it might be said that the leadership, in the light of Toronto, wish to espouse, in the language of the Pastorals, virtues such as εὐσέβεια and σωφροσύνη! Nevertheless, thaumaturgy still has its attractions – there is still a desire amongst the leadership to see more signs and wonders in evidence. It would appear then, in the case of BCF, that the tension between teaching, tradition and thaumaturgy continues to be played out in its development.

This tension between the continuing demand for the charismatic moment and the process of institutionalisation, as borne out by the responses of the interviewees, is also highlighted by the responses to the questionnaire. As stated on page 77, equal numbers of respondents listed the 'Toronto Blessing' and decreasing supernatural expectations as key changes which have taken place in the development of BCF. Despite ranking just above diminishing supernatural expectations in the overall ranking of key changes in Appendix 3, the highly thaumaturgical 'Toronto Blessing' has not reversed the trend of diminishing emphasis on miracles and oracles as far as the respondents to the questionnaire are concerned.

This, on the surface, would appear to indicate that, in the case of BCF, thaumaturgical demand as exemplified by the 'Toronto Blessing' has proved highly ephemeral and has not subverted the institutionalisation process. However, the fact remains that a sufficient number of respondents listed the 'Toronto Blessing' as one of the five key changes impacting the development of BCF to place it sixth in the overall ranking. This perception of the significant impact of the 'Toronto Blessing' despite its seeming failure to halt the declining emphasis on miracles and oracles requires some explanation. One key factor has been the ambivalence of the leadership over the 'Toronto Blessing' as indicated above. The 'Toronto Blessing' has sufficiently affected the lives of a number of people within BCF to be perceived as having a significant impact. Consequently, if the leadership had unequivocally endorsed this movement I have no doubt that the downward trend in connection with the emphasis on miracles and oracles would have been reversed. This is further borne out by the emphasis on revival. Responses indicate that the emphasis on revival has remained consistently high since 1992. The increasing emphasis on revival thus predates the 'Toronto Blessing' but appears to have been sustained by it. It is important to note that, in the context of the 'Toronto Blessing', the expectation of revival is not simply that of significant numbers being converted to Christianity. In the words of John Arnott, senior pastor of TACF, quoted above on page 73, 'Whenever God moves in revival, *there is always an increase in signs and wonders*' (my emphasis). The analysis is thus highly revealing. The effects of institutionalisation are so profoundly felt that there is a general perception that the emphasis on signs and wonders has decreased. Nevertheless, there is a simultaneous increase in the expectation of revival with signs and wonders seen as an integral part of such revival. The increased emphasis on prayer, as I have suggested above, is also directly connected with concern for revival. So, although signs and wonders are apparently not currently experienced in the ongoing life of the church, there is an increasing hope that they will soon be experienced in the context of revival.

The development of BCF over the last twenty-five years clearly demonstrates the process of institutionalisation at work. However, the impact of the 'Toronto Blessing' and the continuing emphasis on revival in its wake suggest that the charismatic moment is still cherished in the life of the church and that thaumaturgical demand remains a significant factor within the congregation.

The evidence of this case study suggests, therefore, that institutionalisation and the intensification of the thaumaturgical response can occur simultaneously within a conversionist sect. In the following chapter I shall argue that this tension between institutionalisation and thaumaturgical demand is present at the time of Ignatius. I shall then argue in Chapter 6 that if this was true of the church of Ignatius' day then it could also be true of the communities addressed by the Pastorals. The Pastorals, I shall argue, emphasise teaching and tradition in the face of what the author perceives to be unacceptable thaumaturgical demand.

Chapter 5

SECOND-CENTURY DEVELOPMENTS: IGNATIUS, PROTO-MONTANISM AND MONTANISM

1. *Introduction*

The notion that the Pastorals reflect increasing institutionalisation and the emergence of 'early catholicism' is widespread in the scholarly literature. Dunn (1998: 598), for example, states: 'It is no surprise, then, that already in the unanticipated second-generation Pauline churches (the Pastorals) we see the familiar second-generation pattern of routinization of charisma and institutionalisation of authority'. If this is considered true of the Pastorals, it is almost universally claimed by New Testament scholars that, by the time of Ignatius, the process of institutionalisation has triumphed over Paul's notion of the church as charismatic community.[1] In chapters three and four I have described a developmental model which suggests that in charismatic communities the inevitable routinisation of charisma over time is accompanied by increased thaumaturgical demand. It remains an open question, as far as this model is concerned, whether this dialectic results in the total subversion of the institutionalising process, the final triumph of institutionalisation, or a continuing tension between the two. In this chapter I shall argue that the tension is still present at the time of Ignatius, that the institutionalising process is later subverted by Montanism and that the emergence of Montanism itself served, in turn, to accelerate institutionalisation.

If the tension between the routinisation and intensification of charisma is still present by the time of Ignatius then, according to the model, it will undoubtedly be present in the Pastorals. I shall then finally be in a position to examine the Pastorals from the perspective of this developmental model.

2. *Ignatius and the Demand for Charisma*

Even a cursory reading of the seven letters of Ignatius comprising the middle recension[2] reveals the importance of the role of the bishop to Ignatius. He has rightly been regarded as an early champion of monepiscopacy. Nevertheless, a sociologically sensitive reading of Ignatius would want to question the scholarly consensus that Ignatius is merely reflecting the contemporary structure of the

---

1. Von Campenhausen (1969) remains one of the classic expositions of this position.
2. Now widely accepted as authentic. See the discussion in Trevett (1992: 9–15).

churches in Syria and Asia. His need to emphasise the priority of the bishop more likely indicates that this was a contested concept and that the Ignatian vision of monepiscopacy was yet to become the norm. Indeed, indications of some tension between bishops and their congregations do appear in the letters.[3] Furthermore, the letter to the Romans does not even mention a bishop.[4]

a. *Ephesians*
I shall argue in Chapter 6 that the Pastorals' address to communities in Ephesus and Crete should be treated as authentic. I shall, therefore, in the light of this, con-centrate on Ignatius' letter to the Ephesians before looking at his letter to the Phila-delphians (which contains the primary evidence for the relevance of my model). It is obvious that there are problems between the congregation and its leadership. Ignatius has to urge them to love their bishop (1.3) and to be 'in tune' with the bishop and the presbytery (4.1–2). Some are apparently meeting together outside of the officially approved meeting place (5.2). In these meetings (which of course are without the bishop being present) they emphasise prayer which has power (5.2; ἰσχύς). Ignatius seeks to deal with this by emphasising how much more power there would be if the bishop and the whole congregation were involved (5.3). However, from what follows, it seems clear that those emphasising 'powerful prayer' are opposed to the bishop (5.3b).

Although Ignatius praises the Ephesian Christians for the fact that no heresy is to be found among them (6.2; 9.1; possibly echoing Rev. 2.2), he is obviously con-cerned, like the author of the Pastorals, about those who 'corrupt households' (16.1; οἱ οἰκοφθόροι). As in the Pastorals, Ignatius appears to be combating opponents from within – they are 'accustomed to carrying about the Name' (7.1). It is possi-ble that those who meet for prayer without the bishop are precisely those whom Ignatius sees as corrupting households. He writes that the former are among the arrogant whom God opposes (5.3).

There are additional connections with the Pastorals. Interestingly, the only occur-rence of the entire σωφρ– word group (σωφροσύνη) in Ignatius is found in 10.3. This word group occurs ten times in the Pastorals. Furthermore, *Ephesians* contains the only reference to magic (μαγεία) in Ignatius (19.3). I shall argue in Chapter 6 that the author of the Pastorals considers the opponents as 'workers of magic'. The most significant connection, however, concerns the emphasis on 'silence' which is also to be found in 1 Tim. 2.11–12.

b. *'Silence' in Ignatius*
Ignatius mentions the 'silent' (σιγάω) bishop in *Eph.* 6.1 and *Phld.* 1.1 and 'si-lence' (σιωπάω/σιγάω/ἡσυχία) more generally in *Ephesians* 15. The meaning of 'silence' in Ignatius has been disputed. Chadwick, for example, argues that for Ignatius God is silence (*Eph.* 19.1; *Magn.* 8.2) and the bishop corresponds to God (*Eph.* 5.3; *Magn.* 6.1; *Trall.* 3.1; *Smyrn.* 8.1–2); therefore, the bishop's silence

---

3.   E.g. *Eph.* 2.2; 5.2; 6; 15; *Magn.* 3–4; 6; 7.1; *Trall.* 2–3; 7.2; *Smyrn.* 8; 9.1.
4.   The most likely explanation of this is that the church in Rome did not have a single-bishop structure when Ignatius wrote. See Trevett (1992: 91–92).

reflects God's silence (and in turn reflects certain Gnostic parallels).[5] Schoedel (1985: 56) suggests that it refers to the bishop's ineloquence resulting in a lack of ability to argue effectively against false teachers. This suggestion fails adequately to account for why Ignatius should praise the bishop's silence. Trevett (1992: 128–29), in my view, provides the most persuasive argument. She notes that in *Phld.* 1.1 the bishop's silence is contrasted with those who talk vainly.[6] Similarly the words and deeds of the teacher are contrasted in *Ephesians* 15. *Eph.* 15.2 is concerned with those who truly apprehend the word of Jesus. Trevett argues that precisely what is at issue is the question: who has the authority to teach? For Trevett, Ignatius is here arguing that Jesus' teaching and example had not always been correctly understood and transmitted. 'Silence', therefore, reflects an attitude of desiring to learn as in 1 Tim. 2.11. The passage thus engages with the debate about teaching and prophecy which was going on in Ignatius' time. Those authorised to teach and prophesy are those who have through 'silence' learned to apprehend the word of Jesus.

Furthermore, the passage concerning the bishop's silence in *Eph.* 6.1 is immediately followed by an endorsement of the bishop as one sent by 'the master of the house to manage his own house'. As such the bishop is to be welcomed just as the one who sent him would be welcomed, and the bishop is to be regarded as the Lord himself. This passage should be compared with *Didache* 11–13. Here it is apostles and prophets who are to be welcomed as the Lord himself would be welcomed. If Trevett's conclusions are right (that the final form of the *Didache* is to be dated to the first quarter of the second century CE and that it is of Syrian provenance), then it is highly likely that Ignatius knew the work in some form.[7] So for Ignatius the silent bishop is to be received in the same way as the Didachist urges for apostles and prophets.

The need for Ignatius to support the bishop's silence in *Eph.* 6.1 and *Phld.* 1.1 suggests that the Ephesian and Philadelphian Christians were unimpressed by it. The support for the bishop's silence in *Eph.* 6.1 comes immediately after reference to gatherings of 'one or two' apart from the bishop offering a 'prayer of power' (*Eph.* 5.2). The bishop's 'silence' must therefore be seen in this context and it is thus likely that those gathering apart from the bishop were unimpressed with his ability to offer powerful prayers. Trevett's conclusion that the bishop's silence 'was understood [by charismatic Christians in the congregations] in terms of failure

---

5.   H. Chadwick, 'The Silence of the Bishops in Ignatius', *HTR* 43 (1950): 169–72; cited in Schoedel (1985: 57) and Trevett (1992: 128–29). Neither Schoedel nor Trevett find this convincing.

6.   'μάταια λαλούντων'; cf. 1 Tim. 1.6; Tit. 1.10.

7.   Niederwimmer (1998: 52–54) finds 'no compelling reasons' to reject the hypothesis that the final form of the *Didache* should be dated around 110 or 120 CE. However, he is not as convinced as Trevett about its Syrian provenance; he is unable to decide between an Egyptian, Syrian or Palestinian origin. Jefford (1995) concludes that it is very plausible that Ignatius knew some early form of the *Didache* and even more likely that he was familiar with materials and traditions used by the Didachist. He considers it only 'remotely possible' that Ignatius knew the *Didache* in its present form.

to provide spiritual leadership and sustenance, especially in terms of prophecy' (1992: 195) is persuasive.

c. *Philadelphians*

It is the letter to the Philadelphians which is of crucial significance in connection with the emergence of proto-Montanism. For Ammia, the female prophet remembered by catholics and Montanists alike, came from Philadelphia.[8] She was, quite probably, a contemporary of Ignatius. Already, in the inscription, Ignatius finds it necessary to single out for praise those who 'are at one with the bishop and the presbyters and deacons who are with him'. The bishop, due to his 'silence', appears to need Ignatius' endorsement (*Phld.* 1.1). There seem to be Philadelphian Christians who celebrate the Eucharist apart from the bishop, much to Ignatius' disapproval (*Philadelphians* 4). The whole letter points to considerable tension in the church at Philadelphia: this is particularly evident in *Philadelphians* 7. Here Ignatius recalls his prophecy that the Philadelphian Christians should 'pay attention to the bishop and to the presbytery and deacons'. Trevett persuasively argues that the letter also indicates considerable strain in the relationship between Ignatius himself and the Philadelphian Christians:

> First, Ignatius did not write of the endurance of Philadelphian Christians, such as we find in the greetings and exhortations of all the other epistles (*Eph.* 3.1; *Magn.* 1.2; *Trall.* 1.1; *Rom.* 10.3; *Smyrn.* 12.1; *Pol.* 3.1f.; 6.2)... Secondly the use of *axio* compounds is interesting. These occurred in his descriptions of other churches but again they were absent from the Philadelphian letter, except for *axiopistoi* in 2.2 (cf. *Pol.* 3.1) describing errorist 'wolves' [who are seemingly trustworthy]... We must assume that given his experience while halted in Philadelphia his less fulsome praise of its church was due to a sense of wrong to himself.[9]

The combination of opposition to the bishop, hostility towards Ignatius, his mention of having prophesied, and his support of the 'silent' bishop suggests to Trevett (1992: 194–99) that Ignatius encountered opposition from charismatic Christians, particularly at Philadelphia, profoundly concerned about his monepiscopal emphasis.[10] Church order was thus by no means a settled issue in Ignatius' time although his view eventually triumphed.

d. *Conclusion*

Ignatius' undoubted championing of monepiscopacy should not be taken as providing evidence of the actual structure of the churches in Asia Minor and Syria addressed. Rather, the writings of Ignatius should be regarded as prescriptive and not descriptive of the prevailing situation. The picture emerges of a church in transition with itinerant apostles and prophets still on the scene but with an increasing emphasis on residential offices. In this transitional climate there was clear suspicion of

---

8. Eusebius, *HE* v. 17.2–3.
9. Trevett (1992: 96).
10. Trevett argues that Ignatius combats three groups in his letters: docetics, judaizing Christians and (Johannine?) charismatics.

residential offices as reflected in *Didache* 15 and in the letters of Ignatius. Ignatius' view of church order was thus contested. The tension that Trevett finds between the hierarchical structure favoured by Ignatius and the views of his charismatic opponents is precisely what the developmental model I have outlined suggests.

3. *Proto-Montanism*

If Trevett's arguments are accepted (1996: 15–45), Montanism emerged in the region east of Philadelphia in the 160s CE.[11] To describe the opponents in the Pastorals as 'proto-Montanist' in the way Ford (1971) does without proper nuancing is, therefore, problematic. Nevertheless, it is appropriate to seek to trace the antecedents to the emergence of Montanism proper on the basis that it is highly unlikely that the movement simply emerged out of nowhere. According to Eusebius' anonymous source, the Montanists regarded themselves as heirs to a prophetic succession traced from Agabus to Judas, Silas, the daughters of Philip, Ammia, Quadratus and on to Priscilla and Maximilla (*HE* v.17.3–4). Quadratus and Ammia are specifically associated with Philadelphia by Eusebius' anonymous source. In this connection it is significant that the church in Philadelphia is addressed by Ignatius in a way which suggests that he encountered some degree of opposition there.

Trevett (1996: 37–42) has persuasively argued that the prime opponents of monepiscopacy as advocated by Ignatius can best be labelled as 'proto-Montanist'. The issues involved in the debate with Ignatius are precisely those which re-emerged in the catholic-Montanist debate several decades later.[12] She concludes:

> I have been arguing for more than a decade that Ignatius was opposing (what he regarded as) false teaching on more than one front. Lines of demarcation are not always easy to draw, yet it seems to me that his letters to Asia witness to the discomforting presence of just the kinds of Christians whose descendants would have welcomed [Montanism]. Most significant of all, *Philadelphia* was where he met strongest opposition, and that town is a common factor linking the Apocalypse, the Ignatian letters and Montanism. According to his letters there were difficulties for Asian bishops in other churches too, notably in Ephesus and Smyrna. It does not seem to me coincidental that these were places to which the Seer had addressed letters.
>
> Montanus' bid for the public sphere half a century or so later must have come in relation to something *which already existed*. Was he part of a tolerated prophetic conventicle whose relations with catholic clergy had been relatively unstrained up to this time…? That is an option I favour (1996: 39).

---

11. Tabbernee (1997: 53) is unconvinced of the Philadelphian origin of Montanism; he suggests that the movement probably originated in Phrygia rather than Lydia. He does, however, suggest that Montanism emerged around 165 CE (1997: 17).

12. Trevett (1996: 38–39) lists: Scripture and the nature and content of the gospel (*Philadelphians* 7–8); the importance of visionary and other charismatic gifts, especially for the bishop (*Eph.* 5.1–2; 20; *Trallians* 4; *Philadelphians* 7; *Pol.* 2.1–2); celibacy (*Polycarp* 5); prophecy (*Philadelphians* 7) and failure to participate fully in the life of congregations gathered round their bishops (*Ephesians* 2–3; 5.2–6.1; *Phld.* 6.3; 8–9; *Polycarp* 6).

Thus the letters of Ignatius, far from providing evidence for a thoroughly institutionalised church, actually suggest an environment in which what was to emerge as
Montanism flourished.

4. *Montanism*

a. *Beginnings*

According to Eusebius' anonymous source, Montanus began prophesying in a
village called Ardabau in Phrygian Mysia (*HE* v.16.7). Montanus is invariably
linked with two prophetesses Priscilla and Maximilla (*Panarion* xlviii.1.3). The
location of Ardabau is unknown and has occasioned lively scholarly debate.[13]
There is no agreement concerning the date Montanism started either. Eusebius dates
its commencement in 172 CE and this is the date favoured by the majority of scholars. Epiphanius, on the other hand, dates the beginning of Montanism to 157 CE
(*Panarion* xlviii.1.2). However, Epiphanius is self-contradictory. Earlier in the
Panarion, Epiphanius appears to favour the decade of the 140s, while his statement
in *Panarion* xlviii.2.7 that 'there have been approximately 290 years from then to
our own time' dates the death of the Montanist prophetess Maximilla at around 85
CE. Furthermore, he states in *Panarion* li.33 that the church in Thyatira succumbed
to Montanism 93 years after Jesus' ascension. This would indicate Montanist
influence in the 120s. Epiphanius' evidence is thus highly problematic but this has
not prevented a number of scholars from accepting his date of 157 CE. Trevett
(1996: 32–45) carefully and convincingly argues the case for a degree of harmoni-
sation of the witness of Eusebius, Epiphanius and others. She suggests that Montanism arose in the decade of the 160s and was initially tolerated within the church,
but subsequently driven out (*HE* v.16.10). Acute confrontation with the movement
began in the 170s.

Montanism spread within its first few decades from Asia Minor to Rome and
North Africa. Tertullian's subsequent conversion to Montanism suggests that it had
reached Carthage by about 200 CE.[14]

b. *Teaching*

According to Apollonius (*HE* v.18.2), Montanus, among other things, taught the
dissolution of marriages (ὁ διδάξας λύσεις γάμων), made laws concerning fasts
(ὁ νηστείας νομοθετήσας), and supplied salaries to those who preached his doctrine so that the teaching of his doctrine might take hold through gluttony (ὁ
σαλάρια χορηγῶν τοῖς κηρύσσουσιν αὐτοῦ τὸν λόγον, ἵνα διὰ τῆς γαστ-
ριμαργίας ἡ διδασκαλία τοῦ λόγου κρατύνηται). These accusations find
parallels in the Pastorals (1 Tim. 4.3; 6.5b; Tit. 1.11).

However, it would appear that it was the way in which Montanus and the
prophetesses prophesied which caused most concern to their opponents. Eusebius'

---

13. See the discussion in Trevett (1996: 21–24). She opts for the general region east of
Philadelphia.

14. See Trevett (1996: 70–72).

anonymous source, for example, speaking of Montanus, states: ἐν ἐπιθυμίᾳ ψυχῆς ἀμέτρῳ φιλοπρωτείας δόντα πάροδον εἰς ἑαυτὸν τῷ ἀντικειμένῳ πνευμα- τοφορηθῆναί τε καὶ αἰφνιδίως ἐν κατοχῇ τινι καὶ παρεκστάσει γενόμενον ἐνθουσιᾶν ἄρξασθαί τε λαλεῖν καὶ ξενοφωνεῖν...[15] Immediately after this the Anonymous states that this was contrary to the *tradition* of the church. Speaking subsequently of Priscilla and Maximilla he states that they too spoke madly (ἐκφρ- όνως), inappropriately (ἀκαίρως) and abnormally (ἀλλοτριοτρόπως) (*HE* v.16.9). Criticism was not just directed at the three main leaders; in *HE* v.16.14 the Anonymous mentions Theodotus who experienced heavenly ascents in an ecstatic state and died after one such experience.

Epiphanius admits that the Montanists were impeccably orthodox in connection with their view of the Scriptures, the resurrection and the doctrine of the Trinity, but insists that they were deceived by paying attention to Montanus, Priscilla and Maximilla and in their mode of prophesying (*Panarion* xlviii.1.3–4). There follows a long discussion in which Epiphanius insists that the prophets and apostles prophe- sied in full possession of their senses and not in an ecstatic state like the Montanists (*Panarion* xlviii.2.5–8.8). Interestingly, in this section Epiphanius alludes to or quotes 1 Tim. 1.19; 4.1, 3. In xlviii.9 he quotes from 1 Tim. 5.11–12 and 5.14. 1 Timothy, at least, proved to be relevant to those opposed to Montanism.

Other Montanist practices, besides their asceticism, were criticised by the 'catho- lic' side.[16] However, undoubtedly the key issues were the ecstatic nature of their prophesying and the threat that their additional revelations from the Spirit posed to the authority of the catholic leadership.[17] Trevett (1996: 147) sums the situation up well:

> I conclude that all followed from the fact of that dangerous entity *prophecy*, and this one of a special kind: inapposite, 'untraditional' and incorporating innovatory discipline. Here was no sober didacticism and no *gravitas* of male catholic lead- ership. Here were 'wild and barbarous' people (Epiphanius *Pan*. xlviii.12,3) defending the message on the basis of cherished scriptural principles.

Additionally, if the comments of Celsus were directed against Montanist prophets, then, after describing the typical content of their prophecies in terms of God's desire to save people from coming judgment, he continues that they also add words which are unintelligible (ἄγνωστα), frenzied (πάροιστρα) and utterly obscure (πάντη ἄδηλα).[18]

Finally, Epiphanius (*Panarion* xlviii.13.1) states that Maximilla claimed to be 'the knowledge and teaching of understanding' (ἡ τῆς παρακολουθίας γνῶσις καὶ διδασκαλία). Interestingly, this combination of παρακολουθέω and διδασ- καλία occurs in the New Testament only in 1 Tim. 4.6 and 2 Tim. 3.10,[19] both of

15. 'In the immense desire of his ambitious soul [Montanus] gave the adversary access to himself and, being possessed by a spirit, and suddenly experiencing some kind of frenzy and false ecstasy, he was inspired and began to speak and say strange things' (*HE* v. 16.7).

16. For a detailed discussion see Trevett (1996: 77–150).

17. So rightly Trevett (1996: 146–49).

18. Origen, *Contra Celsum* 7.9.

19. παρακολουθία itself does not appear in the New Testament. If Mk 16.17 is excluded,

which follow immediately after condemnation of the opponents. It is Paul's teaching, rather than that of the opponents, which Timothy is exhorted to follow.

c. *Women*

The founding of Montanism is linked not just to Montanus but to his two female associates – the prophetesses Prisca/Priscilla and Maximilla. Another prophetess, Quintilla, is mentioned by Epiphanius (*Panarion* xlix.1) who goes on to speak of seven prophesying virgins among the 'Quintillians' who functioned often in congregational settings (*Panarion* xlix.2). The Montanists also ordained women as clergy, appealing to Miriam and Philip's daughters as precedents and also to Gal. 3.28 (ἐν γὰρ Χριστῷ Ἰησοῦ οὔτε ἄρσεν οὔτε θῆλυ) (*Panarion* xlix.2). Women thus featured prominently in Montanism and this also brought condemnation from the catholic side. Here again there are significant parallels with the Pastorals where the opponents enjoy particular success among women and where the author has to forbid women not only from teaching but also from exercising undue authority over men (1 Tim. 2.12).

d. *Subsequent Developments*

It would appear that, although Montanism in Asia Minor was originally orthodox, aberrations occurred fairly early on in its Roman version. As early as Hippolytus we have the following comment:

> But some of them, agreeing with the heresy of the Noetians, say that the Father himself is the Son, and that he has experienced birth, suffering and death.[20]

In Asia Minor Montanism was roundly condemned in the time of Eusebius' anonymous source. This resulted, after careful deliberation, in Montanists being expelled from the church. Although 'the Anonymous' speaks of heresy and false prophecy, it appears that the main issue was ecstatic prophecy, as noted above (*HE* v.16.1–10). The accusation of Sabellianism became widespread in the fourth and fifth centuries.[21] It seems that, whatever Montanus himself taught, some Montanists eventually became Sabellian in doctrine whilst others claimed either that the fullness of the Spirit came with Montanus rather than with the apostles,[22] or that Montanus himself was the Paraclete.[23] Nevertheless, as Trevett (1996: 214–15) rightly reminds us, caution needs to be exercised with these sources as heresy was a frequent way of accusing one's opponents and many later writers based their claims on the copying of earlier writers. Trevett's cautious conclusion is as follows:

παρακολουθέω appears elsewhere only in Lk. 1.3. For an extensive discussion of the semantical development of παρακολουθέω in connection with Lk. 1.3 see Alexander (1993b: 128–30).

20. Hippolytus, Refutatio Omnium Haeresium 8.19.

21. E.g. Didymus, *De trinitate* 2.15; Jerome, *Ep* 41.3, *ad Marcellam*. All references taken from Heine (1989).

22. E.g. Pseudo-Tertullian, *Adversus Omnes Haereses* 7; Filastrius of Brescia, *Diuersarum Haereseon Liber* 49; Augustine, *De haeresibus* 26.

23. Basil of Caesarea, *Epistle* 188.1; Theodoret, *Haereticarum fabularum compendium* 3.2.

The New Prophecy had first found itself squeezed into schism and as matters deteriorated it offered hostility for hostility. Increasingly isolated from the catholic mainstream but having still to defend itself from time to time, speculative theology may have come to the fore... Probably we should believe the consensus view of our sources from the fourth century onwards that *by that time* the Montanist understanding of Father, Son and Spirit was not that of the orthodox, though caution is needed, given that 'Montanism' had split and diversified (1996: 222–23).

Montanism took some time to die out but the Christianising of the empire under Constantine was a decisive factor in its demise.[24] Consequently, although Montanism undoubtedly contributed to the increasing institutionalisation of the church as a result of reaction against its ecstatic nature, the tension between this institutionalisation and the demand for a more thaumaturgical expression persisted for at least two hundred years.

5. *Ecstasy and the Pastorals*

It has become commonplace to assume that the Pastorals reflect the increasing institutionalisation of church authority into a hierarchy consisting of a single bishop, presbytery and diaconate. The Ignatian correspondence is often cited as evidence for such a structure early in the second century CE. However, it has been argued above that the Ignatian hierarchical view of church government was by no means a settled issue in his time. The rise of Montanism as a phenomenon initially *within* the catholic church strongly suggests that some prophetic element continued to be at least tolerated, if not encouraged, well into the second century.[25] We cannot, therefore, assume that this hierarchical structure was the norm at the time the Pastorals were written. It remains to be seen whether the church order advocated in the Pastorals should be understood against a similar background of opposition from charismatic groups.

In this connection an appropriate place to start is with Ford's emphasis that the stress on sobriety and self-control in the Pastorals cannot be aimed against sexual licence and intoxication. For the opponents clearly advocate sexual abstinence and asceticism (1 Tim. 4.1–5). It is instructive to note how often having a sound mind and clear understanding is stressed in anti-Montanist polemic directed against Montanist ecstatic prophecy, particularly in Epiphanius' source in *Panarion* xlviii.1–13. Although the actual words used are not the same (Epiphanius' favoured expression is ἐρρωμένη διανοία) the sentiments are similar. Could it be that the Pastorals' emphasis on σώφρων,[26] σωφροσύνη,[27] σωφρονίζω,[28] σωφρονισμός,[29]

---

24. Trevett (1996: 223).
25. This can be demonstrated too from the evidence of the *Didache*.
26. 4 times in the Pastoral Epistles but nowhere else in the New Testament.
27. Twice in the Pastorals, elsewhere only in Acts 26.25.
28. Once in the Pastorals only.
29. Once in the Pastorals only.

σωφρονέω[30] and ὑγιαίνω/ὑγιής[31] indicates a similar background? On one occasion the text comes tantalisingly close to suggesting a context of ecstasy; in 1 Tim. 6.5 we read διεφθαρμένων ἀνθρώπων τὸν νοῦν. Διαφθείρω when used with νοῦς can mean 'to lose one's mind'[32] rather than 'depraved in mind' as in the NRSV. Ford (1971: 343) thinks that this may indeed be a reference to frenzy, and the references in anti-Montanist passages concerning being out of one's mind in the context of ecstasy make this suggestion highly likely.[33] Furthermore, 1 Tim. 6.5 goes on to talk about financial gain and greed and this was a charge also levied against the Montanists (*HE* v.18.2).

Finally, as in Montanism proper, it would appear that women were both effectively recruited by the heretics (2 Tim. 3.6–9) and were themselves prominent in the heretical movement (1 Tim. 2.9–15). Apollonius, cited in *HE* v.18.4, is concerned that Priscilla 'has received gold and silver and expensive clothes'. This is interesting in the light of 1 Tim. 2.9.

6. Conclusion

The above analysis has sought to demonstrate that Montanism was perceived as an ecstatic movement and that its roots stretched back at least to the time of Ignatius. The Ignatian correspondence has been used to argue that monepiscopacy was by no means a settled issue in his day. Ignatius is not describing the actual church structure of his day but seeking to be prescriptive in a transitional period of the church when there were competing claims for authority between itinerant apostles and prophets, as evidenced by the *Didache*, and residential bishops, presbyters and deacons. If there is evidence of continuing charismatic authority in Ignatius' time it is even more likely that this would be the case when the Pastorals were written. Comparison of the polemic used in the Pastorals with that of anti-Montanists suggests that the opponents addressed in the Pastorals advocated an enthusiastic, even ecstatic, form of Christianity. In the next chapter I shall examine this possibility more closely from the text of the Pastorals.

---

30. Once in the Pastorals, five times elsewhere in the New Testament.

31. Nine times in the Pastorals, fourteen elsewhere.

32. LSJ (s.v.), citing Homer, *Iliad* XV.128 suggests that the perfect tense of διαφθείρω can mean 'to have lost one's wits'. Additionally, LSJ translates διαφθείρω in combination with φρήν as 'loss of one's mind'.

33. E.g., Epiphanius, *Panarion* xlviii.2.8; 3.6, 8; 4.3, 6. Further support comes from Malherbe (1980: 32) who, citing Demosthenes and Plutarch, suggests that τετύφωται in 1 Tim. 6.4 'is quite likely...intended to describe mental illness'.

Chapter 6

TEACHING, TRADITION AND THAUMATURGY

1. *Paraenesis or Polemic?*

a. *Paraenesis and Other Literary Arguments*
i. *Polemic and Personal Example in Paraenesis.* I have dealt with the positions of
Johnson (1978/79) and Fiore (1986) in some detail in Chapter 1 above. Fiore's
impressive examination of the function of personal example both in contemporary
Graeco-Roman literature and in the Pastoral Epistles provides strong evidence for
viewing the Pastorals as personal paraenesis. However, as stated above, I do not
think either Johnson or Fiore take sufficient account of the extent of the polemical
language, nor the actual naming of opponents. Fiore, for example, notes:

> Fictitious, typical or hypothetical examples, as opposed to named historical fig-
> ures, have been admitted since Aristotle... The indefinite pronoun for this type of
> example, usually negative, has been seen in use in Isocrates... Unnamed propo-
> nents of adversary positions appear in Isocrates... Seneca...and the Socratics...
> (1986: 200 n. 22)

This is precisely the point; unlike the negative examples in the paraenetic literature,
many of the opponents are named in the Pastorals. Furthermore, as stated in Chapter 1, a major weakness of a purely literary approach when dealing with polemical
language is that it does not take account of the sociological reality of community
conflict, power struggles and the labelling of deviants.

    ii. *The Social Function of Paraenesis.* Quinn (1990b), whilst arguing that the
Pastorals are paraenetic letters, is sensitive, following Berger and Luckmann
(1967), to the social function of paraenesis 'as a potent instrument of socialization'
(1990b: 195). Quinn argues that paraenesis is particularly appropriate for both primary socialisation (entrance into the community) and secondary socialisation
(entry into special roles within the community). Baptismal, ordination and marriage
liturgies (all of which Quinn finds in the Pastorals)[1] therefore result in paraenesis
which serves to reinforce both group identity and a sense of separation from those
outside the group. Regardless of what one makes of Quinn's examples of liturgical
materials in the Pastorals,[2] he at least recognises the social function of paraenesis.

---

1.   Baptismal in Tit. 2.11–14; 3.4–7; ordination in 1 Tim. 3.1–13; 6.11–16; Tit. 1.6–9; marriage in 1 Tim. 2.11–15; Tit. 2.4–5.
2.   The extent to which tradition has been reworked in each of the passages Quinn cites is
disputed. I find Quinn's references to marriage liturgies particularly unconvincing.

Nevertheless, Quinn does not adequately address the severity of the polemical language used. He apparently sees the function of negative examples as primarily a
foil for the positive, for he states that Christian 'paraenesis looks to the parousia
with its definitive revelation of who is 'in' and who is 'out' of the new world'
(1990b: 197). On Quinn's own terms the Pastorals cannot function as Christian
paraenesis for they clearly do not need to wait for the parousia to define the 'out'
group.[3]

   iii. *Epistolary Novel.* Another illuminating attempt to view the Pastorals from a
literary perspective is that of Pervo (1994). He seeks to read the Pastorals as an
example of an epistolary novel. Using *Chion of Heraclea* as the prime example of
an ancient epistolary novel, Pervo suggests the following characteristic features:
they are pseudonymous by nature; historical in setting; characterological in orientation; philosophical/moral in aim; they constitute a collection and the collection will
present a narrative. Turning to the Socratic Epistles, Pervo notes that they too as
a collection can be classed as an epistolary novel.[4] However, the narrative in the
Socratic Epistles has to be constructed by the reader by filling in the gaps. For this
reason Pervo prefers to see them as standing 'in a penumbra between an organized
collection and something that might be called an epistolary novel proper'. Pervo
then proceeds to read the Pastorals like an epistolary novel, in other words, 'as a
pseudonymous, historical work that tells a coherent story and focuses upon character formation through the promulgation of a moral, ideological message'. He
believes that this reading strategy is most successful in identifying the intended
audience; he sees the Pastorals as 'edification for boys or young men, dealing with
both their own moral development and with the nature of the Church to which they
belong'. However, compared with *Chion*, or even the Socratic Epistles, Pervo notes
that the Pastorals tend to sketch in some blanks of an already well-known story
rather than tell a story in their own right. For this reason he prefers to classify them
'as a collection with some features of the epistolary novel'.

   One of the strengths of Pervo's paper is that he is able to take into account the
naming of some of the opponents. He notes that this is unusual in polemical contexts and that neither the historical Paul nor Ignatius named their opponents. He
suggests that the practice of naming the opponents, together with other prosopog-
raphical data, is more indicative of narrative fiction than early Christian polemic.
In this regard he compares them with the various apocryphal acts and with 3
Corinthians.

   However, from a literary perspective, Pervo's argument is unconvincing. The
apocryphal acts are not in epistolary form and 3 Corinthians is embedded in the
Acts of Paul;[5] furthermore, the portion of 3 Corinthians purporting to be Paul's

---

   3.   E.g. 1 Tim. 1.19–20; 2 Tim. 2.16–18; 3.5b–9; Tit. 1.10–16.
   4.   Rosenmeyer (1994: 151–52) believes that the twenty-one letters of Themistocles have a
better claim to the title 'epistolary novel' than the Socratic Epistles. However, she concludes that
Chion is the only 'extant ancient Greek fictional work developed solely through an exchange of
letters that cohere to form an undeniable artistic whole' (1994: 152).
   5.   For the argument that 3 Corinthians forms part of the original *Acts of Paul*, see Schneemelcher (1965: 341–42).

reply to the Corinthians fails to mention opponents by name. The fact that *Chion* is the only convincing extant example of an epistolary novel means that we should be particularly cautious, especially if there are other literary alternatives to hand such as provided by Johnson and especially Fiore.

b. *Polemic*

i. *As an Explanation of Occasion and Purpose.* Towner (1989) sees the question of the opponents as the most important aspect of the background to the Pastoral Epistles. Recognising the paraenetic function of the letters, he nevertheless argues that the false teaching forms the backdrop to the paraenesis 'at almost every turn'. Consequently, he devotes an introductory chapter to the question of the heresy being addressed. For Fee (1988) the purpose, at least of 1 Timothy, is to combat the false teaching. Bassler (1996), Knight (1992), Marshall (1999) and Young (1994) all also note that the presence of false teaching in the communities is the prime reason for the letters. Nevertheless, none of these scholars regards the Pastorals as polemical through and through. They are prepared to give far more weight to the reality of the opposition encountered than those who advocate a purely literary approach above, but still recognise the paraenetic nature of the letters. Marshall (1999: 41) sums up this position well:

> If anything about the circumstances of the PE is clear, it is that their immediate occasion is the development of groups within the churches which are regarded as opposed to the authority and teaching of Paul. From a negative point of view, the PE may be regarded as basically responses to this situation. This evaluation, however, needs to be amended since by itself it may give the impression that the motive of the author is entirely negative and defensive, simply concerned with the refutation of error. It is clear that the main motivation of the author is the positive one of wishing to maintain the purity and truth of the gospel over against what he saw as distortions of it, because of his conviction that the gospel contains the saving truth by which the church stands.

ii. *The Pastorals as Primarily Polemical Documents.* Goulder (1996) does not opt for the middle ground of the scholars in the preceding section; he argues that the Pastorals are 'pervasively polemical'. He takes as his starting point the vehemence of the language used in addressing the opponents which he describes as 'abusive and uncharitable'. Due to the degree of hostility displayed in the letters Goulder believes it is a mistake to see other statements as unrelated; they should rather be understood in the light of the overtly hostile ones. On this basis he proceeds to engage in a sustained mirror-reading of the Pastorals. In particular he suggests that the opponents had a defective Christology, in the view of the author of the Pastorals, from a mirror-reading of 1 Tim. 3.15–16. He insists that the opponents were visionaries because of the repeated emphasis in the Pastorals that no-one has seen God. Furthermore, he argues from the mention of deceitful spirits and doctrines of demons in 1 Tim. 4.1 that the opponents were interested in angels. 'The Pastor, in his fair-minded way, calls these deceitful spirits and demons, but to the charismatics themselves these were angels'.[6] Goulder also argues that the quali-

---

6. Goulder (1996: 244).

fications for leadership in the church also function polemically to disqualify the opponents from any leadership role. I am substantially in agreement with Goulder's view that the Pastorals should be read as polemical documents. However, in my view, some of his conclusions, particularly the significance of angels, result from an over-ambitious attempt at mirror-reading.[7]

iii. *Status Degradation Ceremony*. The major problem with all of the literary approaches to the opponents in the Pastorals is that they display a profound lack of sociological sensitivity to real conflicts, power struggles, ideological commitments, etc. within Christian communities. Horrell (1993) has demonstrated the fruitfulness of a sociological approach. He is sensitive to the ideological element in the text of the Pastorals and draws attention to the polemic as evidence of a struggle between social groups with conflicting interests. His sociological understanding leads him to the realisation that it is possible that the opponents 'equally saw themselves as exponents of the true gospel, and as faithfully continuing the Pauline tradition' (1993: 97). This is a point which I shall return to below.

As stated in Chapter 2, in Pietersen (1997) I sought to demonstrate, utilising Garfinkel (1956), that the Pastorals function as a literary version of a status degradation ceremony. Such ceremonies involve public denunciation and, if successful, transform the public status of those denounced. According to Garfinkel (1956: 423), an essential aspect of the status degradation process is that the denouncer (a recognised public figure) highlights the core values of the witnesses and delivers the denunciation in the name of those core values. In the Pastorals, no less a public figure than Paul functions as the denouncer and Timothy and Titus (and through them the communities addressed)[8] serve as witnesses to the denunciation. From this perspective the paraenetic elements, which have been so carefully explored by scholars such as Fiore, function as a vital part of the status degradation ceremony. Paraenesis, by its very nature, highlights the core values and urges avoidance of those things which would detract from the core values. Thus paraenesis serves the overall polemical sociological function of the Pastorals.

The use of stereotypical language to describe the opponents, which has been well documented by those utilising literary approaches, draws attention to the use of 'name-calling' or 'labelling'. As outlined in Chapter 2 above, labelling theory, from the symbolic interactionist perspective on the sociology of deviance, highlights the power struggle involved in the labelling of deviants. From a sociological

---

7.   For a balanced approach to mirror-reading polemical letters see Barclay (1987). Barclay warns against the following dangers: being unduly selective in the use of texts; over-interpretation; misunderstanding the extreme nature of polemical language; and latching onto particular phrases as direct echoes of the opponents' vocabulary. In my view, Goulder is at least guilty of over-interpretation at times. Barclay helpfully goes on to list seven criteria which he considers appropriate for the task of mirror-reading, which involve paying attention to: the type of utterance in view (assertion, denial, command or prohibition); tone (emphasis and urgency or casual); frequency; clarity; unfamiliarity (an unfamiliar motif may well reflect the actual situation); consistency (assume a single type of opponent unless there is strong evidence to the contrary); and historical plausibility.

8.   Taking the ὑμῶν of 1 Tim. 6.21; 2 Tim. 4.22 and Tit. 3.15 as original.

perspective, the need to resort to labelling suggests that the opponents had real power in the community. The reference to the teaching function of some elders in 1 Tim. 5.17, the question of entertaining accusations against elders in 1 Tim. 5.19[9] and the evidence from Acts 20.28–30 (which I shall examine below) combine to convince me that the leaders of the opposition, or at least some of them, had previously been elders at Ephesus.[10] The leadership of the opposition thus enjoyed real status within the Christian community and so the author of the Pastorals has to resort to the device of a status degradation ceremony in the context of the power struggle taking place.

Finally, Garfinkel draws attention to the fact that, in any successful status degradation ceremony, the typical, negative characteristics of those being denounced must be appreciated by the witnesses by means of a 'dialectical counterpart'. In this way the community cannot conceive of those denounced without reference to this positive counter conception. In the Pastorals the qualities of bishops, elders and deacons serve as dialectical counterparts to the deeds of the opponents. Thus, for example, the injunction in 1 Tim 1.2 that the bishop should be μιᾶς γυναικὸς ἄνδρα serves as the dialectical counterpart to the opponents who, among other things, κωλυόντων γαμεῖν (1 Tim. 4.3). Goulder is thus right to argue that the qualifications of leadership function polemically.

If the strategy of status degradation is successful then the identity of the opponents will be totally transformed from insiders to outsiders.[11] Furthermore, through the process of retrospective interpretation documented by labelling theory, the communities addressed come to see that the opponents all along were never really 'true' leaders.

In conclusion, seeing the Pastorals as a literary version of a status degradation ceremony recognises both the fact that they are thoroughly polemical documents and the significance of paraenesis within them to highlight the core values which the author wants to uphold. However, recognising the form of the Pastorals in this way only yields the function of transforming previously influential insiders into outsiders. I believe it is possible to reach a greater degree of specificity concerning the opponents utilising the model of the thaumaturgical subversion/transformation of the institutionalising process developed in chapters three to five. In this connection I turn first to the question of the locations addressed.

9.   Marshall (1999: 617) is not convinced that the accusations refer to heretical teaching, but considers that they involve moral misbehaviour, possibly including misuse of money. However, the quotation in 1 Tim. 5.18b is from Luke's version of the saying (Lk. 10.7), rather than Matthew's (Mt. 10.10); Marshall himself accepts that the verbal agreement here requires an authoritative written source. In my view, this provides evidence for the argument that the author of the Pastorals knew Luke (cf. 2 Tim. 4.11). If this is correct, Luke's mention of problems concerning elders at Ephesus in Acts 20.30 is pertinent. Furthermore, the teaching function of elders is specifically mentioned in 1 Tim. 5.17.

10.   See Fee (1988: 7–8) for further arguments concerning the opponents as previous elders in the community.

11.   Garfinkel (1956: 421–22).

2. *The Significance of Ephesus and Crete*

As outlined in Chapter 1, MacDonald (1983) argued that both the Pastoral Epistles and the *Acts of Paul* drew on similar oral legends circulating about Paul. Bauckham (1993), however, has argued that the *Acts of Paul* are literarily dependent upon the Pastorals. Nevertheless, even if literary dependence is granted, the Paul of the *Acts of Paul* is both ascetic and thaumaturgical and very different from the Paul of the Pastorals. Thus, if the *Acts of Paul* has been composed by its author as an imaginative novelistic biography (Bauckham's view of its genre) and not from oral traditions, the fact remains that the author was attracted to a very different image of Paul than the one presented by the author of the Pastorals. Bauckham's argument, therefore, does not exclude the possibility of a battle for the memory of Paul in the immediate post-Pauline era.

The Pastorals locate Timothy in Ephesus and Titus at Crete. Thiessen (1995: 248–341) has convincingly demonstrated the historical likelihood of the connection with Ephesus. In addition, the similarities between 1 Timothy and Titus suggest that it is unlikely that they would be addressed to an identical location. Consequently, given the likelihood of 1 and 2 Timothy being addressed to the Christian community at Ephesus, there is no persuasive reason to doubt that Titus is addressed to Christians in Crete.[12] These two locations function, therefore, within the Pastorals, as the focal points of the opposition addressed. The link is significant and noted by ancient authors. Strabo, for example, in a long digression, speaks of the intermingling of Cretan and Phrygian traditions and rites. He notes, in particular, the mixing of traditions concerning the rearing of Zeus in Crete, the Phrygian orgies in honour of the mother of the gods and Dionysiac and Phrygian frenzied rites.[13] Diodorus too, in his discussion concerning Crete, links Artemis with both Ephesus and Crete (as well as Pontus and Persis) and affirms Crete (rather than Delos) as the birthplace of both Artemis and Apollo.[14] Ephesus was regarded as a centre for magical practices in the first century CE.[15] Tradition also associated Crete with the Idaean Dactyli who, according to Diodorus, were skilful magicians who practised charms, initiatory rites and mysteries (...ὑπάρξαντας δὲ γόητας ἐπιτηδεῦσαι τάς τε ἐπῳδὰς καὶ τελετὰς καὶ μυστήρια, καὶ περὶ Σαμοθρᾴκην διατρίψαντας οὐ μετρίως ἐν τούτοις ἐκπλήττειν τοὺς ἐγχωρίους·).[16]

In Acts 19 Luke presents a thoroughly thaumaturgical Paul at Ephesus. The passage also refers to an encounter involving Jews at Ephesus and these Jews are said to be 'itinerant exorcists' (Acts 19.13). These Jewish exorcists appear to have been impressed by the 'extraordinary miracles' (δυνάμεις τε οὐ τὰς τυχούσας) worked through Paul as they attempt to invoke the name of Jesus in their exorcisms. Thaumaturgy, magic and Jews are all combined in the narrative of Acts 19. In Acts 20

---

12. This point is well made by Marshall (1999: 85–87).
13. Strabo, *Geography* 10.3.7–17.
14. Diodorus Siculus, *Bibliotheca historica* 5.77.6–7.
15. See, for example, Arnold (1989: 14–20).
16. Diodorus Siculus, *Bibliotheca historica* 5.64.4.

Luke's Paul makes no mention of miracle working in his farewell speech to the Ephesian elders at Miletus. He does not mention the disturbance at Ephesus involving devotees of Artemis, but instead focuses on his trials at the hands of the Jews (Acts 20.19). Paul asserts that he 'did not shrink from doing anything helpful' and this appears to consist of 'proclaiming the message…and teaching publicly and from house to house'[17], 'proclaiming the kingdom' and 'declaring the whole purpose of God' (Acts 20.20, 25, 27). Paul's address to the Ephesian elders specifically states that some of the elders themselves will distort 'the truth in order to entice the disciples to follow them' after Paul has gone (Acts 20.29–30). Whether this is a speech of the historical Paul or a Lukan construction, the text demonstrates knowledge of a problem at Ephesus involving some of the elders. Luke's narrative concerning Paul at Ephesus thus combines Paul as thaumaturge, Paul as proclaimer and teacher, problems with Jews and problems with some of the Ephesian church leaders. It appears highly likely to me that we have in this passage the background to the problems addressed in the Pastorals.[18]

According to Acts, the Pauline community at Ephesus originated in a thaumaturgical Paul. Given the mix of magic and religious frenzy associated with both Ephesus and Crete, as described by writers such as Strabo and Diodorus, a miracle-working Paul would have been particularly attractive. Arnold (1989: 123), following a careful analysis of the background of Ephesians, comments:

> A multiplicity of sources attest to the pervasive influence of magic, the Phrygian mystery religions (including the worship of the Ephesian Artemis), and astrology not only among the pagans of Ephesus and western Asia Minor, but also among the Jews.

In Chapters 3 and 4 I have sought to demonstrate that charismatic communities do not simply succumb to the institutionalising process over time. I have argued that there is a continuing demand for revitalised charisma in such communities which serves to subvert the institutionalising process. If the founding myth of the Christian community at Ephesus involved a thaumaturgical Paul, and if the Christian community at Crete were similarly attracted to a miracle-working Paul, then over time the communities, according to my analysis, would display both signs of institutionalisation and signs of a counter-demand for the intensification of charisma. Before examining the Pastorals I will provide further evidence for the model.

---

17. In the Pastorals it is the younger widows and the opponents who go 'from house to house', 1 Tim. 5.13; 2 Tim. 3.6; Tit. 1.11. Schlarb (1990: 32–33) also believes that Acts 19–20 is important for understanding the situation in the Ephesian community at the time Luke was writing. He suggests that Luke's emphasis on Paul proclaiming the entire βουλή of God both publicly and from house to house is directed against heresy that offers secret teaching only in private.

18. This would be even more persuasive if Lukan authorship of the Pastorals is accepted. See Moule (1965), Quinn (1978) and Wilson (1979). Although I am not convinced by the arguments for Lukan authorship, I am persuaded that the Pastorals should be dated at a point not long after Paul's death and certainly not as late as the second century. See Marshall (1999: 83–92). I also believe that there are significant points of contact with Luke–Acts. See n. 9 above.

3. *Thaumaturgy and the Pauline Communities*

In Chapter 5 I argued that the process of both institutionalisation and its potential charismatic subversion is evidenced in the writings of Ignatius. Such subversion clearly took place sometime later with the emergence of Montanism. In Chapter 3 I concurred with Holmberg's refinement of Weber in connection with Paul's ministry. According to Holmberg, Paul's ministry itself displays signs of the routinisation of charisma. Indeed, as I shall seek to show below, Paul himself was concerned to counter what he saw as extreme thaumaturgical demand. In what follows I am taking Pauline Christianity to be a social movement as defined by Blasi (1988), in particular emphasising the importance of connectedness[19] as a facet of any social movement. As such a movement it is appropriate sociologically to analyse its development over time as Blasi does for early Christianity as a whole.

a. *Corinth*
i. *1 Corinthians*. In 2 Tim. 2.17–18 we read of two leaders of the opposition who claim 'that the resurrection has already taken place'. The closeness of the language of 2 Tim. 2.15–18 and 1 Tim. 6.20–21 indicates that at the heart of the false gnosis of the opponents was the claim that the resurrection had already taken place.[20] This understanding of gnosis is in marked contrast to the oft-repeated claims that the opponents must be advocating some form of early Gnosticism based on the use of this word. This stance on the resurrection should also be linked to the asceticism of the opponents mentioned in 1 Tim. 4.3.[21] It is important to note that the opponents did not deny the resurrection; the use of the perfect tense ἤδη γεγονέναι indicates the belief that believers in the present were already experiencing the resurrection. This amounts to a 'spiritualising' of the resurrection and represents some form of realised eschatology.[22] Towner (1987) persuasively argues for a connection between the realised eschatology of the opponents in the Pastorals and the situation Paul counters in 1 Corinthians.[23] Thiselton argues that the presence of such an eschatology suggests charismatic enthusiasm:

19. Connectedness, as part of the cohesion of social movements, suggests that, with appropriate caution, one can proceed on the basis that events affecting say Pauline communities in Corinth and Colossae would not have gone unnoticed in other Pauline communities. Stark (1996) recognises the importance of existing social networks in the growth of early Christianity. Thompson (1998) has demonstrated that the early Christian communities had both 'the motivation and the means to communicate often and in depth with each other' (1998: 68).

20. See Towner (1989: 29–33) and Chapter 1 above.

21. See Towner (1989: 36–38).

22. See Wedderburn (1987: 164–232). Wedderburn concludes that the origins of the idea of a present resurrection are not to be found in either contemporary Judaism or Graeco-Roman ideas but rather within Pauline tradition itself.

23. Litfin (1994) is unconvinced about claims concerning 'over-realised eschatology' in 1 Corinthians or that some in Corinth were 'over-enthusiastic…charismatics' (1994: 244). He persuasively argues that the background to 1 Cor. 1–4 is to be found in the Corinthians' fascination with Greek rhetoric. According to Litfin, many of the Corinthian Christians perceived deficiencies in Paul's preaching when compared to the eloquence of Greek ῥήτορες. Nevertheless, Litfin's

> This is to say that distortions or imbalance in the area of eschatology stand in a direct causal relationship to errors about the gifts and work of the Holy Spirit. Indeed excesses and mis-statements in either area affect the other. In specific terms, *an over-realized eschatology leads to an 'enthusiastic' view of the Spirit.*[24]

The combination of charismatic enthusiasm, abolition of marriages and asceticism is found later in Montanism as highlighted above in chapter five. An emphasis on the present experience of resurrection is also likely to avoid any talk of suffering and persecution – the very things mentioned as Paul's experience in 2 Tim. 3.11. Indeed, the author emphasises that persecution will be the lot of all who seek to 'live a godly life in Christ Jesus' (2 Tim. 3.12).

ii. *2 Corinthians*. In 2 Corinthians Paul is clearly combating some form of Jewish-Christian thaumaturgical movement. In 2 Cor. 10–12 Paul has to defend his apostolic credentials to the Corinthian Christians in the face of inroads into the community made by those he designates as 'super-apostles' (2 Cor. 11.5). He fears that the Corinthians are being deceived by these apostles (2 Cor. 11.3) whom he further describes as 'false apostles, deceitful workers, disguising themselves as apostles of Christ' and 'ministers of Satan' (2 Cor. 11.13–15). Paul's opponents are clearly Jewish (2 Cor. 11.22) and appear to boast, from Paul's responses, about their rhetorical skills (2 Cor. 10.10), visions and revelations (2 Cor. 12.1–10) and thaumaturgical prowess (2 Cor. 12.11–12). In his full scale treatment of the opponents in 2 Corinthians Georgi (1987) argues that they were itinerant preachers of Jewish origin who imitated Jewish missionaries. He suggests that Jewish pneumatics were particularly important for the Jewish mission and concludes:

thesis, whilst proving highly illuminative of 1 Cor. 1–4, does not adequately refute the view concerning the presence of an 'over-realised' eschatology at Corinth. Litfin himself states that it is not his intention 'to draw a comprehensive picture of the Corinthian situation' (1994: 160). Although he rightly argues that too much has been made of 1 Cor. 4.8 in connection with the Corinthians' eschatology, he underplays the significance of theological differences between Paul and some in the Corinthian congregation. He concludes that 'Paul seems to have considered the commitment of the Corinthians to his Gospel to be basically sound and unchanged' (1994: 180). He recognises that 1 Cor. 15 appears to contradict this but insists that Paul could only conduct the argument of 1 Cor. 15 on the basis of shared agreement between him and his readers (1994: 180 n. 10). In the same footnote, however, he recognises that '[t]he problem was that 'some' (15.12) had denied the resurrection of believers'; this is precisely the point – here was a clear theological difference between Paul and at least some of the Corinthians and this difference involved eschatology. Furthermore, Litfin neither engages with the issues addressed in 1 Cor. 12–14 nor with the sustained argument of Thiselton (1978).

24. Thiselton (1978: 512), his emphasis. Thiselton's comments need appropriate nuancing, for he overstates the position. It seems to me more likely that the position is the other way round. Charismatic enthusiasm *may* stand in a direct causal relationship to eschatology. Charismatic enthusiasm in itself does not necessarily lead to a wholly realised eschatology as can be readily established by the varied eschatological perspectives of current charismatic groups. However, a wholly realised eschatology can only be adequately explained by reference to charismatic enthusiasm: in other words, the claim that current experience of the Spirit is so overwhelming that it can only mean that believers are already experiencing the full benefits of resurrection.

> The opponents combined an elaborate concept of tradition with a pronounced self-understanding. An essential link was provided by the θεῖος ἀνήρ christology. Through retrospective views of the past, *demonstrations of the power of the spirit in the present*, and *ecstatic breakthroughs* into the future and the beyond, they augmented their present existence.[25]

Although Georgi's use of the θεῖος ἀνήρ concept has been rightly criticised,[26] his arguments concerning Jewish, ecstatic pneumatics are persuasive.

Ralph Martin, after a careful discussion concerning the identity of Paul's opponents in this section of 2 Corinthians, concludes in his comments on 2 Cor. 11.4:

> 'another Jesus' for the opponents is the *wonder-working Jesus*, rather than Paul's crucified and risen Lord. The alien 'spirit' is *the spirit of power and ecstasy* which these messengers claimed to possess and embody in their ministry, rather than the Spirit of Christ which Paul exemplified. The new 'gospel' is the *message of power and present glory, based on demonstrable tokens of the divine* and evidences of authority in their lives as Christ's servants (v 13), rather than Paul's kerygma of the suffering Christ whose power is displayed incognito and in patient love (13.3, 4).[27]

Sumney (1990) has investigated the methodology used by scholars in identifying Paul's opponents.[28] He divides the major hypotheses concerning the opponents in 2 Corinthians into four groups: (a) Judaizers; (b) Gnostics; (c) Divine Men; and (d) Pneumatics. His own conclusion is that the opponents are pneumatics and that the same kind of opponent appears in 1 Corinthians (1990: 190).

b. *Colossae*

The problems encountered at Colossae appear to be Jewish in origin.[29] There is also an ascetic[30] and mystical[31] element. O'Brien (1982: xxxviii), after examining

---

25. Georgi (1987: 315–16), my emphasis.
26. See, for example, Barnett (1993) and especially du Toit (1997).
27. Martin (1986: 341), my emphasis.
28. Sumney observes that the primary issues of method can be grouped into three main categories: (a) issues that involve reconstructions of the history of early Christianity; (b) issues that involve the use of sources other than the primary text to identify the opponents; and (c) issues that involve assessing types of passages within the primary text to identify the opponents. He recognises some overlap between the categories and identifies in further detail the issues involved. Questions connected with reconstructions of early Christianity are: (a) what materials are valid as sources for constructing the history of the movement?; (b) what is the proper function of a reconstruction when identifying the opponents in view in a particular letter?; and (c) what bearing does the possibility that Paul misunderstood his opponents have on the process of identifying those opponents from his letters? The issues involving the use of sources other than the primary text are: (a) should a given Pauline letter be analysed individually or in conjunction with other Pauline letters?; (b) what are the valid ways to identify parallel passages in the Pauline corpus and in non-Pauline material?; and (c) what is the legitimate use of parallels found in the Pauline corpus and in non-Pauline material? Finally, the issues involved in assessing passages within the primary texts are: (a) do some kind of passages yield better information about the opponents than other types (e.g. explicit statements or perceived allusions)? and (b) what is the appropriate use of mirror-reading?
29. Food and sabbath regulations are mentioned in Col. 2.16.
30. Col. 2.21.
31. Col. 2.18.

the various proposals concerning the nature of the Colossian heresy, cautiously concludes:

[I]t does appear that recent scholarly work on the Jewish-Christian ascetic and mystical background has been helpful in illuminating the meaning of several of these difficult expressions in the polemical sections of Colossians (2.16–23).

Furthermore, O'Brien, following Francis (1975a) and (1975b), argues that Col. 2.18 refers to the practice of fasting and other bodily disciplines in order to receive visions of the heavenly mysteries. He translates Col. 2.18a as: 'Let no one condemn you, delighting in humility[32] and the angelic worship [of God],[33] which he has seen upon entering [the heavenly realm]'.

Francis' (1975a) and (1975b) argument that the opposition at Colossae advocated a form of Jewish mysticism involving ascetic practices as a preparation for visionary experiences of ascent into heaven has been widely accepted.[34] Arnold (1995) has recently questioned this interpretation.[35] He argues that ἐμβατεύων in Col. 2.18 should be taken in a technical sense as referring to initiation into a mystery cult and that τῶν ἀγγέλων should be taken as an objective genitive. Utilising local inscriptional evidence together with Jewish literature which displays an interest in angels, Arnold concludes that the opponents combined Jewish, Christian and Phrygian elements within a general framework of magic and folk religion. Arnold also highlights the importance of both magic and ecstatic forms of worship in the local, Lydian-Phrygian context. Arnold and Francis both agree, therefore, that the opposition involved an emphasis on ecstatic, visionary experiences. Francis sees this in the context of Jewish mysticism whereas Arnold sees this in the context of syncretistic Jewish-Christian-Phrygian thaumaturgical practice.

Lincoln (1999: 108) helpfully points out the significance of the household code in Colossians in the context of the opposing 'philosophy':

What I am suggesting here is that from the writer's perspective the philosophy has a wisdom that takes its starting point from below and moves to the above by means of ascetic rigour and visionary experiences involving angels. The wisdom of the Christian gospel, he asserts, is that believers are already related to the above through union with Christ and that this relationship is to be worked out on earth… Having a Lord in heaven does not direct attention away from the earthly. Rather it is meant to provide the motivation for taking earthly relationships with all seriousness and living distinctively within them. Adapting the household code is an

---

32. According to Francis, the technique of 'humility' (ταπεινοφροσύνη) as a prerequisite for receiving visions is widespread in Jewish and Christian sources.

33. Taking τῶν ἀγγέλων as a subjective genitive.

34. See the bibliography in Arnold (1995: 9 n. 7).

35. See too DeMaris (1994), who argues that the opponents were pagans who combined Jewish and Christian elements with popular middle Platonism. Arnold (1995: 206–207) points out that a significant weakness of DeMaris' position is that he fails to demonstrate the influence of Middle Platonism in western Anatolia at that time. Van Broekhoven (1997: 89) also notes, in connection with the Colossian problem, that it 'is not necessary…to posit…the influence of specific but elusive philosophical schools'.

effective means of making such a point over against those who emphasized visionary experiences and ascetic practices that could detract from the importance of the earthly and of everyday life.[36]

c. *Conclusion*

It would appear that Paul himself encountered opposition from itinerant, charismatic, Jewish-Christian missionaries. Paul's experiences at Corinth draw attention to the thaumaturgical demand prevalent at the time. Problems at Colossae too indicate the influence either of some form of Jewish-Christian, ascetic, visionary mysticism or of syncretistic magical practices in the Pauline community there. There were thus thaumaturgical elements around in Paul's ministry, at Colossae and later with Ignatius flowering subsequently into Montanism. The fact that we have evidence of such demand highlights the pressure on the Pauline communities to be transformed from conversionist sects into thaumaturgical ones according to the sociological model developed in chapters three and four above. It is highly likely, therefore, that we will find this process at work in the Pastorals. So far I have utilised evidence from Acts to show that this was the case, at least as far as Ephesus is concerned. It is now time to turn to the text of the Pastorals itself.

4. *Thaumaturgy and the Pastoral Epistles*

a. *Realised Eschatology*

The clearest indication of the opponents' position is found in 2 Tim. 2.18. As stated above in note 24, in my view the only adequate explanation for the presence of realised eschatology is some form of 'enthusiasm'.[37] Theologically, the position may have arisen from a reinterpretation of Paul's teaching on rising with Christ as Marshall (1999: 753) advocates. However, it is hard to see how such a theological reinterpretation could have arisen without prior enthusiastic experience of having been raised with Christ. Marshall (1999: 754) mentions the possibility of enthusiasm but rejects it because he finds 'it hard to see any evidence for such 'enthusiasm' among the opposition, and certainly not for a special possession of the Spirit'. I shall argue below that there is indeed evidence for an enthusiastic outlook among the opponents. Interestingly, Towner (Marshall's collaborator on his commentary) has no problem in identifying the eschatological outlook with 'enthusiasm'. He speaks of 'the pervasive effect of the enthusiastic eschatology in Ephesus' (1989: 44).

Quinn and Wacker (2000: 679–83) claim that the opponents only recognise the resurrection of Jesus and deny any resurrection of believers and thus 'have struck a

---

36. Lincoln's observations are important in the light of the appearance of the *Haustafeln* in the Pastorals. Lincoln (1999: 109) goes on to note the significance of thanksgiving in Colossians and explicitly links this with the Pastorals' emphasis on thanksgiving as an antidote to asceticism (1 Tim. 4.3–5).

37. Johnson, commenting on the similarities with 1 Cor. 15.12, notes that the Corinthian position opposed by Paul was 'based on the certainty that the power of new life already enjoyed by believers was already the realized end-time, the full *basileia* of God: they were already filled, already rich, already ruling (1 Cor. 4.8)' (2001: 303).

reasonable compromise with the drastic, materialistic pessimism of Greek culture' (2000: 682). They appear to misinterpret the evidence. They cite Justin, *Apol.* 1.26.4; Irenaeus, *Adv. haer.* 1.23.5 and the Letter to Rheginus 45.23; 49.15–16. However, these texts all refer to various assertions that there is no future general resurrection because believers have already experienced resurrection. These texts do not deny resurrection, only future resurrection; they claim resurrection as present experience. 2 Tim. 2.18 refers to a similar claim.

Further evidence connecting enthusiasm with a realised eschatology can be found in the Latter Rain Movement, mentioned in Chapter 4, which has profoundly influenced 'New Churches' in the United Kingdom. This movement was highly enthusiastic and believed that there would be some among their number whose current experience of the Spirit would lead to them experiencing bodily resurrection within their lifetime and prior to the general resurrection of all believers. The quotation from Charles Schmitt on page 61 above highlights this using the concept of 'first fruits'. Admittedly the eschatology of the Latter Rain Movement still allowed for a future general resurrection and the movement recognised that even the resurrection of the 'manifest sons of God' was still future. Nevertheless, their teaching that current experience of the Spirit could be so strong that it leads to resurrection ahead of time provides a clear link between charismatic enthusiasm and resurrection teaching.

b. *Asceticism*
The ascetic nature of the opponents' teaching is found in 1 Tim. 4.1–3. The combination of fasting and celibacy, as noted in chapter five, was practised later by at least some Montanists in Phrygia. Asceticism was also a feature of the Colossian heresy as noted above. In Colossae ascetic practice was probably linked to preparation for visionary experiences.[38] Here Goulder's approach is important. Arguing that the opponents were Jewish-Christian visionaries, he notes the threefold denial that anyone has seen God in 1 Tim. 6.16 and suggests that this repetition of the denial most likely indicates that the opponents claimed to have had visions of God:

> It is the repetition of the denial which implies the claim: light *unapproachable*, ἀπρόσιτον, whom *no one of men* has seen, οὐδεὶς ἀνθρώπων, *nor can see*, οὐδὲ ἰδεῖν δύναται.[39]

Thus it would appear possible that the enthusiasts were also Jewish-Christian visionaries.

Arguably, further evidence for the charismatic nature of the opponents may be provided by the formula introducing their ascetic emphasis. The author of the Pastorals begins this section with Τὸ δὲ πνεῦμα ῥητῶς λέγει... (1 Tim. 4.1). This formula is never used by Paul and is only found elsewhere in the New Testament in Acts 21.11 and in Revelation. In Acts the formula introduces a prophecy by the prophet Agabus. In Revelation the formula represents the words of the Spirit of

---

38. See n. 32 above.
39. Goulder (1996: 246), his emphasis.

prophecy to the seven churches.[40] Aune (1983: 289–90) classifies 1 Tim. 4.1–3 as a prophetic oracle. The use of ῥητῶς, a New Testament hapax, may be a deliberate attempt by the author to oppose the prophesying of the opponents. For, as Aune (1983: 290) points out, 'early Christian prophetic speech is...frequently attributed to the Spirit of God'. It may well be that the opponents couched their language in terms of τὸ πνεῦμα λέγει to which our author replies τὸ δὲ πνεῦμα ῥητῶς λέγει. The author claims this as true prophecy over and against the false prophecy of the opponents.

c. *Meaningless Talk*

On several occasions the opponents are said to engage in meaningless talk (ματα-ιολογία)[41] and profane chatter (βεβήλος κενοφωνία).[42] They are described as idle talkers (ματαιολόγοι).[43] Marshall (1999: 372) suggests that this battery of terms simply describes false teaching as 'vain, empty talk'. Karris (1973: 553) includes these phrases in his list of stock language used against the sophists.[44] However, these words too may serve to reinforce the possibility that the opponents were Jewish-Christian ecstatics. Eusebius' anonymous source mentions that Montanus, after having some kind of ecstatic experience 'began to speak and say strange things' and pronounced 'spurious utterances'.[45] Epiphanius, speaking of the Montanists, states: 'But these people set forth things which they profess to prophesy neither with steadfastness nor in possession of the persuasion of reason. For their sayings are ambiguous, devious and incorrect'.[46] Celsus, speaking of ecstatic prophets in Phoenicia and Palestine, states:

> After they have brandished these words, they subsequently add words that are unintelligible, and frenzied, and totally obscure, whose meaning no intelligent person could discover, for they are obscure and void of meaning, but they afford opportunity to every fool or sorcerer (γόης) to appropriate what was said concerning anything in whatever way he wishes.[47]

The language of meaningless talk, although admittedly using different terminology from that used in the Pastorals, was thus used by later writers to describe ecstatic prophecy. It may well be that the author of the Pastorals uses the language in this way. This is not to deny that his rhetoric also functions as a 'stock' charge against the opponents, seeking to discredit their teaching as idle speculation.

In addition, the opponents engage in disputes about words (λογομαχία),[48] specu-lations (ἐκζήτησις)[49] and controversies (ζήτησις).[50] In 1 Tim. 1.4 and Tit. 3.9 the

40. See Aune (1997: 151).
41. 1 Tim. 1.6.
42. 1 Tim. 6.20; 2 Tim. 2.16.
43. Tit. 1.10.
44. See too Johnson (2001: 166, 311).
45. Eusebius, *HE* 5.16.7–8.
46. Epiphanius, *Panarion* 48.3.11
47. Origen, *Contra Celsum* 7.9.
48. 1 Tim. 6.4, cf. 2 Tim. 2.14.
49. 1 Tim. 1.4.
50. 1 Tim. 6.4; 2 Tim. 2.23; Tit. 3.9.

latter two words occur in conjunction with 'genealogies'. It would appear therefore that, whatever the preoccupation with genealogies precisely means, it gave rise to intense debate and speculation.

d. *Myths and Genealogies*

The first clue that the writer gives us concerning the false teaching involves 'myths and endless genealogies' (μύθοις καὶ γενεαλογίαις ἀπεράντοις) (1 Tim. 1.4). Kelly (1963: 44) notes: 'These words come tantalizingly near disclosing the content of the heresy, but their interpretation is far from clear'. He goes on to note that many commentators have sought to identify this phrase with the fully developed Gnostic notion of emanations or aeons but rightly rejects this interpretation. As noted in Chapter 1, the idea that the Pastorals are combating some form of fully developed Gnosticism is highly problematic. Plato uses the terms in connection with myths about origins. He states: 'and [Solon] went on to tell the myth about Deucalion and Pyrrha after the flood, and how they survived it, and to give the genealogy of their descendants' (καὶ μετὰ τὸν κατακλυσμὸν αὖ περὶ Δευκαλίωνος καὶ Πύρρας ὡς διεγένοντο μυθολογεῖν, καὶ τοὺς ἐξ αὐτῶν γενεαλογεῖν).[51] Polybius speaks of other historians attracting many different kinds of readers by dealing with every branch of history. In particular, he writes, those who deal with genealogies appeal to readers who are fond of a story (τὸν μὲν γὰρ φιλήκοον ὁ γενεαλογικὸς τρόπος ἐπισπᾶται).[52] In contrast to those who write about 'genealogies and myths' (περὶ τὰς γενεαλογίας καὶ μύθους) among other things, Polybius states: 'I decided on writing in a systematic manner' (ὁ δὲ πραγματικὸς τρόπος ἐνεκρίθη). He is conscious that by taking this route he is appealing to only one class of reader; nevertheless, he states his clear intention:

> My aim, therefore, being not so much to entertain readers as to benefit those who pay careful attention, I disregarded other matters and was led to write this kind of history. The best testimony to the truth of what I say will be that of those who study this work with due application.[53]

For Polybius, therefore, writing about myths and genealogies is a form of entertainment rather than 'serious history' which he believes he is writing.[54] For the author of the Pastorals, a concern for myths and genealogies promotes speculations rather than οἰκονομίαν θεοῦ τὴν ἐν πίστει (1 Tim. 1.4). Later he makes clear that his purpose in writing is that his readers might know how to behave ἐν οἴκῳ θεοῦ (1 Tim. 3.15). Like Polybius, the author of the Pastorals is concerned about 'serious' matters (God's administration, behaviour in God's household, sound doctrine)

51. Plato, *Timaeus* 22a.7–22b.2.
52. Polybius, *Histories* IX.1.4.
53. Polybius, *Histories* IX.2.1, 4, 6–7.
54. This statement is, of course, part of a much wider topos in ancient historiography in which ancient historians seek to present themselves as detached and impartial observers. Thucydides, for example, states: 'Still, it is safer to draw substantially the conclusions that I have drawn from the evidence that I have cited, as contrasted with the poets' exaggerated rhapsodies or the entertaining rather than accurate compositions of the genealogists (λογογράφοι)', Thuc. I.21.1.

rather than 'myths' which serve to fuel speculation or suit the desires of the listeners (cf. 1 Tim. 4.7; 2 Tim. 4.4).

However, it would be a mistake merely to assume that the phrase is a stock phrase used to emphasise that which is serious over against that which is trivial. In Tit. 1.14 the myths are specifically described as 'Jewish' and in Tit. 3.9 'genealogies' appears in connection with 'quarrels about the law'.[55] The preoccupation with 'myths and genealogies' which is being opposed here has a particularly Jewish dimension. Furthermore, in 1 Tim. 1.7 the opponents are described as desiring to be teachers of the law and in Tit. 1.10 those of the circumcision are mentioned. Ignatius simply equates Judaism with 'strange doctrines and antiquated myths' (Μὴ πλανᾶσθε ταῖς ἑτεροδοξίαις μηδὲ μυθεύμασιν τοῖς παλαιοῖς ἀνωφελέσιν οὖσιν, εἰ γὰρ μέχρι νῦν κατὰ νόμον ζῶμεν, ὁμολογοῦμεν χάριν μὴ εἰληφέναι).[56] It has been plausibly suggested that the author is referring to the kind of preoccupation with creation myths and genealogies displayed in writings such as Philo's *Questions and Answers on Genesis*, Pseudo-Philo's *Book of Biblical Antiquities* or the *Book of Jubilees*.[57] A particularly interesting passage in Pseudo-Philo links the question of genealogy with a prophecy made by a woman:

> Now Reu took as his wife Melcha the daughter of Ruth, and she bore to him Serug. And when the day of his delivery came, she said, 'From him there will be born in the fourth generation one [Abraham] who will set his dwelling on high and will be called perfect and blameless; and he will be the father of nations, and his covenant will not be broken, and his seed will be multiplied forever'.[58]

It is unlikely that 'genealogies' refers to an obsession with tracing prophetic succession as evidenced later by the Montanists, as suggested by Ford (1971). However, it could refer to attempts to trace lineage back to Abraham. Paul's opponents in 2 Corinthians boast of being σπέρμα Ἀβραάμ (2 Cor. 11.22). Georgi (1987: 58–59, 236–37) emphasises Philo's presentation of Abraham as a pneumatic and θεῖος ἀνήρ. In the text from Pseudo-Philo above, the concern is to trace a genealogy forward to Abraham. These are possibilities[59] but, at the end of the day, as Fee (1988: 42) states:

---

55. Schlarb (1990: 83–93) highlights the importance of the 'triad' μῦθοι, γενεαλογίαι and ἐντολαί/νόμος. After noting the references to 'myths and genealogies' in Plato and Polybius he goes on to suggest a close connection between this phrase and the law and, drawing on the use of cosmogony and genealogy in Philo's *Life of Moses*, argues that the opponents were attracted to a particular exegesis of passages in the early chapters of Genesis.

56. *Magn* 8.1.

57. See the comments in Knight (1992: 73–74), Karris (1979: 54–57) and Quinn (1990a: 110–11). Marshall (1999: 366) suggests either this Philonic use or speculation based on genealogies found in the Old Testament.

58. Pseudo-Philo, *Biblical Antiquities* 4.11 (*OTP*).

59. Interestingly, some contemporary practitioners of so-called 'deliverance ministry' (exorcism) pay particular attention to genealogies. They seek to trace how perceived demonic influences on the person being exorcised have been passed down through his or her ancestors. Graham and Shirley Powell, after citing Exod. 20.5, typically assert: 'Bondages are from generation to generation: lines of hatred, anger, physical or mental diseases, the inability to believe, and so on. If forebears have been involved in forms of witchcraft, there is almost certainly some

It must finally be admitted that we simply do not know, because [the author] does not give us enough clues.

On the other hand, it is interesting to note that Hippolytus, in his attack on the Montanists of his day, does not hesitate to echo the language of the Pastorals:

> These things happen to uneducated and simple people who do not give careful attention to the Scriptures, but rather [gladly] listen to human traditions, their own errors and dreams, fables (μυθολογίαις), and silly tales (λόγοις γραῴδεσι).[60]

5. *The Opponents' Success with Households*

1 Tim. 1.6; 2 Tim. 3.6 and Tit. 1.11 indicate the success the opponents had in infiltrating households within the Christian communities at Ephesus and Crete. In particular, they appeared to be particularly successful among women and, to some extent, slaves. In this context the author envisages the Christian community as the household of God (1 Tim. 3.15), insists that community leaders must manage their own households well (1 Tim. 3.4, 12), utilises the traditional *Haustafel* topos[61] and addresses women in particular.

a. *Household Emphasis*
The Pastoral Epistles use οἶκος eight times[62] and οἰκία three times.[63] In addition believers are urged to provide for family members (οἰκεῖος, 1 Tim. 5.8), and younger widows to manage their households (οἰκοδεσποτέω, 1 Tim. 5.14); older women are exhorted to encourage young women to be good managers of the household (οἰκουργός, Tit. 2.5). The understanding of the church as the household of God (1 Tim. 3.15)[64] is both central to the Pastorals[65] and serves the author's overall polemic. If the church is seen as God's household then the opponents' disruption of Christian households (Tit. 1.11) is a direct assault on 'the church of

---

inherited bondage… There are also bondages that exist at a national level – national traits that are carried down from generation to generation' (1983: 52). I am not arguing that this specific practice is directly relevant to the opponents' interest in 'myths and genealogies' in the Pastorals. However, the contemporary connection between interest in genealogies and thaumaturgical practice suggests that it is not out of the question that this phrase in the Pastorals has to do with thaumaturgy.

60. Hippolytus, *Commentary on Daniel* 4.20, echoing 1 Tim. 4.7.

61. For the Pastoral's emphasis on the household see especially Verner (1983). For the use of *Haustafeln* in the New Testament see Crouch (1973), Lührmann (1980) and Balch (1981). Marshall (1999: 231–36) has an extensive bibliography and argues, as does Verner, that it is better to talk of 'station codes' rather than 'household codes' in the Pastorals because the instructions are structured in terms of positions in society and lack the reciprocal household relationships of the *Haustafeln*.

62. 1 Tim. 3.4, 5, 12, 15; 5.4; 2 Tim. 1.16; 4.19; Tit. 1.11.

63. 1 Tim. 5.13; 2 Tim. 2.20; 3.6.

64. Marshall (1999: 507–509) rightly argues that it is the concept of the church as God's household rather than God's temple which is primary in 1 Tim. 3.15.

65. This is clearly seen by Marshall (1999: 497–99), at least as far as 1 Timothy is concerned.

the living God, the pillar and bulwark of the truth' (1 Tim. 3.15). In this connection, it would appear that the author particularly implicated women in the disruption of households.

b. *Libertarian Women*

In Pietersen (1998b) and (1998c) I have argued, drawing heavily on Bassler (1984), (1988) and (1996), that the teaching of the opponents proved particularly attractive to women in the community who had taken vows of celibacy.[66] 1 Tim. 5.3–16 is the key text in this respect. The length devoted to the question of widows and their support suggests that this was a very important issue as far as the author is concerned. Commentators are divided as to whether only one group of widows is addressed throughout or whether a separate group of enrolled widows is referred to in vv. 9–15. In my view, the passage refers to one group throughout. The section is framed by the concern for those who are really widows in vv. 3 and 16 (ὄντως χήρας) and there are no obvious breaks.[67] The whole passage is concerned with those whom the church should support financially as 'real widows'. It would appear that the support of widows was proving a drain on the community's resources and so the author wants to restrict support to those without family support (vv. 4, 8, 16), who are over sixty, have been 'the wife of one husband'[68] and are well attested for good works (vv. 9–10).[69] It would appear that the group of widows supported by the church had grown too large and included younger women who had also taken a vow of chastity.[70] The author of the Pastorals is particularly concerned about the behaviour of these younger widows.

> These younger widows were revelling in their freedom from the constraints of the traditional household structure. Having already taken the celibate route, they were

66. 1 Tim. 5.12 appears to refer to a vow of chastity. Marshall (1999: 599–600) argues that πίστις here has its usual meaning of 'faith'; however, πίστις together with the verb ἀθετέω is used in the sense of breaking a pledge in Diodorus Siculus 21.20; 32.7 and Polybius 8.36.6; 11.29.3; 22.16.1; 36.9.17, therefore this is the most likely meaning here. For the view that the pledge refers to the vow to remain a widow see, for example, Bassler (1996: 93–94), Kelly (1963: 117) and Knight (1992: 222–27).

67. So Bassler (1996: 92–93), Dibelius/Conzelmann (1972: 73–74), Knight (1992: 230–31) and Marshall (1999: 580–81). For the opposite view see Verner (1983: 161–66) who notes other scholars holding this position on page 161 n. 109.

68. The meaning of ἑνὸς ἀνδρὸς γυνή is disputed; it is unlikely to be proscribing polyandry and so the choice appears to be between 'married only once' (Bassler (1996: 96–97), Fee (1984: 119), Kelly (1963: 115–16)) and 'faithful to her husband' (Dibelius/Conzelmann (1972: 75), Knight (1992: 223), Marshall (1999: 593–94)).

69. It is highly unlikely that 'enrolment' in v. 9 refers to an official order of widows. In my view the whole passage is concerned with the support of widows – a concern rooted in Jewish tradition (Exod. 22.22; Deut. 24.17–22). This view is carefully argued by Marshall (1999: 576–81).

70. An extension of χήρα to include virgins is found in Ign. *Smyrn.* 13.1, 'I greet the households of my brothers with their wives and children, and the virgins who are called widows'. See Schoedel (1985: 252). Bassler (1984: 35) also points out that the references to marriage of the younger widows in vv. 11 and 14 'provide no linguistic indication that the author actually had *re*-marriage in mind, it appears that the widows' circle had evolved to the point that chastity, not widowhood, was the determinative factor'.

also particularly vulnerable to false teachers who were forbidding marriage. If they were enjoying the freedom that celibacy brought, it would not be a huge step to embrace teaching that actually opposed marriage.[71]

The author's solution to the problem is to insist that these 'younger widows marry, *bear children*[72] and manage their households' (1 Tim. 5.14). The constraints of household management would thus serve to counter the freedom these women were enjoying which enabled them, according to the author, to go from house to house gossiping and engaging in some form of thaumaturgical practice which included 'saying what they should not say' (1 Tim. 5.13).[73]

I have argued (1998) that it is the role of the younger widows in spreading the false teaching and the propensity for women, in the author's view, to succumb to the opponents' teaching (2 Tim. 3.6–7), that forms the background to the prohibition of women from teaching in 1 Tim. 2.12. 1 Tim. 2.9–15 is concerned with women, but v. 9 begins with ὡσαύτως thus linking it to v. 8. 1 Tim. 2.8–15 is therefore concerned with the way both men and women conduct themselves in 'the household of God'. I suggested above that the younger widows addressed in 1 Tim. 5 were particularly attracted to the false teaching as it provided them with freedom from the constraints of the patriarchal family structure. In this context, therefore, the author addresses women in a way which reinforces the traditional family values of both Jewish and Graeco-Roman cultures.[74] The emphasis on σωφροσύνη (vv. 9 and 15) frames the section on women. In v. 9 it is linked with αἰδώς, a combination which occurs regularly in classical literature to suggest the idea of modesty.[75] In v. 15, σωφροσύνη occurs on its own and the emphasis here is probably on self-control.[76]

In verses 11–12 the author clearly prohibits women from exercising a teaching role in the community. This can be seen from the chiastic structure, which places the emphasis on 'I do not permit a woman to teach':

71. Pietersen (1998b: 11).
72. Τεκνογονεῖν, cf. τῆς τεκνογονίας in 1 Tim. 2.15.
73. Most interpreters translate περίεργοι as 'busybodies' due to the connection here with φλύαροι and the use of περιεργάζομαι with this meaning in 2 Thess. 3.11. See Marshall (1999: 603). This view is persuasive but does not do full justice to the following λαλοῦσαι τὰ μὴ δέοντα which is paralleled by διδάσκοντες ἃ μὴ δεῖ in Tit. 1.11. The fact that the young widows in Ephesus are saying 'things which ought not be said' and the opponents in Crete are teaching 'what ought not be taught' suggests that the author views the content as sinister. This should be combined with the only other use of περίεργος in the New Testament in Acts 19.19, where it specifically refers to things belonging to magic. Furthermore, mention of the opponents' success in persuading women in 2 Tim. 3.6–7 is immediately followed by a reference to Jannes and Jambres which, I shall argue below, makes the magic link explicit. The view that περίεργοι refers to magic and that τὰ μὴ δέοντα refers to charms, incantations and magic formulae is considered possible by Kelly (1963: 118) and specifically argued by Kroeger and Kroeger (1992: 62–63, 203–11).
74. The contrast between external adornment and moral virtue for women was a regular feature of traditional paraenesis. See the discussion in Marshall (1999: 448–51).
75. See *TDNT* I, 169–71; Marshall (1999: 448–49).
76. Marshall (1999: 471).

γυνὴ ἐν ἡσυχίᾳ μανθανέτω
   ἐν πάσῃ ὑποταγῇ
         διδάσκειν δὲ γυναικὶ οὐκ ἐπιτρέπω
   οὐδὲ αὐθεντεῖν ἀνδρός
ἀλλ᾽ εἶναι ἐν ἡσυχίᾳ

The reason for this is clearly due to the fact that women have proved particularly vulnerable to the false teaching of the opponents. This can be seen by the way the author continues by grounding his prohibition on women teaching and having authority over men[77] in the creation account. The Genesis account provides a two-fold warrant for the author. First, the sequence of creation – Adam, then Eve – draws on 'the widespread [contemporary] assumption that the first born…has superior status and rightful authority over younger siblings'.[78] This supports his contention that a woman should not exercise authority over a man. Second, the author relies on Gen. 3.13 to argue that Eve, not Adam, was deceived and this enables him to draw a parallel with the situation facing the communities addressed in which women, as far as the author is concerned, were prone to deception. As Bassler (1996: 60–61) states:

> The author's reasoning is that the deception of Eve and not Adam reveals this to be a weakness peculiar to women, and the particular success of the opponents with women confirms it. Thus women must not be permitted to exercise the crucial role of teacher lest their vulnerability to deception permit the spread of false teachings in the church (cf. 5.13).

1 Tim. 2.15 has been a notoriously difficult verse to interpret as commentators have argued over the meaning of σωθήσεται and τεκνογονία, how they are related to each other and how this verse relates to the preceding verses.[79] The connection between this passage and 1 Tim. 5.11–14 is made explicit in 1 Tim. 2.15 by the use of τεκνογονία. The author's exhortation that younger widows should marry and bear children (τεκνογονέω) in 1 Tim. 5.14 makes the popular suggestion that τεκνογονία in 1 Tim. 2.15 refers to the birth of Jesus highly unlikely.[80] Τεκνογονία is used here in its ordinary sense of childbirth. Furthermore, διά with the genitive, as Marshall (1999: 468) notes, should be taken in an instrumental sense to denote 'by means of'.[81] The author thus states that women will be saved by means of childbirth. The question remains, therefore, as to what 'salvation' means in this context. In my view, commentators have had difficulty at this point because they consistently equate σῴζω with spiritual salvation. Marshall (1999), for example, states that 'σῴζω consistently refers to salvation from sin in the [Pastoral

---

77. I do not intend to enter into the debate over αὐθεντέω here. It seems to me that some form of domineering authority is the most likely nuance of the word. See the extended discussion and bibliography in Marshall (1999: 456–60).

78. Bassler (1996: 60).

79. See Marshall (1999: 467).

80. So, rightly, Marshall (1999: 469).

81. So too Knight (1992: 147).

Epistles]'. However, Marshall does not do justice to the use of σώζω in 1 Tim. 4.16 where Timothy is exhorted to pay close attention to himself and his teaching and, by persisting in them, thereby save both himself and his hearers. Marshall (1999: 571) argues that σώζω here is to do with final salvation. However, the context of 1 Tim. 4 concerns the refutation of false teaching. It is much more likely, therefore, that the author is concerned that Timothy and his hearers should be saved *from error*. This usage of σώζω makes perfect sense of 1 Tim. 2.15. In the context of opponents who forbid marriage, and younger widows who have taken a vow of celibacy being attracted to this false teaching, the author insists that women will be saved from error by means of childbearing. Those women who adopt the traditional role of mother are unlikely to be affected by the false teaching. Of course, the author recognises that childbearing alone is no guarantee against error so he insists that the traditional role must be accompanied by 'faith, love and holiness with self-control'. Bassler (1988: 55–56) sums this up well:

> The reference to bearing children has an obvious anti-ascetic and thus anti-heretical thrust. It may be that because of the Pastor's concern to reject the celibate lifestyle advocated by his opponents, he sought here to *counter* the suggestion of Genesis that childbirth is a curse, an idea that would play into the hands of the heretics. Indeed, the heretics, who were skilled in manipulating Jewish myths [Tit. 1.14], may have already exploited the potential of this idea. The Pastor then polemically transformed the Genesis curse into a Christian blessing, which may have operated on two levels. A woman will be saved *from the allure of the heretical message* by bearing children, and because she thus avoids making a shipwreck of her faith [1 Tim. 1.19], she will also be saved in the absolute sense of the word, provided, of course, she continues in faith, love, and holiness.[82]

Holmes (2000: 102) notes that the view of libertarian women espoused above has 'widespread and increasing support'. She believes that this view is erroneous and seeks, in Part II of her monograph, to refute the claim that a reconstruction of the background concerning false teachers and their effect on women is significant for the exegesis of 1 Tim. 2.9–15. She acknowledges that false teaching is a major concern but concludes that 'there is no convincing evidence in those passages that the Author believes that significant numbers of Christian women…are rejecting traditional female roles' (2000: 186). Holmes argues that every attempt at such reconstruction is 'based upon some combination of six erroneous views about 1 Timothy and the other Pastoral Epistles' (2000: 104). These are: the view that the Pastorals should be treated as 'church manuals'; the view that false teaching is the most influential background factor; treating the Pastorals as a composite document and thus failing to recognise distinctive characteristics; misunderstanding of the letters' purpose; treating the opponents as a more or less unified group arising from within the communities; and assuming that paraenesis on women specifically addresses problems at the place of address.

There are significant problems with Holmes' treatment. She rightly argues that the Pastorals should not be treated as 'church manuals'and that all three letters are

---

82. Her emphasis.

personal with a concern for the addressees' commission but she underplays the importance of combating false teaching as a vital component of that commission. She argues that it is '*the foolish and godless chatter and controversy* from which heresy emerges' that is more significant than the false teaching itself (2000: 108, her emphasis). However, as Towner rightly notes, godless chatter is directly linked to both γνῶσις (1 Tim. 6.20) and the false teaching concerning the resurrection (2 Tim. 2.16–18).[83] It seems to me that false teaching remains both the most significant background factor and the prime purpose of the letters. Holmes fails to notice their pervasive polemical character and her comments concerning paraenesis do not address the question as to whether paraenesis is employed in the Pastorals to emphasise core values as part of the strategy of a status degradation ceremony, as argued above on page 111. Holmes' analysis suffers from a lack of attention to sociological factors in the letters in the same way as other literary approaches.

c. Ecstatic Women

The problem with women in the Pastorals concerns more than just their desire for freedom from the constraints of the family patriarchal structure. If women were not teaching in the community, or at least aspiring to teach, there would be no need for any specific prohibition. According to 1 Tim. 5.13 the younger widows are guilty of dispersing the false teaching by 'gadding from house to house'; in 2 Tim. 3.6 households are infiltrated by the opponents and women in particular prove vulnerable to their teaching. Furthermore, 2 Tim. 2.16–17 speaks of the 'profane chatter' spreading 'like gangrene'. The picture is of false teaching disseminating through the community first, by the proponents gaining entrance to households and attracting women especially, and second, by female recruits subsequently spreading the teaching from house to house. Significantly, it is in this context that the content of the teaching is mentioned in 2 Tim. 2.18. It would appear that women were particularly attracted by the teaching that the resurrection had already taken place. Realised eschatology proving attractive to women brings us once again to the relevance of 1 Corinthians for understanding what is happening in the Pastorals. This can be seen immediately from the close relationship between 1 Tim. 2.11–12 and 1 Cor. 14.34–35. Fee has argued on text-critical grounds that 1 Cor. 14.34–35 is an interpolation probably based on 1 Tim. 2.11–12.[84] However, Wire (1990: 149–52) mounts a strong case for the text being part of the original letter to the Corinthians.[85] In this case the author of 1 Timothy is either applying 1 Cor. 14.34–35 to the situation at hand or, more likely, draws

---

83. See page 9 above.

84. See Fee (1987: 699–708), especially 699 n. 6.

85. Niccum (1997), in a careful sifting of the textual evidence, thoroughly refutes Fee's claim that the transposed order (which places vv. 34–35 after v. 40) is supported by the entire Western tradition. Niccum demonstrates that the transposed order 'occurs in only a few, closely related MSS from northern Italy spread abroad in the Middle Ages by Irish monastics' (1997: 254). No extant MS omits 1 Cor. 14.34–35 (Niccum convincingly argues against Payne's claim (1995) that codices Vaticanus and Fuldensis provide evidence for such an omission) and the overwhelming textual evidence thus favours the authenticity of 1 Cor. 14.34–35 in its traditional location.

upon known Pauline tradition.[86] Wire's entire thesis is that women prophets at Corinth form a significant challenge to Paul's authority there. She argues force-fully that Paul's strategy in 1 Corinthians leads to the final silencing of women in ch. 14 and that 1 Cor. 11 is an initial restriction on women's prophecy, on the way as it were to ch. 14, rather than permission for women to prophesy.[87] Although Wire overstates her case,[88] nevertheless she does succeed in highlighting the signi-ficance of women in the opposition to Paul at Corinth. Whatever the specific interpretation of 1 Cor. 14.34–35, it is interesting that both the situation at Corinth and the situation at Ephesus required the silencing of women in some way.

I have already argued above that the presence of realised eschatology can only be adequately accounted for by some form of charismatic enthusiasm. In the Pas-

---

86. See Marshall (1999: 439–40).

87. See especially Wire (1990: 152–58, 229–32).

88. Even if 1 Cor. 11 functions as a restriction on women prophets in the way envisaged by Wire, it is highly unlikely that Paul would call for the silencing in ch. 14 of what he has permitted in ch. 11. Of course, it is the apparent contradiction between 1 Cor. 11.2–16 and 1 Cor. 14.34–35 which informs the view that the latter is an interpolation. Horrell (1996: 186), who favours the interpolation theory, rightly insists that those who accept the authenticity of 1 Cor. 14.34–35 must be able to harmonise it convincingly with 1 Cor. 11.2–16. In my view, a case can be made for seeing the prohibition in 1 Cor. 14.34–35 in terms of those claiming to be women prophets. The immediate context concerns prophets and prophecy and the wider context concerns order in public worship. Charismatic exegesis distinguishes between 'prophets' and 'those who prophesy' on the basis of 1 Cor. 12.28–29; 14.1, 5, 29, 31–32. Charismatic praxis, based on 1 Cor. 14, recognises that all in the congregation may prophesy but not all are called to the ministry of prophet. Fee (1987: 693–96), in his exegesis of 1 Cor. 14.29–32, fails to engage with this charismatic under-standing. He simply interacts with those who argue that 'prophets' refers to a special group of people in the community who have been given the gift of prophecy. No contemporary charismatic would equate those with the gift of prophecy with prophets. Fee rightly argues that Paul envisages that *all* may prophesy but then wrongly concludes on this basis that the 'two or three prophets' referred to in 1 Cor. 14.29 are the same as the 'all' who can prophesy in 1 Cor. 14.31. By making this equation Fee is forced to argue that Paul is recommending that there can be no more than two or three prophecies at a time before the prophecies are weighed, after that there can be a further sequence of three prophecies and so on. Fee does not do sufficient justice to the relationship between 1 Cor. 12: 29–30; 14.5 and 14.27, 29. Paul insists that not all are prophets and not all speak in tongues, wants all to speak in tongues and prophesy, and limits to a maximum of three the number of contributions from tongue-speakers and prophets in any congregational gathering. It seems to me that charismatic praxis makes the most sense of the entire passage. Namely, that although all can speak in tongues in private (cf. 1 Cor. 14.18–19), only some exercise the public gift of tongues (just as there are recognised 'interpreters' [1 Cor. 12.30; 14.28]); furthermore, although all can prophesy, only some are prophets.

This distinction between 'prophets' and 'those who prophesy' enables women to be included in the 'all who prophesy' of 1 Cor. 14.31 yet excluded from the company of prophets by virtue of 1 Cor. 14.34–35. Women can thus prophesy, so there is no contradiction with 1 Cor. 11.2–16, but are silenced in terms of the presumably authoritative pronouncements of the prophets and in terms of judging those pronouncements publicly. This prohibition on women prophets strongly suggests that there is a problem with women claiming to be prophets in the Corinthian situation. In my view, therefore, Wire is right to draw attention to the problem of women prophets at Corinth but wrong to conclude that Paul really intends to silence women altogether. For the view that Paul, in 1 Cor. 14.34–35, is seeking to prohibit women from judging prophecies see Grudem (1988: 217–25) and Liefeld (1987: 148–51).

torals, therefore, we have evidence of at least some enthusiastic women. Wire's work on women prophets at Corinth is particularly helpful in this respect. Both Wire (1990) and Fee (1987) recognise that speaking in tongues was highly prized by the Corinthian Christians. In addition, Paul's emphasis on order in worship in 1 Cor. 14.26–40 indicates that Corinthian worship tended to be ecstatic and thus out of control.[89] This may well be the issue in the notoriously difficult 1 Cor. 11.2–16.[90] If ἀκατακάλυπτος in 1 Cor. 11.5 refers to loosed hair, and a strong case can be made for this,[91] then the issue of shame can be related to long, dishevelled hair which was typical of the frenzied worship of women in the cults of Dionysus, Cybele and Isis.[92] The silencing of women prophets, as I have argued above for 1 Cor. 14.34–35, in the context of orderly worship, may be due to such women prophesying and/or speaking in tongues in a manner reminiscent of ecstatic, pagan cultic activities. Wire (1990: 237–69) provides a selection of texts from the first century BCE to the second century CE, illustrating 'women who speak for the divine'. These illustrate the comment of Strabo:

> All regard women as the prime movers when it comes to religion. It is they who incite the men to the more devoted worship of the gods, to festivals and to wild outcries. One rarely finds such a behaviour pattern in a man living by himself.[93]

A passage from Irenaeus demonstrates that similar issues to those addressed in the Pastorals were still affecting the church a century or so later. He speaks of the heretic Marcus who, by means of 'magical impostures', succeeds in attracting a following which includes a number of women. According to Irenaeus 'he is regarded by his senseless and cracked-brain followers as working miracles'. Marcus' strategy is to devote 'himself especially to women, and those such as are well-bred, and elegantly attired, and of great wealth, whom he frequently seeks to draw after him'. He encourages these women to participate in his 'Charis' by urging them to prophesy. As far as Irenaeus is concerned, the resulting prophecies

---

89. So, rightly, Fee (1987: 713).

90. Commentators are divided on this point. The majority view is that Paul is concerned here to combat the view of some of the Corinthians that differences of gender and sexuality are no longer of any significance. Instead, Paul insists, although women do indeed have authority to pray or prophesy they, unlike men, must wear some form of head-covering as a sign of that authority. 'Women must pray and prophesy as women, and men as men', Horrell (1996: 173). See too Meeks (1974: 199–203), Fee (1987: 497–98) and especially Hooker (1964). Others view the issue as Paul's concern to distinguish Christian worship from ecstatic, mystery cult worship. See Fiorenza (1983: 227–30) and Kroeger and Kroeger (1978). Fee (1987: 498 n. 23) sees this as a tempting possibility.

91. See the discussion in Fee (1987: 508–10). Fee favours the view that ἀκατακάλυπτος refers to the lack of some external covering but recognises that 'the linguistic ties with the LXX and the parallels from pagan ecstasy offer a truly viable alternative in favor of hairstyle' (1987: 510).

92. Fee (1987: 509–10 n. 75). The available evidence suggests that women did not form a majority of the adherents of the various cults but that they were more involved in the oriental cults, and specifically the Isis cult, than in the traditional state religions, Heyob (1975: 87). Women involved in the Isis cult of the imperial period tended to have 'long hair with a band on the forehead and curls falling on the shoulder', Heyob (1975: 60).

93. Strabo, *Geography* 7.3.3. See too Kroeger and Kroeger (1992: 70–74).

are meaningless but result in the duped women regarding themselves as prophet-esses thereafter. Irenaeus continues by relating how Marcus, whom he calls a magician, is received into the house of one of the church deacons and succeeds in seducing the deacon's wife who then travels with him for a long period. Speaking of Marcus' disciples, Irenaeus concludes that 'they have deceived many silly women' and that, in his own district of the Rhone, 'they have deluded many women who have their consciences seared as with a hot iron'.[94]

Here we have the case of someone who apparently is able to make his way into households, is regarded as a magician, has a following and is able to attract many women, particularly by encouraging them to prophesy. Although there are impor-tant differences (Marcus' teachings are decidedly Gnostic), there are remarkable similarities with the situation addressed by the Pastorals.[95] This comparison is given further weight by Lewis' (1989) conclusions concerning the persistence of ecstasy in 'peripheral possession cults' highlighted in Chapter 3 above. As noted there, it is particularly significant for the Pastorals that Lewis finds evidence that it is women who tend to be involved in such possession cults. It is thus highly likely that women were attracted to the opponents in the Pastorals due to their thauma-turgical emphasis.

6. *The Opponents as 'Magicians'*

a. *Jannes and Jambres*
Further evidence for the thaumaturgical nature of the opposition comes from their comparison with Jannes and Jambres in 2 Tim. 3.8. This follows immediately after the author's accusation that the opponents 'make their way into households and captivate silly women'. Here we are explicitly in the realm of magic. Dibelius/Con-zelmann (1972: 117) cite a number of ancient texts referring to the brothers Jannes and Jambres as the magicians who opposed Moses in Exod. 7–9.[96] These texts regard the brothers as eminent magicians and wonder-workers. Given this tradition, it seems to me highly likely that they are specifically referred to, not just as exam-ples of those who oppose the truth,[97] but because of the thaumaturgical activities of the opponents. Karris (1973: 560–61), citing Philo, *Det. Pot. Ins.* 38–39 and *Migr. Abr.* 76–85, argues that the use of Jannes and Jambres here forms part of the

---

94. Irenaeus, *Against Heresies* I 13.1–7 (ANF), echoing in several places the language of the Pastorals.

95. Irenaeus' account, of course, must be read critically; he uses exaggerated polemical lan-guage. Nevertheless, it seems likely that Marcus and his followers did have particular impact among women and that thaumaturgy played a part in this. Chadwick (1967: 80) is able to say that Irenaeus, 'even after the numerous recent discoveries of Gnostic documents, remain[s] an essential and remarkably fair-minded source for the history of the second-century sects'.

96. CD V.17–19; Pliny, *Hist. Nat* 30.2.11; Apuleius, *Apologia* 90; Numenius as cited in Eusebius, *Praep. Ev.* 9.8.1; the targum *Pseudo-Jonathan*; the midrash *Tanḥuma*, commenting on Exod. 32.1; *Evangelium Nicodemi* (*Acta Pilati* A) 5; *Mart. Pt. et Pl.* 34.

97. *Pace* Towner (1989: 264 n. 37), Knight (1992: 435) and Marshall (1999: 769, 778). Apart from CD V.17–19, which does seem to mention 'Jannes and his brother' simply as those who opposed Moses and Aaron, the texts emphasise their role as magicians.

traditional polemic against sophists. It is, therefore, a stock charge and should not be taken as descriptive of the actual activities of the opponents. Philo's account certainly identifies the magicians with sophistry, but significantly, Philo does not name the magicians, as Karris recognises. It is by no means certain, therefore, that the author is drawing on Philonic material here.[98] Karris himself is forced to speculate: 'it might be conjectured that they [Jannes and Jambres] were introduced into a tradition similar to that of Philo at a later date with the purpose of embellishing the story' (1973: 561). The naming of the magicians here makes it far more likely that the author is specifically drawing on material that highlights their role as magicians.[99] In the text from Irenaeus cited above, Marcus is specifically described as a magician. Interestingly, the author here, who elsewhere accuses the opponents of occupying themselves with 'myths and genealogies', is not afraid to use, as Marshall (1999: 779) notes, 'Jewish embellishments of the story of Moses and legends that were circulating in his day'.

b. *The use of* γόης
The above interpretation of the reference to Jannes and Jambres is reinforced by the use of γόητες in 2 Tim. 3.13. The NRSV translates this as 'impostors' with which Towner (1989: 264 n. 37) concurs. However, the word can mean 'sorcerer', 'impostor/charlatan' or 'juggler' depending on the context.[100] As this is a New Testament hapax[101] it is worth looking at how the word is used in other contexts. In Appendix 1 I have set out extracts, as provided by the *TLG* CD-ROM, from various passages in which a word from the γοη– group occurs. I have concentrated on non-Christian authors from the fifth century BCE through to the second century CE. The search yielded 359 references for this period. Although the majority of references do not concern sorcery or magic, it is clear that context is all important when determining which of the nuances of γόης is appropriate. Whenever the context involves magic or wonder-working of some kind the appropriate translation is magician/sorcerer. Of course, if the author is not predisposed towards magic then the term is used pejoratively and, in the author's eyes, is tantamount to being an impostor.

---

98. This is not to say that elsewhere the Pastorals do not draw on Philonic material. See Hitchcock (1940) and Mott (1978).

99. The reference in Pliny's *Natural History* demonstrates that the name Jannes was associated with magic at a time roughly contemporary with the Pastorals. Fee (1988: 272) dates the naming of Jannes and Jambres to 'at least 150 BCE', although it is not clear where he gets this date from. Spicq (1969: 104–10) is one of the few scholars who takes both the reference to Jannes and Jambres and the mention of γόητες in v. 13 as alluding to magical practices. I agree with Spicq on this, although he makes too much of CD V.17–19 in arguing that esoteric Judaism of the Qumran type provides the background for the opponents in the Pastorals. Fee (1988: 272) entertains the possibility that the opponents practised magic but does not think γόητες should be translated as 'magicians' in v. 13.

100. Marshall (1999: 786–87) is open to the possibility that magic practices are alluded to here. Kelly (1963: 200) states: 'Again as in [verse] 8, there is conceivably an allusion to their dabbling in magic arts'.

101. γοητεία occurs once in the LXX at 2 Macc. 12.24 speaking of the 'guile' of Timothy.

In the writings of Plato, γοητεία appears to refer to sorcery in *Symp.* 203a as it appears in the context of the spiritual realm between mortals and the divine through which are conveyed divination, priestcraft, incantations, soothsaying and γοητεία. Similarly, in *Meno* 80a; 80b, γοητεύω, although used metaphorically of Socrates bewitching Meno with his spells and incantations, nevertheless has the connotations of magic for Socrates, in any other city, would be taken as a γόης. Finally, in *Laws* 933a, Plato distinguishes between injuries caused naturally and those attempted by sorceries, incantations and spells; here too γοητεύω must refer to magic.

In Euripides, *Bacchae* 234 γόης refers to a sorcerer/conjuror. In Herodotus, *Histories* 4.105.1 γόης also refers to magic for Herodotus speaks of the power of the Neuri to change into wolves. Although he himself is sceptical, nevertheless he states that it might be the case that they are γόητες. Philo, *On Dreams* 1.221.1 probably uses γοητεύω in the context of magic for he speaks of the sophists of Egypt, including augurs and soothsayers who are proficient in charming and bewitching. Josephus certainly uses γοητεία this way in *Antiquities* 2.286.4; 2.320.2 where the magic arts of Moses are compared to those of the Egyptian magicians. Γόης occurs in the context of signs and wonders in *Antiquities* 20.167.2. In Diodorus Siculus 5.55.3 γόης refers to the Telchines as magicians who could change the weather and change their natural shapes, and in 5.64.4 the Idaean Dactyli of Crete are described as γόητες because they practise charms, initiatory rites and mysteries. Strabo regularly uses γόης and γοητεία to refer to magicians and magic. Particularly significant is *Geography* 10.3.23 where, in the context of a discussion about the Idaean Dactyli, Strabo refers to γοητεία as being closely related to religious frenzies, worship and divination.

Plutarch in particular demonstrates the various nuances of the γοη– word group. In many of the references cited the context indicates the word group carries the sense of deceit; however in several texts he speaks of women using potions, drugs and γοητεία on their husbands, or of γοητεία in the context of spells.[102] He speaks of Proteus who can change his shape by γοητεία and of certain γόητες in Thessaly who, by means of γοητεία, are able to call up and banish ghosts.[103]

Although Lucian almost invariably uses γόης in the sense of impostor/charlatan it seems to me that at least in *Alexander* 5.5 and 6.8 he uses γόης/γοητεύω in the sense of magician/sorcery. Of course, Lucian still thinks of Alexander as an impostor but in these two texts the contexts concern enchantments, incantations and sorcery. Karris (1973: 560 n. 47), who in my view considerably overplays the equation of γόης with charlatan, admits that γόης can be synonymous with μάγος in Lucian.

Cassius Dio uses the word group in the context of magic in 52.36.3 and 57.15.7, 8. Finally Philostratus, not surprisingly due to his subject matter, consistently uses the word group in the context of thaumaturgy.

---

102. Advice About Keeping Well 126.A.6; Advice to Bride and Groom 139.A.3; Superstition 171.B.1; Bravery of Women 256.C.6; 256.E.3.
103. On Having Many Friends 97.A.5; Fragments 126.2, 3.

As context is all important, in our text the reference to Jannes and Jambres several verses earlier thus makes it highly likely that γόητες should be translated 'sorcerers'.[104] The reference to 'deceiving others and being deceived' makes the opponents like the 'super-apostles' Paul describes as 'deceitful workers' in 2 Cor. 11.13. The opponents' emphasis on thaumaturgy is, in the view of the author of the Pastorals, sorcery of a kind similar to that of Jannes and Jambres. In an environment in which magic was highly valued (Acts 19.19) and where Pliny can link Jannes with Moses and Jewish magic,[105] the author makes it clear that such practices are unacceptable in the community.

7. A Composite Picture of the Opponents

From the analysis above it would appear that the opponents:

- were Jewish-Christians;
- have as some of their leaders those who had previously been elders at Ephesus;
- like those encountered in 1 Corinthians, argue that present experience of the Spirit means that the resurrection has already taken place. Consequently Christians 'neither marry nor are given in marriage...because they are like angels...';[106]
- like those encountered in Colossians, are ascetic and practise asceticism primarily as preparation for visionary and ecstatic experiences of God;
- probably, again like those in 1 Corinthians, prize glossolalia which the author of the Pastorals dismisses as 'meaningless talk';
- with their realised eschatology find success particularly among women who, casting aside the restrictions of marriage, urge others to do likewise;
- encourage women, recognised in antiquity as particularly sensitive to the divine, to work miracles and to spread the message from house to house;
- as a result attract prominent women who are in a position to teach others in the community;
- like those encountered in 2 Corinthians, boast of their visions and their miracle-working.

The above summary does not lead to the conclusion that the opponents were early Gnostics, nor does it mean that the opponents saw themselves as practising magic. The sociological, developmental model I have highlighted in chapters three to five suggests that there will be a continuing demand for thaumaturgy in charismatic communities in the process of institutionalising. It is much more likely, given this model and the above mix, that the opponents were able to attract whole households (Tit. 1.11) precisely because of this process. In communities such as Ephesus,

104. The LXX does not help as ἐπαοιδός is consistently used of the magicians in Exodus.
105. Pliny, *Hist. Nat.* 30.2.11, 'There is yet another branch of magic, derived from Moses, Jannes, Lotapes and the Jews...'
106. Lk. 20.35–36; I am suggesting that this saying of Jesus was known to the Corinthian and Ephesian Christians.

which would have begun to demonstrate the process of institutionalisation, influential leaders who advocated a return to charismatic enthusiasm would inevitably prove attractive to certain sections of the church. These leaders could appeal particularly to Paul as a thaumaturge as portrayed in Acts 19. This is a claim that the author of the Pastorals vigorously opposes.

8. *The Author's Strategy*

If the author is seeking to combat what he sees as a dangerous demand for the intensification of charisma rooted in the memory of a wonder-working Paul, then he would not, I suggest, be able to tackle the problem by directly refuting such an image of Paul. For it is clear from Acts that at least some early Christian communities saw Paul in this way. Furthermore, Paul himself speaks of performing signs and wonders (2 Cor. 12.12). The author, who sees himself standing in the Pauline tradition, cannot, therefore, deny the charismatic dimension. Instead he adopts the following strategy:

First, as Karris (1973), Johnson (1978/79), Fiore (1986) and others have noted, he employs stereotypical language to describe the opponents. This literary device does not function, I have already argued, merely as a foil to serve an overall hortatory purpose or as an anti-type to the exemplary teacher. Rather, the stereotypical language is used to label the opponents as outsiders and the language, therefore, functions as a literary form of a status degradation ceremony. If the strategy is successful then the opponents, even though some had previously been leaders in the community, will be perceived by the community as having always been in reality 'outsiders' through the process of retrospective interpretation.

Second, the qualifications for leadership in the community contained in 1 Timothy and Titus serve a dual purpose. As well as highlighting the standards expected of community leaders they also function polemically to disqualify the opponents. Elders and deacons are to be 'husbands of one wife' (1 Tim. 3.2, 12; Tit. 1.6) thus disqualifying the opponents who forbid marriage (1 Tim. 4.3). They must demonstrate that they can manage their own households well (1 Tim. 3.4, 12) in contrast to the opponents who make their way into households and upset whole families (2 Tim. 3.6; Tit. 1.11).

Thirdly, to counter the success the opponents seem to have had amongst women (2 Tim. 3.6–7), the author wants younger widows to marry (1 Tim. 5.14) and denies any public teaching role to women, insisting that they will be saved (from error) by embracing their traditional childbearing role (1 Tim. 2.8–15).[107]

Fourthly, some room is given to charisma. The author seeks to deal with the charismatic problem by being seen to embrace spiritual gifts. Timothy is exhorted not to neglect the gift received through prophecy (1 Tim. 4.14) and to rekindle the gift within (2 Tim. 1.6). The Spirit is said to be richly poured out on the believing community (Tit. 3.6). However, this charismatic dimension is placed within certain boundaries. Timothy's gift is received through officially sanctioned channels – the elders and Paul. The abundance of the Spirit leads to good works, not ecstatic

---

107. For a detailed discussion of 1 Tim. 2.8–15 see Pietersen (1998b) and (1998c).

experience, and the avoidance of the controversies, genealogies, etc. which occupy the opponents (Tit. 3.8–9).

Fifthly, the Pastorals contain a massive emphasis on sobriety, moderation, soundness of mind, sound teaching, etc.[108] In an important article Malherbe (1980) highlights the pervasive nature of medical imagery in the Pastorals. He argues that the function of the imagery is thoroughly polemical:

> In sum, the author's use of the medical images is part of his overall perception of the heretics. The author describes them as intellectually inferior, having diseased minds which produce violent preaching and contaminate those who accept their teaching (1980: 23).

Malherbe suggests that the language best describes a certain type of Cynic wandering teacher. In the second half of his article he provides impressive evidence for his position. However, I am not convinced that Pauline communities in Ephesus and Crete would have been particularly persuaded by Cynic preachers. I have already demonstrated in Chapter 5 above how this language was taken up subsequently by writers opposing Montanist ecstasy. For example, Hippolytus, speaking of Montanists, states 'Those who possess a sound mind (ὑγιαίνοντα νοῦν) need not pay any attention to them'.[109] Given the association of Ephesus particularly with magical practices I would suggest that preachers advocating some sort of ecstatic and thaumaturgical spirituality would prove more attractive to the Christian community than wandering Cynics.

The author considers the opponents to be mentally deranged,[110] depraved in mind[111] and to have corrupted minds and consciences (Tit. 1.15). This is very similar language to that used subsequently by Epiphanius in his attack on Montanism in *Panarion* 48.1–13. Epiphanius is at pains to stress that true prophets prophesy in full possession of their understanding and intellect and in control of their powers of reasoning in contrast to Montanist ecstatic prophecy which he regards as foolish and deranged.

Sixthly, Paul is presented as a teacher (1 Tim. 2.7; 2 Tim. 1.11), a term Paul nowhere uses of himself, and the emphasis falls on teaching. The overseer must be adept at teaching (1 Tim. 3.2; Tit. 1.9). Sound teaching is contrasted with profane myths and old wives' tales (1 Tim. 4.6–7). Timothy is to pay attention to teaching (1 Tim. 4.13, 16). The elders who work hard at preaching and teaching are to be especially honoured (1 Tim. 5.17) and so on. In the entire Pauline corpus διδάσκαλος, διδάσκω, διδαχή or διδασκαλία occur 48 times; the Pastorals contain 25 of these.[112] Teaching is of considerable importance to the author.

---

108. σωφρονέω Tit. 2.6; σωφρονίζω Tit. 2.4; σωφρονισμός 2 Tim. 1.7; σωφρόνως Tit. 2.12; σωφροσύνη 1 Tim. 2.9, 15; σώφρων 1 Tim. 3.2; Tit. 1.8; 2.2, 5; ὑγιαίνω 1 Tim. 1.10; 6.3; 2 Tim. 1.13; 4.3; Tit. 1.9, 13; 2.1, 2; ὑγιής Tit. 2.8.

109. *Refutation of all Heresies* 8.19.

110. Malherbe (1980: 31 n. 7) argues the case for translating τετύφωται in 1 Tim. 6.4 as 'mentally ill'.

111. διεφθαρμένων (1 Tim. 6.5); ἄνθρωποι κατεφθαρμένοι τὸν νοῦν (2 Tim 3.8).

112. Romans (8), 1 Corinthians (6), Galatians (1), Ephesians (3), Colossians (4), 2 Thessalonians (1), 1 Timothy (12), 2 Timothy (7), Titus (6).

Finally, the author emphasises tradition. Timothy and Titus function as the bearers of the true Pauline tradition. If Timothy instructs the community in such a way that the false teaching is rejected he will have been nourished on the sound teaching which he has followed (1 Tim. 4.4–6). He is to guard what has been entrusted to him (1 Tim. 6.20; 2 Tim. 1.14), holding to the standard of sound teaching received from Paul (2 Tim. 1.13). He is to continue in what he has learned and firmly believed (2 Tim. 3.14). Titus, like Timothy, is Paul's 'loyal child in the faith' (1 Tim. 1.2; Tit. 1.4), and is to teach what is consistent with sound teaching (Tit. 2.1). Nowhere is the concept of Pauline tradition more pronounced than in 2 Tim. 2.2. Here four generations are envisaged in the passing on of the tradition: Paul, Timothy, faithful people and those taught by the faithful people.

9. *Conclusion*

In order to combat the opponents' ecstatic spirituality the author highlights teaching and tradition. The sense of guarding a tradition, holding on to it and passing it on faithfully is paramount. Teaching produces a good conscience (1 Tim. 1.5) which Timothy will possess if he follows Paul's instructions (1 Tim. 1.18–19), for Paul himself has a clear conscience (2 Tim. 1.3); deacons too must have a clear conscience (1 Tim. 2.9). The opponents, however, have seared (1 Tim. 4.2) and corrupt (Tit. 1.15) consciences.

Paul is the great teacher; Timothy and Titus function as true community leaders who have faithfully received Paul's teaching, guard and pass on the Pauline tradition. Through teaching and tradition, thaumaturgy is combated.

Two recent discussions on the opponents in the Pastoral Epistles have produced very different conclusions. Marshall, in his monumental commentary, concludes that they were Jewish-Christian ascetics but finds no evidence that they claimed any special endowment of the Spirit and so cannot be called 'enthusiasts' (1999: 51). Goulder (1996), on the other hand, argues that they were Jewish-Christian, visionary, charismatics who embraced a proto-Gnostic myth concerning the aeons which was similar to that of the Barbeliots.

I agree with Marshall (1999: 51) that 'the identification of the heresy in the PE as a form of Gnosticism is not only an unnecessary hypothesis but also a distortion of the evidence'. Too much has been made of the occurrence of γνῶσις in 1 Tim. 6.20 and μύθοις καὶ γενεαλογίαις in 1 Tim. 1.4 has too readily been identified with Gnostic systems of aeons standing in genealogical relationship. In Chapter 6 above I have listed several possibilities for the interpretation of 'myths and genealogies', none of which resort to Gnosticism. Furthermore, as mentioned in Chapter 1, Towner (1989) has persuasively argued that γνῶσις in 1 Tim. 6.20 refers to the opponents' over-realised eschatology. However, Marshall fails adequately to deal with the over-realised eschatology of the opponents. In commenting on 2 Tim. 2.18 he notes the possibility that their eschatology may have been the result of their 'enthusiasm' but dismisses this with the remark that 'it is hard to see any evidence for such 'enthusiasm' among the opposition, and certainly not for a special possession of the Spirit' (1999: 754). I have argued in Chapter 6 that the only adequate way to account for the presence of an over-realised eschatology is an enthusiastic version of Christianity and demonstrated this by reference to the Latter Rain Movement. I, therefore, concur with Goulder that the opponents were Jewish-Christian, visionary, charismatics although I do not think that they were Gnostic.

I have suggested that the Pastorals should be seen as part of a continuum stretching from early Pauline Christianity through Ignatius to full blown Montanism at the end of the second century CE. Along with the majority of scholars, I regard the Pastorals as post-Pauline but earlier than Ignatius.[1] I have argued that Paul encountered opposition from charismatic enthusiasts during his lifetime, that this was true too of Ignatius and that charismatic enthusiasm became manifest *within initially orthodox circles* with the arrival of Montanism. If this is true of Paul, Ignatius and the orthodox opponents of Montanism (who did not hesitate to use the language of

---

1.   As argued in Chapter 2 for different reasons, I agree with Marshall that the Pastorals were written in the period immediately following the death of Paul and thus in the lifetime of Timothy and Titus.

the Pastorals to condemn the Montanists of their day), then I suggest it is also true of the Pastorals.

I have sought to ground the above position by combining insights from both the sociology of deviance and the sociology of religion. Recognising that the author of the Pastorals has to resort to name-calling in dealing with the opponents, I have utilised labelling theory to argue that the rhetorical strategy of the Pastorals is that of the status degradation ceremony which transforms the status of previously influential 'insiders' to that of 'outsiders' in the eyes of the communities addressed. The fact that the author has to use status degradation suggests that there was a real power struggle taking place within the community. I have argued that some of the leaders of the opposition had previously been elders at Ephesus. The fact that the denouncer in the Pastorals is no less a figure than Paul himself suggests that the opponents too would acknowledge Paul's authority. If this were not the case then the author's strategy of using Paul as the prime denouncer would be meaningless. Hope is held out that the opponents may repent (2 Tim. 2.25–26). The use of Paul in this way strongly suggests a battle for the memory of Paul in the communities addressed. The author clearly sees Paul as a κῆρυξ and διδάσκαλος (two terms which Paul never uses of himself), as well as an ἀπόστολος (1 Tim. 1.7; 2 Tim. 1.11). The emphasis in the Pastorals on Paul as teacher, together with the teaching roles urged upon Timothy and Titus, suggest that the opponents had a very different view of Paul. I propose that they viewed Paul as primarily a thaumaturge.

1. *Paul as Thaumaturge*

The main evidence for this proposal comes, admittedly, not directly from the Pastorals, but from Acts 19–20. It is the Paul of Acts 19.11–12 who is presented as a thaumaturge *par excellence* at Ephesus. I have already suggested that 1 Tim. 5.18b is dependent upon the Lukan rather than the Matthean dominical saying. I have also argued that Acts 20.17–38 provides important background information for the setting of the Pastorals. Furthermore, Luke is specifically mentioned in 2 Tim. 4.11. Differences in style count as much against Lukan authorship of the Pastorals as they do against Pauline authorship, as Marshall (1999: 87) correctly notes. Nevertheless, the significant points of contact between Luke–Acts and the Pastorals mentioned by Moule (1965), Quinn (1978) and Wilson (1979) should be taken seriously. It is, of course, rightly maintained that Acts should not be taken as primary evidence for the epistles. Nevertheless, Still (1999: 61–82) has mounted a persuasive argument for the substantial reliability, despite obvious Lukan stylisation, of Acts 17.1–10a as background for Paul and the Thessalonian church. I wish to argue similarly for the substantial reliability of Acts 19–20 in connection with Paul at Ephesus.

According to Acts 19.8–10, Paul remained for at least two years and three months in Ephesus.[2] As far as the data in Acts is concerned this is the longest

---

2.   Three years according to Acts 20.31.

period Paul stayed in any one place.[3] Paul wrote 1 Corinthians from Ephesus where he notes that 'a wide door for effective work has opened up to me, and there are many adversaries' (1 Cor. 16.9). In Ephesus Paul suffered some kind of life-threatening affliction (2 Cor. 1.8–11). The length of stay in Ephesus would have made Paul a particularly significant figure for the Christian community in Ephesus. Furthermore, Acts 19–20 combine images of Paul as both an extraordinary thaumaturge (Acts 19: 11–20) and a gifted teacher (Acts 19.8–10; 20.20, 27, 31). Paul speaks of teaching both 'publicly and from house to house' (Acts 20.20). If Acts 19–20 forms a reliable account of Paul's ministry at Ephesus then it would not be at all surprising if members of the Christian community there subsequently cherished different aspects of Paul's ministry. The length of stay at Ephesus, combined with what we know of Paul from his genuine letters, makes the image of Paul as teacher highly credible; but what about Paul as thaumaturge? Lüdemann (1989: 212), citing Conzelmann, thinks that the depiction of Paul as thaumaturge here is unhistorical and drawn from a later time.[4] He also believes that the incident involving the Jewish exorcists in Acts 19.13–16 is legendary. However, he does regard the detail that Paul worked in Ephesus for two years in Acts 19.10 as 'historically credible' (1989: 214). Both Arnold (1989) and Trebilco (1994), on the other hand, provide evidence for Ephesus as a centre for magical practices and particularly for the cult of the Ephesian Artemis.[5] In addition, Trebilco's analysis provides a persuasive argument for the overall historical plausibility of the account of the riot in Ephesus in Acts 19.21–41. Finally, Trebilco (1994: 312–14) notes the widespread interest in healing in the ancient world together with the extensive belief that 'the bodies of particular people, or whatever touched them, had thaumaturgical powers'. Arnold's work too draws attention to the importance of thaumaturgy in order to attract potential converts in Ephesus. The historical plausibility of Acts 19.18–41, the widespread interest in healing and the relevance of the Ephesian background all combine to make the image of a thaumaturgical Paul at Ephesus highly likely. Additional evidence comes from 2 Cor. 12.12 where Paul, writing after his experience at Ephesus,[6] speaks of his thaumaturgical prowess.

It is highly likely, therefore, that the Christian community at Ephesus was founded on the basis of a thaumaturgical Paul. I have argued that the Pastorals should be viewed as a literary version of a status degradation ceremony in form. This requires, as argued in Chapter 2, a historical situation in the lifetime of Timothy and Titus. If this is accepted then Ephesus and Crete must also be regarded as

---

3. See Alexander (1993a) for a discussion of the chronology of Paul in Acts and in the Pauline letters. Alexander states that '[t]he two sets of data are remarkably coherent'.

4. Schreiber (1996: 99–107) is also unconvinced of the historicity of this material.

5. Interestingly, Artemidorus, *Onir.* 2.35, notes that Artemis makes people healthy (ὑγιής) – a term which is used in the Pastorals. Furthermore, Trebilco (1994: 318) notes that one of her titles, found on inscriptions, is 'most manifest' (ἐπιφανεστάτη). Of the six occurrences of ἐπιφάνεια in the New Testament, five are found in the Pastorals.

6. Even the most extreme partition theory of Schmithals concerning the Corinthian correspondence places 2 Cor. 10–13 after the latest section of 1 Corinthians. See Martin (1986: xli) for details.

reliable destinations for the letters.[7] Despite the arguments of Prior (1989) and Murphy-O'Connor (1991), I am persuaded by the view that all three letters are by the same author[8] and that therefore there would be no need for both 1 Timothy and Titus if the letters were all intended for the same destination.[9] 1 and 2 Timothy are thus addressed to Christians at Ephesus whereas Titus is addressed to Christians at Crete facing similar problems to those encountered at Ephesus.[10] The Ephesian destination of 1 and 2 Timothy, combined with the historical plausibility of Acts 19, suggest that the image of Paul as thaumaturge is highly relevant to the background of the Pastoral Epistles.

I have not mentioned the historical plausibility of the account of Paul and the Ephesian elders at Miletus in Acts 20.17–38. In my view it does not matter whether the text contains a substantially accurate account of the historical Paul's address to the elders. What matters, even if this is entirely a Lukan construction, is that Luke subsequently knows of problems at Ephesus involving some of the Ephesian elders 'distorting the truth' and enticing others to follow them. Lüdemann, who does not think the speech can make any claims to historicity, nevertheless is happy to see this as a historical reference to false teachers arising in and/or around Ephesus in Luke's day (1989: 226–30). I am, therefore, persuaded that Acts 20.17–38 refers to the problems addressed in the Pastorals.[11]

2. *Institutionalisation and Thaumaturgical Persistence*

The fact that the Ephesian community addressed in 1 and 2 Tim. could look to a thaumaturgical Paul as founder and that the Cretan community addressed in Titus could look to Titus as the appointed delegate of such a Paul leads naturally to the Weberian problem of succession following the death of a charismatic founder. I have argued in Chapter 3 that the process of institutionalisation is inevitable but that that process, as suggested by O'Dea's dilemmas of institutionalisation and confirmed by the analyses of MacMullen, Lewis and Wilson, does not necessarily lead to the extinguishing of O'Dea's 'charismatic moment'. In the process I suggested a developmental model whereby organisations founded in a charismatic moment simultaneously display the process of institutionalisation accompanied by a persistent demand for thaumaturgy. I have demonstrated this model in Chapter 4 by considering the development of a contemporary Christian NRM founded in a

7. This is argued by Thiessen (1995) and accepted by Marshall (1999).

8. All three letters share similar language and style, and similar terminology is used of the opponents as argued in Chapter 1. See Marshall (1999: 1).

9. So, rightly, Marshall (1999: 1–2). Johnson (2001) also agrees that each letter's particular situation must be taken seriously.

10. Tit. 1.5 does not require Paul's previous presence in Crete. If ἀπολείπω here means 'leave behind' this would either require a Pauline mission to Crete, which is otherwise unattested, or it forms part of a literary fiction. However, if, as I have argued, the Pastorals were written soon after Paul's death then it becomes highly improbable to regard this as literary fiction; otherwise the Cretan Christians would have very short memories! It is much more likely that ἀπολείπω should be translated as 'dispatched', 'deployed' or 'assigned' as suggested by Marshall (1999: 150).

11. So, rightly, Fee (1984: 7–8, 29 n.16).

'charismatic moment'. In Chapter 5 I have sought to show that my developmental model of simultaneous institutionalisation and thaumaturgical persistence is relevant to the second century in connection with both Ignatius and the subsequent rise of Montanism.

Having grounded my model in Chapter 4 and established its relevance for Christian communities in the second century in Chapter 5, I finally turned to the Pastorals in Chapter 6. Engaging in a form of mirror-reading, informed by my model, I argued that the opponents were Jewish-Christian visionaries and wonder workers who were successful particularly in attracting women within the community.

The Pastorals have consistently been read as reflecting an institutionalised Pauline Christianity. What has been missing in such readings has been an analysis of the sociological factors at work within the communities addressed which led to the author's stance. The opponents are dividing the community and the author has to take drastic action. We read the Pastorals from the author's perspective. What can appear, therefore, to be signs of straightforward institutionalisation may, in fact, be reactions to what the author sees as an inappropriate demand for the 'charismatic moment'. As stated in Chapter 2, social control theory is a useful device for examining the author's strategy. The very factors which have been read as marks of institutionalisation, or as literary devices of the author for the sake of paraenesis, can be seen to be the author's attempts to reinforce the social bonds between members of the community and thus make deviance less likely. For the author, members of the community should recognise that they are all members of one household and learn how to behave appropriately as members (1 Tim. 3.15) thus avoiding those who upset whole families (Tit. 1.11). Leaders should be those qualified to lead by virtue of their character rather than their thaumaturgical prowess (1 Tim. 3.1–13; Tit. 1.5–9). However, leaders should be able to teach (1 Tim. 3.2; Tit. 1.9). In this connection, 1 Timothy 4 is particularly instructive.

3. *1 Timothy 4*

The polemic of 1 Tim. 4.1–2 is interesting. Those advocating a literary approach have drawn attention to the stock charges of philosophers against the sophists. However, Aune (1983: 229) draws attention to the charges brought in early Christianity against those perceived as false prophets:

> Unlike false teachers, false prophets were particularly difficult to deal with since they appealed to the divine authority which stood behind their pronouncements. Two basic types of charges, often combined, were used to discredit prophets regarded as a threat: *they were deceivers or they were possessed by evil spirits* (my italics).

1 Tim. 4.1–2 appears to fall into this category and so the author may, by virtue of the device of prophecy, be branding the opponents as false prophets. To combat the ascetic nature of the false teaching the author draws attention to the doctrine of creation (1 Tim. 4.3–5). The author rejects this stance as contrary to God's intention in creation. However, I would suggest that this emphasis on creation is a

necessary move by the author for a much wider theological reason: *thaumaturgical demand is the result of an inadequate view of creation*. As far as the author is concerned, the persistent demand for supernatural acts of God, either in miracle or oracle, is the result of a failure to appreciate everyday life as a gift of the creator. Young expresses this point well (albeit with regard to what she calls 'radicalism' rather than thaumaturgy):

> If [the view that the Pastorals reflect a comfortable Christianity is] valid, and there have been a number of studies suggesting on several grounds that it is hardly fair, such a criticism fails to take account of the sacredness of the ordinary and the dangers of radicalism. The context of the Pastorals would appear to be reaction against the kind of radicalism that rejects the world and its ties. To live as if heaven were already here, without any appreciation of the material world, its food and wine, its social and community structures, is treated as flouting the goodness of the Creator God... The stance of the Pastorals would appear to be that...for most people most of the time, loyalty to Christ is expressed in everyday living according to the highest, indeed universal, human values of peace, integrity, thankfulness and respect for the 'given-ness' of life, loyalty to others and to the truth, generosity and the obligations of love in the community (1994: 152).

The author then goes on to stress the importance of the Pauline tradition (1 Tim. 4.6) and the necessity for ongoing teaching (1 Tim. 4.11–16). It is teaching and tradition that are important to the author, not thaumaturgical demand.

Appendix 1

USES OF THE ΓΟΗ– WORD GROUP

I set out below the results of a *Thesaurus Linguae Graecae* search on the γοη-word group from the fifth century BCE to the second century CE, excluding Christian authors. The Greek extracts appear exactly as extracted from the *TLG* CD-ROM.

Euripides Trag.Hipp 1038 {Θη.} ἆρ' οὐκ ἐπῳδὸς καὶ γόης πέφυχ' ὅδε,
Ba 234 γόης ἐπῳδὸς Λυδίας ἀπὸ χθονός,
Number of matches: 2

Herodotus Hist.Hist 2.33.4 ἀνθρώπους, γόητας εἶναι ἅπαντας.
Hist 4.105.7 ἄνθρωποι οὗτοι γόητες εἶναι. Λέγονται γὰρ ὑπὸ Σκυθέων
Number of matches: 2

Xenophon Hist.Anab 5.7.9.2 ὑμᾶς ἐξαπατηθέντας καὶ γοητευθέντας ὑπ' ἐμοῦ
ἥκειν εἰς
Number of matches: 1

Plato Phil.Phaed 81.b.3 πεύουσα καὶ ἐρῶσα καὶ γοητευομένη ὑπ' αὐτοῦ ὑπό τε
τῶν
Soph 234.c.5 ἀφεστῶτας διὰ τῶν ὤτων τοῖς λόγοις γοητεύειν, δεικνύντας
Soph 235.a.1 σαφές, ὅτι τῶν γοήτων ἐστί τις, μιμητὴς ὢν τῶν ὄντων, ἢ
Soph 235.a.8 [ΞΕ.] Γόητα μὲν δὴ καὶ μιμητὴν ἄρα θετέον αὐτόν τινα.
Soph 241.b.7 γοήτων τέχνη τιθέντες, ὁρᾷς ὡς εὔποροι καὶ πολλαί.
Polit 291.c.3 [ΞΕ.] Τὸν πάντων τῶν σοφιστῶν μέγιστον γόητα καὶ
Polit 303.c.4 μιμητὰς καὶ γόητας μεγίστους γίγνεσθαι τῶν σοφιστῶν
Phileb 44.c.8 οὐδὲν ὑγιές, ὥστε καὶ αὐτὸ τοῦτο αὐτῆς τὸ ἐπαγωγὸν γοήτευμα
Symp 203.a.1 καὶ τὰς ἐπῳδὰς καὶ τὴν μαντείαν πᾶσαν καὶ γοητείαν. θεὸς
Symp 203.d.8 δεινὸς γόης καὶ φαρμακεὺς καὶ σοφιστής· καὶ οὔτε ὡς
Euthd 288.b.8 Πρωτέα μιμεῖσθον τὸν Αἰγύπτιον σοφιστὴν γοητεύοντε ἡμᾶς.
Gorg 483.e.6 λέοντας, κατεπᾴδοντές τε καὶ γοητεύοντες καταδουλούμεθα
Men 80.a.2 ἄλλους ποιεῖς ἀπορεῖν· καὶ νῦν, ὡς γέ μοι δοκεῖς, γοητεύεις
Men 80.b.6 γὰρ ξένος ἐν ἄλλῃ πόλει τοιαῦτα ποιοῖς, τάχ' ἂν ὡς γόης
HpMi 371.a.3 σθαι, ὃς ἦν οὕτω γόης καὶ ἐπίβουλος πρὸς τῇ ἀλαζονείᾳ,
Menex 235.a.2 τοῖς ὀνόμασι ποικίλλοντες, γοητεύουσιν ἡμῶν τὰς ψυχάς,
Resp 380.d.1 Τί δὲ δὴ ὁ δεύτερος ὅδε; ἆρα γόητα τὸν θεὸν οἴει εἶναι

Resp 381.e.10 φαίνεσθαι, ἐξαπατῶντες καὶ γοητεύοντες;
Resp 383.a.3 δεῖ περὶ θεῶν καὶ λέγειν καὶ ποιεῖν, ὡς μήτε αὐτοὺς γόητας
Resp 412.e.7 γοητευόμενοι μήτε βιαζόμενοι ἐκβάλλουσιν ἐπιλανθανόμενοι
Resp 413.b.1 Οὐκοῦν κλαπέντες ἢ γοητευθέντες ἢ βιασθέντες τοῦτο
Resp 413.c.1 Τοὺς μὴν γοητευθέντας, ὡς ἐγῷμαι, κἂν σὺ φαίης εἶναι
Resp 413.c.4´ Ἔοικε γάρ, ἦ δ᾽ ὅς, γοητεύειν πάντα ὅσα ἀπατᾷ.
Resp 413.d.7 Οὐκοῦν, ἦν δ᾽ ἐγώ, καὶ τρίτου εἴδους τούτοις γοητείας
Resp 584.a.10 ἀλήθειαν, ἀλλὰ γοητεία τις.
Resp 598.d.3 γόητί τινι καὶ μιμητῇ ἐξηπατήθη, ὥστε ἔδοξεν αὐτῷ
Resp 602.d.2 τῆς φύσεως ἡ σκιαγραφία ἐπιθεμένη γοητείας οὐδὲν
Leg 649.a.4 τοὺς γὰρ γόητας οὐκ ἐν θοίνῃ λέγω–τῆς δὲ ἀφοβίας καὶ
Leg 909.b.5 ἐπῳδαῖς γοητεύοντες, ἰδιώτας τε καὶ ὅλας οἰκίας καὶ πόλεις
Leg 933.a.5 τούτων δυναμένων γοητεύειν βλάπτονται. ταῦτ᾽ οὖν καὶ
Number of matches: 30

Timotheus Lyr.Fragmenta 15, col3.102 στερνοκτύπωι γοηταὶ
Number of matches: 1

Aristomenes Comic.Fragmenta tit 5–10.1 [1ΓΟΗΤΕΣ]1
Fragmenta Goe.tit.1 [120ΓΟΗΤΕΣ.20]1
Tituli 16.3 Γότηε]ς
Number of matches: 3

Hellanicus Hist.Fragmenta 1a,4,F.89.4 τριάκοντα δύο. γόητες δὲ ἦσαν καὶ
φαρμακεῖς· καὶ δημιουργοὶ σιδήρου
Fragmenta 1a,4,F.89.6 τῆς μητρὸς Ἴδης, ἀριστεροὶ μὲν αὐτῶν, ὥς φησι
Φερεκύδης, οἱ γόητες, οι,
Fragmenta 1a,4,F.89.11 τὴν Φορωνίδα συνθεὶς [F 2 Ki] γράφει οὕτως· ʼ3ἔνθα
γόητες Ἰδαῖοι Φρύγες
Number of matches: 3

Gorgias Rhet. et Soph.Testimonia 3.4 αὐτὸς παρείη τῶι Ἐμπεδοκλεῖ γοητεύοντι.
Fragmenta 11.62 δῆς ἔθελξε καὶ ἔπεισε καὶ μετέστησεν αὐτὴν γοητείαι.
γοητείας δὲ
Fragmenta 11.62 δῆς ἔθελξε καὶ ἔπεισε καὶ μετέστησεν αὐτὴν γοητείαι.
γοητείας δὲ
Number of matches: 3

Empedocles Poet. Phil.Testimonia 1.68 γοητεύοντι. ἀλλὰ καὶ αὐτὸν διὰ τῶν
ποιημάτων ἐπαγγέλλεσθαι τοῦτό τε καὶ ἄλλα
Number of matches: 1

Demosthenes Orat.Cor 276.4 γόητα καὶ σοφιστὴν καὶ τὰ τοιαῦτ᾽ ὀνομάζων,
ὡς ἐὰν πρότερός
Or19 102.5 που ὅτι πράξει ταῦτα καὶ ποιήσει, ἢ εἰ μὴ τοῦτο, γοητευθέντα

Or19 109.7 φυλάττεσθε· ἄπιστος, γόης, πονηρός. οὐχ ὁρᾶθ' οἷα
Or29 32.2 εἴ τις ἂν ὑμῖν ἢ ῥήτωρ ἢ σοφιστὴς ἢ γόης οὕτω θαυμάσιος
Ex 52.1.9 δύνησθε φυλάττεσθαι· τοσαῦται τέχναι καὶ γοητεῖαι καὶ
Number of matches: 5

Aeschines Orat.Fals Leg 124.1 Τίνες οὖν ἦσαν αἱ ἀπάται, ταῦτα γὰρ τοῦ
γόητος
Fals Leg 153.2 ἀνθρώπῳ γόητι καὶ πονηρῷ, ὃς οὐδ' ἂν ἄκων ἀληθὲς οὐδὲν
Ctes 137.3 καὶ γόης ἐγένετο, ὅς, ὦ γῆ καὶ θεοὶ καὶ δαίμονες καὶ
Ctes 207.3 δίκαιός εἰμι προειπεῖν. Ἐπεισάξει γὰρ τὸν γόητα καὶ
Number of matches: 4

Dinarchus Orat.Dem 66.4 τούτου γοητείας; τίσιν ὀφθαλμοῖς ἕκαστος ὑμῶν
τὴν
Dem 92.5 τοῦ μιαροῦ καὶ γόητος τούτου δεήσεσιν, οὐδὲ
Dem 95.6 μάρτυρές ἐστε. γόης οὗτος ἄνδρες Ἀθηναῖοι καὶ μιαρὸς
Number of matches: 3

Aristoteles Phil. et CorFragmenta varia 1.3.36.16 καὶ ἀπῄσθιον. τὴν δὲ γοητικὴν
μαγείαν οὐδ' ἔγνωσαν, φησὶν
Number of matches: 1

Alexis Comic.Fragmenta 222.7 χάρις· ἀλλ' ἐπὰν δὴ τὸν γόητα Θεόδοτον,
Fragmenta Tar.4.7 χάρις· ἀλλ' ἐπὰν δὴ τὸν γόητα Θεόδοτον,
Number of matches: 2

Callimachus Philol.Fragmenta Aet.75.64 ἐν δ' ὕβριν θάνατόν τε κεραύνιον, ἐν
δὲ γόητας
Number of matches: 1

Demades Orat. et Rhet.Fragmenta 75.17 ὁ βδελυρὸς καὶ βάναυσος"3.20 καὶ
πάλιν 20"3πλάνης, γόης,
Fragmenta 89.4 καὶ πάλιν· 20"3κόλαξ,20 πού φησι, 20καὶ ἄνθρωπος δὲ γόης
Number of matches: 2

Ephorus Hist.Fragmenta 2a,70,F.8.3 οὐδαμῶς ἁρμόζοντα λόγον αὐτῶι ῥίψας,
ἐπ' ἀπάτηι καὶ γοητείαι
Fragmenta 2a,70,F.104.3 βῆναι δὲ μετὰ Μυγδόνος εἰς τὴν Εὐρώπην.
ὑπάρξαντας δὲ γόητας
Number of matches: 2

Philochorus Hist.Fragmenta 3b,328,F.101.4 δὲ τὸ βλάπτειν λέγουσιν.20
Ἐρατοσθένης [241 F 41] δέ, ἐπεὶ γόητες ὄντες
Number of matches: 1

Hecataeus Abderita Hist.Fragmenta 3a,264,F.25.1164 τῆς ὑποκρίσεως γοητείαν καὶ τὰ τῶν κινδυνευόντων δάκρυα πολλοὺς προτρέπεσθαι
Number of matches: 1

Timon Phil.Fragmenta et tituli 831.1 Πυθαγόρην τε γόητας ἀποκλίνοντ᾽ ἐπὶ δόξας
Number of matches: 1

Polybius Hist.Hist 4.20.5.3 λόγον αὐτῷ ῥίψας, ἐπ᾽ ἀπάτς καὶ γοητεια
Hist 15.17.2.2 φαίνηται γοητείας χάριν καὶ καθ᾽ ὑπόκρισιν
Hist 33.18.11.2 ταῖς Ηρακλείδου γοητείαις συγκατηνέχθησαν ἐπὶ τὸ
Number of matches: 3

Aristophanes Gramm.Epit 2.320.2 κατὰ νύκτα καὶ μεμνῆσθαί πως γοητείαν ὑπὸ τῆς φύσεως. ὅθεν δὴ νυκτὸς
Epit 2.384.2 ἐκαλεῖτο, καὶ ὅτι ἦν γόης καὶ φαρμακίς, καὶ ὅτι δεινῶς ἀκόλαστος ἦν καὶ
Epit 2.384.13 κόπτει. Καὶ ὑπὲρ μὲν τούτων τοὺς γόητάς τε καὶ φαρμακέας Ἄρει φίλω
Paroemiae 5.4 τὴν τῶν ἑταιρῶν γοητείαν. [ἐσπούδαζον γὰρ περὶ τοῦτο
Number of matches: 4

Chrysippus Phil.Fragmenta moralia 394.15 νισμοὶ καὶ γοητεῖαι καὶ τὰ ὅμοια· 20ὑπὸ δὲ τὸν φόβον20 ὄκνοι καὶ ἀγωνίαι
Fragmenta moralia 401.8 20Γοητεία20 δὲ ἡδονὴ κατ᾽ ἀπάτην ἢ διὰ μαγείας.
Fragmenta moralia 402.2 τρίοις κακοῖς· 20ἀσμενισμὸς20 δὲ ἡδονὴ ἐπὶ ἀπροσδοκήτοις· 20γοητεία20 δὲ ἡδονὴ
Number of matches: 3

Posidonius Phil.Fragmenta 60.20 43. Τὸ μὲν οὖν συμβαῖνον τοιοῦτον· γόητας δὲ ὄντας σκήπτεσθαί
1052 003 2a,87,F.70.104 ἕκαστος δύναται. [43] τὸ μὲν οὖν συμβαῖνον τοιοῦτον· γόητας δὲ ὄντας
Number of matches: 2

Philo Judaeus Phil.Opif 2.3 μεστὸν γοητείας, παγκάλην καὶ σεμνοτάτην ἀρχὴν ἐποιήσατο τῶν νόμων,
Opif 165.1 Τὰς δὲ γοητείας καὶ ἀπάτας αὐτῆς ἡδονὴ τω μὲν ἀνδρὶ οὐ
Sac 32.11 φωνος [ἄπιστος] ἀπειθὴς ἀφηνιαστὴς γόης εἴρων κέρκωψ δυσυπονόητος
Post 101.9 ἀσκητῶν θίασος διῆθλει, τὰς τιθασοὺς τῆς ἡδονῆς γοητείας
Plant 105.1 ἐραστὰς γοητεῖαι, πρὸς τοὺς κολακευομένους οἰκοσίτων ἀπάται. τὰς γὰρ
Plant 106.7 οὖν εἰρωνείας καὶ γοητείας καθάπερ ἐπιφυομένας κῆρας τῷ φιλίας φυτῷ

Ebr 71.6 τὰς "1πλησίον"2 καὶ ἀγχιθύρους αἰσθήσεις γοητειῶν, τῶν κατὰ τὸν "1ἔγγιστα"2

Heres 302.4 ἀπίστως τῇ δούσῃ προσενεχθέντες. οὖτοι δέ εἰσιν οἱ γόητες,

Som 1.221.1 καὶ γοητεῦσαι, ὦν τὰς ἐπιβούλους τέχνας μέγα ἔργον διεκδῦναι. διὸ καὶ

Som 2.40.2 λοχῶντας ἀπάτης, φενακισμοῦ, γοητείας, σοφισμάτων, προσποιήσεως,

Mos 1.301.3 ταῖς γοητείαις πρὸς ἀσέβειαν, ἕως υἱὸς τοῦ ἀρχιερέως Φινεὲς ἐπὶ τοῖς

Decal 126.1 γοητείαις τισὶ καὶ ἀπάταις. ἀναστάτους γε μὴν τρεῖς ἀποδεικνύουσιν

Spec 1.315.4 γόης γὰρ ἀλλ᾽ οὐ προφήτης ἐστὶν ὁ τοιοῦτος, ἐπειδὴ ψευδόμενος λόγια

De praemiis et poenis Œ De exsecrationibus 8.6 μύθου πλάσμα ὂν ἀπολελείφθω σοφιστείαν πρὸ σοφίας καὶ γοητείαν πρὸ

De praemiis et poenis Œ De exsecrationibus 25.1 καταποικίλλεται πρὸς ἀπάτην τῶν ὁρώνταν. οὖτός ἐστιν ὁ γόης, ὁ τὰ

Legat 162.4 πίνην ἐπιθυμίας βεβαίωσιν· δεινοὶ γάρ εἰσι τὰς κολακείας καὶ γοητείας

Hypothetica 191.26 καὶ ἐλοιδόρουν γόητα καὶ κέρκωπα λόγων. καλῆς μέντοι

Hypothetica 192.1 γοητείας καὶ πανουργίας, ἐξ ἧς τόν γε λαὸν ἅπαντα ἐν ἀνυδρίᾳ

Hypothetica 192.10 συμβησομένων, ἐπὶ τὸν γόητα ἐκεῖνον ἐπῆρε τοὺς

Hypothetica 199.25 γοητείαις ὑπάγεσθαι. 15. μελετήσασα γὰρ θῶπας λόγους
Number of matches: 20

Diodorus Siculus Hist.Bibliotheca historica 1.76.1.5 τῶν ῥητόρων καὶ τὴν τῆς ὑποκρίσεως γοητείαν καὶ

Bibliotheca historica 3.74.4.7 τῶν Ἰδαίων ὄντα Δακτύλων καὶ γενόμενον γόητα

Bibliotheca historica 5.55.3.1 χινίαν. λέγονται δ᾽ οὖτοι καὶ γόητες γεγονέναι καὶ

Bibliotheca historica 5.64.4.4 νος εἰς τὴν Εὐρώπην· ὑπάρξαντας δὲ γόητας

Bibliotheca historica 5.64.7.4 καὶ περιάμματα ποιεῖν, ὡς γεγονότος αὐτοῦ γόητος

Bibliotheca historica 20.8.1.4 ἀρχῇ μὲν γὰρ ὑπὸ τῆς Ἀγαθοκλέους γοητείας
Number of matches: 6

Dionysius Halicarnassensis Antiq Rom 11.25.4.5 καὶ τῇ γοητείᾳ τῶν λόγων οὐ συνειδὼς ὡς ἐξ

Antiq Rom 12.12.1.7 τις εἶναι καὶ γόης ὁ Τυρρηνὸς καὶ καταψεύδεσθαι

Is 4.12 περὶ αὐτοῦ δόξα παρὰ τοῖς τότε γοητείας καὶ ἀπάτης,

Dem 35.40 γοητευθέντες, ὥστε καὶ τῶν φανερῶν αὐτὸν

Dem 39.11 κυριώτατον τῶν γοητεύειν δυναμένων καὶ κηλεῖν

Th 6.22 ἄψαι, μηδ᾽ εἰς ἀπάτην καὶ γοητείαν τῶν πολλῶν

Th 7.15 θεατρικὰς γοητείας οὐδὲ πρὸς τὴν ἀπάτην ἁρμόττεσθαι
De compositione verborum 11.31 καὶ γοητεύεται, ὑφ᾽ ἑτέρας δέ τινος οὐδὲν
πάσχει
De compositione verborum 12.54 αὐτὴν γοητεύειν, ὥστε ὑπὸ τῆς ἐκείνων
χάριτος
De compositione verborum 11.12 γοητεύεται, ὑφ᾽ ἑτέρας δέ τινος οὐδὲν πάσχει
τοιοῦτον;
Number of matches: 10

Strabo Geogr.Geog 1.2.5.10 τῶν θαυματοποιῶν, γοητεύειν μόνον καὶ
κολακεύειν
Geog 7.3.11.14 συναγωνιστὴν ἔσχε Δεκαίνεον ἄνδρα γόητα,
Geog 7a.1.18.3 φησι τὸν Κίκονα, ἄνδρα γόητα, ἀπὸ μουσικῆς ἅμα καὶ
Geog 10.3.22.16 πάντες δὲ καὶ γόητας ὑπειλήφασι καὶ περὶ τὴν μητέρα
Geog 10.3.23.20 καὶ γοητεία ἐγγύς. τοιοῦτον δὲ καὶ τὸ φιλότεχνον
Geog 13.1.16.7 σπείων καλουμένων ἐπῶν, ἀνὴρ γόης εἴ τις ἄλλος.
Geog 14.2.7.3 νῆσον, οὓς οἱ μὲν βασκάνους φασὶ καὶ γόητας * θείῳ
Geog 15.1.70.9 γοητείας καὶ ἐπῳδῶν καὶ περιάπτων. τοὺς δὲ γυμνήτας
Geog 16.2.43.1 Τὸ μὲν οὖν συμβαῖνον τοιοῦτον· γόητας δὲ ὄντας
Number of matches: 9

Plutarchus Biogr. et Phil. Num 8.5.8 Πυθαγόρην δὲ γόητας ἀποκλίνοντ᾽ ἐπὶ
δόξας
Num 15.3.9 τῆς περὶ τὰ θεῖα γοητείας λέγονται ταυτὰ τοῖς
Sull 28.2.6 μένοις πρὸς ἀπάτην καὶ γοητείαν ἅπασαν ὥσπερ
Crass 22.3.5 πρὸς ἡμᾶς; τίσι δὲ φαρμάκοις ἢ γοητείαις ἔπεισας
Cic 17.5.3 τινὲς καὶ γόητες, ἔπη πεπλασμένα καὶ χρησμοὺς ᾄδοντες
Ant 37.6.4 φαρμάκων τινῶν ἢ γοητείας παπταίνοντα πρὸς ἐκείνην
Quomodo adolescens poetas audire debeat 16.D.7 περὶ τὸ ψεῦδος γοητείαν καὶ
δυνάμενος λέγειν
Quomodo adolescens poetas audire debeat 19.F.8 γοητείας ἀέρος τινὰ κάθαρσιν
εἶναι βούλονται τῷ
Quomodo adolescens poetas audire debeat 20.B.1 Ἥρας ἄριστα τὴν ἀπὸ
φαρμάκων καὶ γοητείας
Quomodo adulator ab amico internoscatur 63.B.4 ἀνελευθέρους καὶ γόητας οὐ
μόνον ʻκλήθρων καὶ
De amicorum multitudine 97.A.5 τὸ ἔργον, ἀλλ᾽ ὑπὸ γοητείας ἑαυτὸν εἰς
ἕτερον
De tuenda sanitate praecepta 126.A.6 κας ὅσαι φίλτρα μηχανῶνται καὶ
γοητείας ἐπὶ τοὺς
Conjugalia praecepta 139.A.3 καὶ φαῦλον· οὕτως αἱ φίλτρα τινὰ καὶ γοητείας
De superstitione 166.A.3 σιν, εἰς ἀγύρτας καὶ γόητας ἐμπεσόντες λέγοντας
De superstitione 171.B.1 ματα καὶ γοητεῖαι καὶ μαγεῖαι καὶ περιδρομαὶ καὶ
Mulierum virtutes 256.C.6 ἄξια· πλὴν εἰ κριτῇ σοι δόξειε φίλτρων ἕνεκα καὶ
γοητείας

Mulierum virtutes 256.E.3 ἐστὶ χρησαμένην γοητείᾳ καὶ φαρμάκοις ἐπὶ τῇ κόρῃ τὴν
Aetia Romana et Graeca 278.F.10 κασιν, ἐκκλήσεις εἰσὶ καὶ γοητεῖαι θεῶν, αἷς νομίζοντες
Aetia Romana et Graeca 290.F.4 ὀχούντων δεόμενον, σκιᾷ δὲ καὶ χλωρότητος ὄψει γοητεύοντα
De Pythiae oraculis 407.C.7 κοῦσα κοινὴν ἐμπαρέχειν ἑαυτὴν ἀπατεῶσι καὶ γόησιν
De defectu oraculorum 417.A.3 ναικός, ἐν ἐκλείψει σελήνης ἀεὶ προσποιουμένης γοητεύειν
Quaestiones convivales 663.C.8 "3ἀλλὰ νὴ Δία τὸ ποικίλον ἐξάγει καὶ γοητεύει τὴν ὄρεξιν
Quaestiones convivales 693.C.5 γοητείας, περιεργία τὸ χρῆμα καὶ λαμυρία μὴ πρέπουσα
Quaestiones convivales 747.A.2 σύνην μὴ κήλησιν εἶναι, τὸ δὲ μὴ γοητείαν ἀλλὰ τέρψιν.
Amatorius 764.E.2 τὴν διάνοιαν, χάριτι καὶ λαμπρότητι τῆς ὄψεως γοητεύων
An seni respublica gerenda sit 792.C.3 γοητεύμασιν, ἄχρι οὗ Μάρκος ὁ ἀδελφὸς ἀπελάσας
De sollertia animalium 961.D.9 δὲ δι᾽ ὀμμάτων γοητεία· χρῶνται δ᾽ ἑκατέροις ἐπὶ τὰ
De sollertia animalium 961.E.4 ὦτος αὖ πάλιν ἁλίσκεται γοητευόμενος, ὀρχουμένων ἐν
Bruta animalia ratione uti 990.C.6 θήλειαι καὶ προϊσχόμεναι τῆς ἐπιθυμίας ἀπάτας καὶ γοητείας
Fragmenta 126.2 Ψυχαγωγοί τινες γόητες ἐν Θετταλίᾳ οὕτω καλούμενοι,
Fragmenta 126.3 οἵτινες καθαρμοῖς τισι καὶ γοητείαις τὰ εἴδωλα ἐπάγουσί
Number of matches: 31

Flavius Arrianus Hist. et Bithynicorum fragmenta 39.11 γυναῖκα γοητευτρίαν.
Fragmenta 2b,156,F.61b.2 δίκην τινὰ Ἱστορεῖ οὐδὲν ἧττον γυναῖκα γοητευτριαν.
Number of matches: 2

Josephus Hist. AJ 2.286.4 τὰ θεῖα τῶν ἀνθρωπίνων διαφέρει. Δείξω δὲ οὐ κατὰ γοητείαν
AJ 2.320.2 τοῦ βασιλέως δεινῶς φέροντος ὡς κατὰ γοητείαν τὴν Μωυσέος
AJ 20.p.47 ὡς ἐπιδημήσαντος Αἰγυπτίου τινὸς γόητος καὶ πολλῶν Ἰουδαίων
AJ 20.97.1 Φάδου δὲ τῆς Ἰουδαίας ἐπιτροπεύοντος γόης τις ἀνὴρ
AJ 20.161.1 καὶ γοήτων ἀνθρώπων, οἳ τὸν ὄχλον ἠπάτων. ἀλλὰ τούτους μὲν
AJ 20.167.2 τὴν πόλιν, οἱ δὲ γόητες καὶ ἀπατεῶνες ἄνθρωποι τὸν ὄχλον
AJ 20.188.2 καὶ πεζικὴν ἐπὶ τοὺς ἀπατηθέντας ὑπό τινος ἀνθρώπου γόητος
Vit 40.2 δημαγωγεῖν καὶ τῶν ἀντιλεγόντων τὰ βελτίω περιεῖναι γοητείᾳ καὶ

Ap 2.145.4 πεποίηνται λόγους οὔτε δικαίους οὔτε ἀληθεῖς, τὸν μὲν ὡς γόητα

Ap 2.161.2 νομοθέτης, οὐ γόης οὐδ᾽ ἀπατεών, ἅπερ λοιδοροῦντες λέγουσιν

BJ 2.261.2 ψευδοπροφήτης· παραγενόμενος γὰρ εἰς τὴν χώραν ἄνθρωπος γόης

BJ 2.264.2 πάλιν ἕτερον μέρος ἐφλέγμαινεν. οἱ γὰρ γόητες καὶ ληστρικοὶ

BJ 2.565.1 κατ᾽ ὀλίγον γε μὴν ἥ τε χρεία τῶν χρημάτων καὶ γοητεύων

BJ 4.85.2 τὴν ἀπόστασιν καὶ συνεκρότει Ληίου τινὸς υἱὸς Ἰωάννης, γόης ἀνήρ

BJ 5.317.2 τὴν ἑλέπολιν, ἐν ᾧ τῶν Ἰουδαίων τις ἀνὴρ γόης ὄνομα Κάστωρ
Number of matches: 15

Epictetus Phil. Dissertationes ab Arriano digestae 2.20.27.6 γοητείας.

Gnomologium Epicteteum 40.3 μῶν ἐστιν ἐπίκαιρος γοητεία, τὸ δὲ σύμφυτος καὶ ἀνεξάλειπτος

Gnomologium Epicteteum 67.2 Ὥσπερ ὁ ἥλιος οὐ περιμένει λιτὰς καὶ γοητείας, ἵν᾽
Number of matches: 3

Dio Chrysostomus Soph. Orationes 2.18.7 ἀναγκάζει καὶ ἀντιλέγειν Δημοσθένει, μάλα δεινῷ ῥήτορι καὶ γόητι,

Orationes 4.129.6 θεσαν, οὕτως ἡ τοῦδε ἀπάτη, ἀλλ᾽ ἐπάδουσα καὶ γοητεύουσά φησι

Orationes 5.16.6 τοὺς ἀνοήτους ἀπάτς καὶ γοητεία, διαφθείρουσιν οἴκτιστα καὶ

Orationes 8.20.3 [οὐκ ἄντικρυς βιαζομένην, ἀλλ᾽ ἐξαπατῶσαν καὶ γοητεύουσαν

Orationes 8.21.3 ἡδονήν,] ἀλλ᾽ [ἐξαπατᾶν καὶ γοητεύειν δεινοῖς φαρμάκοις,] ὥσπερ

Orationes 16.1.2 κηλούμενοι γὰρ καὶ γοητευόμενοι παρὰ ταύτη μένουσι· τὸ δὲ λύπη

Orationes 18.14.11 μὴ λόγων δεινότητι μόνον, ἀλλὰ καὶ γοητεία ἐοικέναι τὴν δύναμιν.

Orationes 32.12.12 δρῶν, ἀφθονίᾳ δὲ κολάκων καὶ γοήτων καὶ σοφιστῶν.

Orationes 32.39.3 ἐμαυτόν. δεινοὶ γὰρ ἐκεῖνοι καὶ μεγάλοι σοφισταὶ καὶ γόητες· τὰ

Orationes 36.41.5 ματος οὕτως ὀνομάζουσιν ἀνθρώπους γόητας. ἐκεῖνοι δὲ τά τε

Orationes 77/78.34.1 τρόπον, κόλαξ καὶ γόης ἀντὶ γενναίου καὶ ἀληθοῦς φανείς.
Number of matches: 11

Harpocration Gramm.Lex 302.12 τος ἐλέγετο ἡ φορίνη καΐ Ἀριστομένης ἐν Γόησι δῆλον ποιεῖ.
Number of matches: 1

Suetonius Hist. et Gramm. Περὶ βλασφημιῶν καὶ πόθεν ἑκάστη 4.31 Τελχῖνες· οἱ <φθονεροὶ καιὶ> ψογεροὶ καὶ γόητες καὶ φαρμακεῖς.
Περὶ βλασφημιῶν καὶ πόθεν ἑκάστη
4.38 ἔχειν ἐν ᾧ ῥίζας κυκῶντες ἐφάρμασσον γοητευτικῶς.' Ἀνατίθεται δὲ αὐτοῖς
Number of matches: 2

Athenaeus Soph.Deipn 4.12.9 χάρις· ἀλλ' ἐπὰν δὴ τὸν γόητα Θεόδοτον
Deipn 6.61.18 πατρον ἄνθρωπον γόητα Νικόλαος ὁ περιπατητικός
Deipn 7.28.19 Γόησι [I 691 K]·
Deipn 9.33.18 Γόησιν οὕτως [I 691 K]· Ⅱ.. καὶ ὄρχεις ἤσθιον, οὓς
Deipn 11.119.30 κυριεύσαντες διὰ γοητείαν νῦν εἰσιν περίβλεπτοι· ὥσπερ
Deipn 14.22.3 [FHG I 234], ἐπὶ ἀπάτς καὶ γοητείᾳ παρεισῆχθαι τοῖς
Deipn 14.75.18 καὶ ἐν Γόησιν [ib. 691]·
Deipnosophistae 2,1.35.38 ἀγενείοις ἴσως ἔπεστί τις χάρις· ἀλλ' ἐπὰν δὴ τὸν γόητα Θεόδοτον ἢ 20τόν20·
Deipnosophistae 2,1.100.2ί Ῥόδιος χρηματίσας. Μιθριδάτου δὲ κόλαξ Σωσίπατρος ἄνθρωπος γόης.
Deipnosophistae 2,2.72.29 χρημάτων γὰρ ἐξ ἀσεβείας καὶ παρὰ φύσιν κυριεύσαντες διὰ γοητείαν νῦν
Deipnosophistae 2,2.131.22 οὐ παραληπτέον δὲ ἐπὶ ἀπάτῃ καὶ γοητείᾳ τὴν μουσικὴν παρεισῆχθαι
Number of matches: 11

Herodianus Hist.Ab excessu divi Marci 4.12.4.1 τὴν γοητείαν ταύτην ὑπισχνουμένων· ὑποπτεύων
Number of matches: 1

Galenus Med.Adhortatio ad artes addiscendas 9.2 μάθησιν ὡρμήσθε· μή τις ὑμᾶς ἀπατεὼν καὶ γόης ἀνὴρ παρακρουσάμενός
Quod optimus medicus sit quoque philosophus 1.55.1 τοσοῦτον ἐσπουδάκασιν, ὥστ', εἴ τις αἱμορραγίαν ἢ Ἱδρῶτα προείποι, | γόητά
Quod optimus medicus sit quoque philosophus 1.61.3 γάρ, ἃ τολμῶσιν ἀδίκως ἄνθρωποι, φιλοχρηματίας ἀναπειθούσης ἢ γοητευούσης
De simplicium medicamentorum temperamentis ac facultatibus l 11.792.12 μύθους γραῶν τινας ἐξετράπετο καὶ τινας γοητείας
De simplicium medicamentorum temperamentis ac facultatibus l 11.793.15 γοητείας οὐκ ἀπηλλαγμένος. ὁ δέ γε Πάμφιλος ὁ τὰ περὶ
De simplicium medicamentorum temperamentis ac facultatibus l 11.794.6 προσγράφων, ἑτέρας τε γοητείας τοιαύτας ληρώδεις.
De simplicium medicamentorum temperamentis ac facultatibus l 11.795.16 ἄνευ γοητείας τε καὶ ἀλαζονείας, ἣν ὕστερον Ανδρέας
De simplicium medicamentorum temperamentis ac facultatibus l 11.797.10 βοτάνας ἀνάσχοιτ' ἄν; ὅτι γὰρ γόητες ἄνθρωποι
De simplicium medicamentorum temperamentis ac facultatibus l 12.263.9 γοητείας δόξαν ἀπενέγκασθαι, φθανόντων ἤδη τῶν βασκάνων

De simplicium medicamentorum temperamentis ac facultatibus 1 12.269.12 ἀληθεύουσιν. ἕτερα δέ τινα γοητείας ἐχόμενα γράφουσιν περί

De simplicium medicamentorum temperamentis ac facultatibus l 12.283.8 περιέργων τινὰ μᾶλλον, ἃ γοητείας ἔχεται. καὶ χωρὶς δὲ τῶν

De simplicium medicamentorum temperamentis ac facultatibus l 12.290.12 δεινοῖς ἅμα γοητείαις τισίν. ἡ μέντοι κόπρος ἕν τι τῶν ἐν

De simplicium medicamentorum temperamentis ac facultatibus l 12.297.6 βάρβαρα, καθάπερ εἰώθασιν ἔνιοι τῶν γοήτων, ἐπείτοι καὶ

De simplicium medicamentorum temperamentis ac facultatibus l 12.306.7 μάκου. οἱ δέ γε οὕτως εἰσὶ ληρώδεις ἢ γόητες ἢ οὐκ οἶδ᾽

De simplicium medicamentorum temperamentis ac facultatibus l 12.307.15 γινωσκόντων ὡς περιέργου τε καὶ γόητος ὃς ἂν ταῦτα

De praenotione ad Posthumum (Epigenem) 14.601.10 ὥστε ἀγαπήσειεν ἄν, εἰ μὴ καὶ γόης τις εἶναι δόξειεν.

De praenotione ad Posthumum (Epigenem) 14.602.1 τοιοῦτο γεγράφθαι, γόητα δ᾽ εἶναι τὸν ἐπιδεικνύμενον

De praenotione ad Posthumum (Epigenem) 14.602.9 ξάνει μὲν τὴν τῆς γοητείας ὑποψίαν αὐτῷ τῷ μέλλειν ἀεί,

De praenotione ad Posthumum (Epigenem) 14.603.3 προσδοκῶντα, πρὸς τῷ καὶ τὴν τῆς γοητείας

De praenotione ad Posthumum (Epigenem) 14.655.17 σῶσι, γόητά τε καὶ μάντιν ἕτερά τε κατ᾽ ἐμοῦ τοιαῦτα

Number of matches: 20

Pseudo-Lucianus Soph.Philopatr 23.2 τὸν κακοδαίμονα εἰς γόητας ἀνθρώπους Philopatr 25.13 εἰ δέ γε μαντεῖαι καὶ γοητεῖαι ὑμᾶς παρέπεισαν, *Number of matches: 2*

Lucianus Soph.Nigr 15.7 γοητείας καὶ ἀπάτης καὶ ψευδολογίας, ἢ ὅστις ἀκούων τέρπεται

Symp 32.4 σοφοῦντος᾽, Ετοιμοκλέους τοῦ γόητος, μετρεῖτε τὸν Κλεάνθην καὶ J Tr 31.20 γόητα μὲν εἶναι τοῦτον, ὑμᾶς δὲ ὄνους κανθηλίους

Gall 4.11 γόρου Εὔφορβος γένοιτο; γόητά φασι καὶ

Gall 28.22 Ελελήθεις με, ὦ ἀλεκτρυών, καὶ σὺ γόης ὤν.

Tim 55.12 προχειρότατα, καὶ ἡ γοητεία προηγεῖται καὶ ἡ ἀναισχυντία

Vit Auct 2.13 τρίαν, μουσικήν, γοητείαν. μάντιν ἄκρον βλέπεις.

Pisc 15.15 γόητας ἄνδρας ἐπὶ τῷ ἡμετέρῳ ὀνόματι πολλὰ

Pisc 25.13 παύεται αὐτὸς μὲν ἀγορεύων κακῶς γόητας καὶ

Pisc 29.9 ρυττον καὶ κακῶς ἠγόρευον ἀλαζόνας καὶ γόητας

Pisc 42.21 γὰρ οἱ γόητες οὗτοι πολλάκις τῶν ἀληθῶς

Pisc 44.8 τοὺς γόητας δὲ καὶ οὐδὲν ἡμῖν προσήκοντας κακοὺς

Bis Acc 1.6 ἀνδρὶ τυφλῷ καὶ γόητι, μάκαρας ἡμᾶς καλοῦντι

Philops 5.18 δὲ ὡς γόης ὢν ἄρα τοσοῦτον χρόνον ἐλελήθει με

Philops 8.21 ὡς φατε, καὶ γοητείας τινὸς ἐνεργεῖν καὶ τὴν

Rh Pr 5.23 οὐκ ἐπίστευσεν, ἀλλὰ γόητα ᾤετο εἶναι τὸν

Alex 1.3 Ἀλεξάνδρου σοι τοῦ Ἀβωνοτειχίτου γόητος βίον

Alex 5.5 τις αὐτὸν ἐραστὴς γόης τῶν μαγείας καὶ ἐπδὰς
Alex 6.8 περιῄεσαν γοητεύοντες καὶ μαγγανεύοντες καὶ
Alex 25.19 γὰρ ἂν ἄλλῳ δικαιότερον προσεπολέμει γόης
Alex 60.7 μοτῶν ἐκείνων καὶ γοήτων, ὅσοι κορυφαῖοι ἦσαν,
Pro Imag 1.7 ἀλλά μοι δοκοῦσιν οἱ τοιοῦτοι γόητες εἶναι καὶ
Pro Imag 22.5 ὁμοίαν, γόης ἂν καὶ τοῦ Κυναίθου κολακικώτερος
Peregr 13.22 γόης καὶ τεχνίτης ἄνθρωπος καὶ πράγμασιν
Fug 17.6 τοιαύτης μισθαρνίας, ἀργοὺς δὲ καὶ γόητας
Fug 27.5 ὦ βελτίστη, εἴ τινας τρεῖς γόητας ἅμα εἴδετε καὶ
Salt 63.8 τοῖς περὶ τὸ πρᾶγμα γοητευομένων, ἐσθῆτι
Astrol 10.5 φάος τὸν λόγον προήνεγκεν, ἀλλ᾽ ἐς γοητείην καὶ
Pseudol 17.12 ἔργων αὐτῶν ὀνομαζόμενον, ἀπατεῶνα, γόητα,
Deor Conc 12.4 Κιλικίᾳ, ψευδόμενος τὰ πολλὰ καὶ γοητεύων τοῖν
Deor Conc 12.8 στεφάνους ἔχῃ καὶ γόητος ἀνδρὸς εὐπορήσς,
D Mort 10.2.5 ὥσπερ ἡμεῖς μόνς τῇ γοητείᾳ διαφέρων; ἀλλὰ πρὸς
D Mort 12.5.11 ὁρῶσιν, ἢ καὶ ὁ Ἄμμων γόης καὶ ψευδόμαντις
D Mort 13.5.9 αὐτὸς λαμβάνων· γόης, ὦ Διόγενες, ἄνθρωπος καὶ
D Mort 20.8.5 Φιλόσοφός τις, ὦ Ἑρμῆ, μᾶλλον δὲ γόης καὶ
Number of matches: 35

Herodianus et Pseudo-Her De prosodia catholica 3,1.112.19 διάστασιν ἔχει. τὸ δὲ 20γόαος᾽ ἐκ τοῦ γόης γέγονε. Τὸ δὲ 20Θήβαος,
De prosodia catholica 3,1.150.4 καθαρμῷ τῆς πόλεως τελευτῶν, 20φάρμακος20 δὲ ὁ γόης. Σεσημείωται
De prosodia catholica 3,1.291.11 λεία, γοητεία, δυναστεία, λαγνεία,
Περὶ ὀρθογραφίας 3,2.452.15 ἀριστεία ἐκ τοῦ ἀριστεύς, ἀλητεία, βουλεία ἡ βούλευσις, γοητεία,
Περὶ ὀρθογραφίας 3,2.590.1 20τερθρεία20 γοητεία, περιπάθεια. παρὰ τὸ τέρας τέρατος τερατεύω
Περὶ παρωνύμων 3,2.852.38 Arc. 38, 14™ τὸ γόαος ἐκ τοῦ γόης γέγονε.
Partitiones 16.15 ἡ γέννησις· γονορρυὴς, ὁ ῥοὴν σπέρματος νοσῶν· γόης,
Partitiones 16.16 μάγος· γοητεύω· γοητεία, ἡ μαγεία· Γόμορρα, τόπος·
Partitiones 183.16 ὁ τραυματίας· ὁ γοητίας. Καὶ ἐπὶ θηλυκοῦ· ἡ νεανεία,
Partitiones 183.18 τῆς τραυματείας· ἡ γοητεία, τῆς γοητείας· καὶ
Partitiones 265.15 Νεανείας, ἀλαζονείας, τραυματείας, γοητείας, Παρεκβολαὶ τοῦ μεγάλου ῥήματος 22.28 γοῶ 20γοήσω,20 τὰ δὲ δύο τῷ α, οἷον ἀκροῶ 20ἀκροάσω,20 μακκοῶ 20μακκοάσω.20
Number of matches: 12

Aelius Aristides Rhet.Συμμαχικὸς ά 487.17 ληκε, καὶ τοσαύτς φαρμάκων περιουσίᾳ καὶ γοητείᾳ
Πρὸς Πλάτωνα ὑπὲρ τῶν τεττάρων 292.14 νέοις, ἀλλὰ ὄντα γόητα καὶ τοῦ πρὸς ἡδονὴν θηρευτὴν,
Περὶ τοῦ παραφθέγματος 367.21 ἐκεῖνον τὸν ἀλαζόνα καὶ γόητα, καὶ ὅ τι τοιοῦτον βούλει
Number of matches: 3

Cassius Dio Hist.Historiae Romanae 46.4.1.1 διὰ μὲν δὴ ταῦτα φυλάττεσθε τὸν ἄνθρωπον. γόης γάρ ἐστι

Historiae Romanae 49.33.4.5 καὶ ὁ μὲν ἔτι καὶ μᾶλλον τῷ τε ἔρωτι καὶ τῇ γοητείᾳ τῇ τῆς

Historiae Romanae 49.43.5.2 μὲν δὴ ταῦτά τε ἐποίει, καὶ τοὺς ἀστρολόγους τούς τε γόητας ἐκ

Historiae Romanae 52.36.3.1 ἀθέῳ τινὶ μήτε γόητι συγχωρήσῃς εἶναι. μαντικὴ μὲν γὰρ ἀναγκαία

Historiae Romanae 57.15.7.5 τε ὅτι δαίμων τις ἐκ γοητείας οἱ ἐπιπέμπεται καὶ τὸν ἄνθρωπον

Historiae Romanae 57.15.8.2 γόητας, εἴ τέ τινα ἕτερον καὶ ὁποιονοῦν τρόπον ἐμαντεύετό τις, τοὺς

Historiae Romanae 61.11.3.4 τὸν Κλαύδιον ἐς ἔρωτα αὐτῆς ταῖς τε γοητείαις ταῖς τε

Historiae Romanae 69.22.1.Ι Ἀδριανὸς δὲ μαγγανείαις μέν τισι καὶ γοητείαις ἐκενοῦτό ποτε

Historiae Romanae 71.9.3.1 ουσίαις καὶ γοητείαις ὁ Μάρκος χαίρειν Ἰστόρηται. ἔστι δὲ ὃ λέγω τοιοῦτον.

Historiae Romanae 77.17.2.5 ὄνομα ΣεμπρωΩνιος Ῥοῦφος, τὸν δὲ δὴ τρόπον φαρμακεὺς καὶ γόης,

Historiae Romanae 77.18.4.3 μετὰ τῶν ἐξελευθέρων ἐδαπάνα. Τοῖς δὲ μάγοις καὶ γόησιν οὕτως

Historiae Romanae 77.18.4.5 νοῦ ἀνθήσαντα ἐπαινεῖν καὶ τιμᾶν, ὅστις καὶ γόης καὶ μάγος

Historiae Romanae 62.13.1.17 μοιχείας καὶ γοητείας

Historiae Romanae 65.1.4.5 νόμους, ὕστερον δὲ καὶ τοὺς γόητας

Historiae Romanae 71.23 τε ἀστρολόγους καὶ τοὺς γόητας ἐκ τῆς πόλεως ἐξήλασε. Καὶ

Historiae Romanae 133.15 καὶ προσέτι καὶ ὑπάτευσε. τοὺς μέντοι ἀστρολόγους καὶ τοὺς γόητας

Historiae Romanae 133.21 γοητείας αὐτῷ ἐπιπέμπεται καὶ τὸν ἄνθρωπον ἀποκτεῖναι.

Historiae Romanae S152.25 διον ἐς ἔρωτα αὐτῆς ταῖς τε γοητείαις ταῖς τε ἀκολασίαις

Historiae Romanae S254.24 μαγγανείαις μέν τισι καὶ γοητείαις ἐκενοῦτό ποτε τοῦ ὑγροῦ, πάλιν

Historiae Romanae S260.31 ἀλλ᾽ οὐχ ὁ Ἀρνοῦφις ὁ μάγος· οὐδὲ γὰρ μάγων συνουσίαις καὶ γοητείαις

Historiae Romanae S334.11 γόης, ἐφ᾽ ᾧ δὴ καὶ ὑπὸ Σευήρου ἐς νῆσον κατε-κέκλειστο,

Historiae Romanae S335.7 μάγοις καὶ γόησιν οὕτως ἔχαιρεν ὡς καὶ Ἀπολ-λώνιον τὸν

Historiae Romanae S335.9 καὶ γόης καὶ μάγος ἀκριβὴς ἐγένετο, καὶ ἡρῷον αὐτῷ κατασκευάσαι.

Historiae Romanae 186.3 μανεν, ὑπονοήσας εἶναι τοῦτο ἐκ γοητείας, ἔν τινι ἡμέρᾳ

Historiae Romanae 765.15 γραμμα τοὺς γόητας καὶ ἀστρολόγους ἐντὸς ῥητῆς ἡμέρας
Historiae Romanae 1.3 ἔρωτι καὶ τῇ γοητείᾳ τῆς
Number of matches: 26

Achilles Tatius Scr. Erot.Leucippe et Clitophon 5.25.3.1 ὦ ζεῦγος κατ᾽ ἐμοῦ γοήτων,
Leucippe et Clitophon 6.7.4.3 τοσούτῳ καὶ γοητότερον. ἐὰν δὲ ἡ δακρύουσα ᾖ καὶ καλὴ καὶ ὁ
Leucippe et Clitophon 7.11.1.6 ζεσθε δὲ γόητος ἀκούοντες πιθανῶς μὲν ὑποκρινομένου, πιθανῶς δὲ
Number of matches: 3

Sextus Empiricus Phil.Pyrr 1.46.2 γόητες χρίοντες τὰς θρυαλλίδας ἰῷ χαλκοῦ καὶ θολῷ
Math 2.28.3 κόν τε καὶ γόητα τυγχάνειν καὶ χειρίστοις ἐντεθραμμένον
Number of matches: 2

Aelianus Soph.NA 1.29.6 γοητείας ὑπεσπαρμένης αἱμύλου τε καὶ θελκτικῆς
NA 1.35.1 Βασκάνων ὀφθαλμοὺς καὶ γοήτων φυλάττεται
NA 3.17.13 καὶ οἱ γόητες τὰ τοιαῦτά φασιν ὁρμάς τινας
NA 3.17.16 ἀνθρώπους μεταλαγχάνειν τοῦ γοητεύματος τοῦδε,
NA 5.2.18 ἡμερώσαντες ἄγουσιν ἐς θαῦμα οἵδε οἱ γόητες
NA 7.48.42 γόης, ἐφείθη οἱ καὶ πάρδαλις. ὁρμώσης δὲ αὐτῆς
NA 12.42.4 γὰρ αὐτοῖς ὁ σκάρος γοητευόμενος ὥσπερ ἡδύσμασι.
NA 15.11.2 ὅτι τοῦτο ἐκαλεῖτο, καὶ ὅτι ἦν γόης καὶ φαρμακίς,
NA 15.11.18 τούτων τοὺς γόητάς τε καὶ φαρμακέας ᾿Άρει φίλῳ
Number of matches: 9

Marcus Aurelius Antoninus Τὰ εἰς ἑαυτόν 1.6.1.2 τῶν τερατευομένων καὶ γοήτων περὶ ἐπῳδῶν καὶ [περὶ] δαιμόνων
Number of matches: 1

Aspasius Phil.In ethica Nichomachea commentaria 54.13 ὅλως τῶν γοήτων τοῦτο ἐχόντων τὸ ὄνομα. οὗτος δὲ [πάντας] τοὺς ἐπὶ τὸ
Number of matches: 1

Polyaenus Rhet.Fragmenta 3c,639,F.1.3 Περσῶν τέμνει, νομίζων εἶναι γοητείαν ἐν αὐτῶι, ὡς Πολύαινος ὁ Αθηναῖος Ἱστορεῖ
Number of matches: 1

Flavius Philostratus Soph.VA 4.18.11 γὰρ ἄν ποτε μυῆσαι γόητα, μηδὲ τὴν Ἐλευσῖνα
VA 5.12.2 ἐγίγνωσκε καὶ ὅτι τοῖς γόητα τὸν ἄνδρα ἡγουμένοις
VA 5.12.4 σκεψώμεθα δὲ κἀκεῖνα· οἱ γόητες, ἡγοῦμαι

VA 5.12.11 ἀνάγκη γενέσθαι αὐτά, προεγίγνωσκε δὲ οὐ γοητεύων
VA 7.17.5 τος ὡς γόητι καὶ ἱκανῳ τὴν τέχνην ὁ μὲν Αἰλιανὸς
VA 7.17.7 τούτου φύλαττε,"2 ὁ δ' Ἀπολλώνιος "1εἰ μὲν γόης"2
VA 7.17.8 ἔφη "1ἐγώ, πῶς κρίνομαι; εἰ δὲ κρίνομαι, πῶς γόης
VA 7.17.10 φησιν, ὡς μηδὲ τῶν γοητευόντων ἡττᾶσθαι αὐτό.
VA 7.33.15 νους μήθ' ὡς γόης εἶ, φάναι, μήθ' ὡς ἴτης μήθ'
VA 7.34.6 δὲ τῶν δεσμῶν "1εἰ μὲν γόητά με ἡγῇ,"2 ἔφη "1πῶς
VA 7.34.7 δήσεις; εἰ δὲ δήσεις, πῶς γόητα εἶναι φήσεις;"2 "1καὶ
VA 7.39.2 πων ἐς τοὺς γόητας ἀναφέρουσι ταῦτα, πεπόνθασι
VA 7.39.14 νους τῷ γόητι, τὰ δὲ ἄτοπα τῇ αὐτῶν φειδοῖ καὶ τῳ
VA 8.3.11 ρος"2 ὦ βασιλεῦ, "1πληγὰς"2 ἔφη "1ἀπειλεῖ μοι ὁ γόης,
VA 8.3.13 μᾶλλον γόης, ἃ γὰρ μὴ ἐγὼ πέπεικά πω τὸν βασιλέα,
VA 8.7.67 οἶδα, γοητεύειν με φήσουσι καὶ τὸν οὐρανὸν ἐς τὴν
VA 8.7.89 αὐτός τε μέγας ἤρθη καὶ ὑμᾶς ἦρεν· εἰ δὲ γόητά
VA 8.7.98 δημοσίᾳ διελέχθην ἐν ἱερῷ, γοήτων δὲ ξυνουσίαι
VA 8.7.106 ἀνδρῶν σοφῶν ἢ μεταποιουμένων γε σοφίας ἐς γόητας
VA 8.7.109 σθαι; καὶ οἱ λόγοι ἦσαν ἐναντιούμενοι τοῖς γόησι·
VA 8.7.111 λείας ἐρῶντα γόησι μᾶλλον ἢ ἑαυτῷ πιστεῦσαι καὶ
VA 8.7.118 πᾶσιν ἐναντίον χρῆμα οἱ γόητες, εἰ γὰρ ἰσχύοι ταῦτα,
VA 8.7.133 οὔπω οἶδα, ἀλλὰ τοὺς γόητας ψευδοσόφους φημί·
VA 8.7.171 δος, ἀλλ' οὕτως ἀνόητος αὐτῷ δοκῶ τις, ὡς γοητεύειν
VA 8.7.174 προκηρύττων τοιαύτην· ἴτε, ὦ ἀνόητοι, γοητεύω γὰρ,
VA 8.7.221 γορος ὡς πολλοῦ ἀξίαν τοῖς γόησι. καίτοι ἀφελόντι
VA 8.7.382 οὐκ ἂν ἐφικέσθαι με, εἰ μὴ γόης τε ἦν καὶ
VA 8.7.387 ειπόντε; ἢ γοητεύοντε προειπεῖν ταῦτα; καὶ μὴν καὶ
VA 8.7.389 καὶ οὐδαμοῦ τῶν αἰτιῶν εἴρηται γόητας εἶναι σφᾶς,
VA 8.7.422 μενος γόης φαίνεσθαι θεῷ ἀναθεῖναι, ὃ αὐτὸς
VA 8.7.425 σθαι γόης ὤν; τὰ γὰρ τοιαῦτα οἱ κακοδαίμονες
VA 8.19.23 τοὺς πολλοὺς λεγόντων, μὴ ἄν ποτε γόητι ἀνθρώπῳ
VA 8.30.23 ἱεροῦ προϊστάμενοι ξυλλαβόντες αὐτὸν ὡς γόητα
VS 1.523.14 γραφόμενος, ὡς γοητεύων ἐν μειρακίοις διαβάλλειν
VS 2.590.7 πολλοῖς γόης δόξαι· ὅτι μὲν οὖν ἀνὴρ πεπαιδευμένος
VS 2.590.8 οὐκ ἂν ποτε ἐς γοήτων ὑπαχθείη τέχνας, ἱκανῶς ἐν
Number of matches: 36

Alexander Aphrodisiensis P De anima libri mantissa 180.14 ἐπιβοῶνται τὴν
εἱμαρμένην. εἰσι δέ τινες καὶ γόητες ἄνθρωποι, οἵτινες
Number of matches: 1

Vettius Valens Astrol.Anthologiarum libri ix 108.9 δεις γοητείας αὐτὰ τὰ
κεφάλαια προέταξα τοῖς μάλιστα περὶ τὰ
Anthologiarum libri ix 238.26 περὶ αὐτῶν γοητείας τε καὶ τόλμης. τὰ γὰρ
ἀποπτώματα μὴ
Anthologiarum libri ix 301.16 μοι ἀπερείσια χρήματα ἐξανάλωσα πειθόμενος
γόησι καὶ

Anthologiarum libri ix 340.3 ἢ ἐπιβλαβής· καὶ οὐχ ὥς τινες γόητες πάντα τὰ πράγματα ἀπὸ
Number of matches: 4

Total number of matches: 359

Appendix 2

QUESTIONNAIRE

Return to: Lloyd Pietersen

Name (only give this if you are happy to be contacted for an interview lasting between 30 minutes to one hour)	
How long have you been a member of BCF?	
What were your reasons for joining BCF?	
Are those initial reasons still valid today?	
If not, what are your reasons for remaining a member of BCF? **List up to five key changes (in order of significance to you) which have taken place in BCF since you joined**	

To what extent do you think these changes have been 'owned' by the church?	*Very much*	*To some extent*	*Not really*	*Not at all*
Change 1	☐	☐	☐	☐
Change 2	☐	☐	☐	☐
Change 3	☐	☐	☐	☐
Change 4	☐	☐	☐	☐
Change 5	☐	☐	☐	☐

What are your own feelings about each of these changes?

BCF is a church with its roots in the charismatic 'House Church Movement'. What, in your opinion, is the degree of emphasis given to the following areas?
Use the scale:
    1—Little or no emphasis
    2—Some emphasis
    3—Moderate emphasis
    4—Great emphasis
    5—Very great emphasis

	When you joined	*Mid-way between then and now*	*Now*
Apostles and prophets	☐	☐	☐
Commitment to BCF	☐	☐	☐
Corporate worship	☐	☐	☐
Deliverance from demons	☐	☐	☐
Discipleship	☐	☐	☐
Evangelism	☐	☐	☐

General prophecy	☐	☐	☐
Importance of the Church in God's 'end-time' purposes	☐	☐	☐
Leadership	☐	☐	☐
Miracles	☐	☐	☐
Pastoral care	☐	☐	☐
Physical healing	☐	☐	☐
Prayer	☐	☐	☐
Prophecy to individuals	☐	☐	☐
Revival	☐	☐	☐
'Second Coming' of Jesus	☐	☐	☐
Serving	☐	☐	☐
Social justice	☐	☐	☐
Speaking in tongues	☐	☐	☐
Teaching	☐	☐	☐
Words of knowledge	☐	☐	☐
Do you think we are on the verge of significant revival in the UK?			
Please give reasons for your answer to the last question			

Thank you so much for taking the time to fill in this questionnaire. Please return it in the envelope provided as soon as possible and by 30 September 1999 at the latest.

Appendix 3

RANKING OF KEY CHANGES

Change	%	Mean Significance	Ranking
Cell church	71.13	2.42	1
Changes from Community to Regions	57.73	2.52	2
Eldership/Leadership changes	32.99	2.13	3
Pioneer	22.68	3.73	4
People leaving	12.37	2.58	5
Toronto blessing	10.31	2.5	6
Diminishing supernatural expectations	10.31	3.2	7
Growth	9.28	1.8	8
Emphasis on mission	9.28	2.8	9
Greater emphasis on youth	9.28	3.3	10
Professionalisation of worship	8.25	3	11
Patchway meetings	8.25	3.3	12
Links with other churches	8.25	3.4	13
Increase in prayer emphasis	7.22	2.3	14
Women in leadership	7.22	3	15
Institutionalisation	7.22	3.6	16
Soundwell joining BCF	6.19	1.8	17
Loss of sound teaching	5.15	2.6	18
Oak Hill School	5.15	2.8	19
Age shift	5.15	3	20
Possibility of travel	4.12	2.5	21
Loss of core values	4.12	3.3	22
Pastoral care & accountability	4.12	3.8	23
Apostolic school/Antioch vision	3.09	2	24=
Differing styles of corporate meetings	3.09	2	24=
Less emphasis on evangelism	3.09	2.3	26
De-centralisation of leadership	3.09	2.33	27
Centralisation of leadership	3.09	3.7	28=
Lack of students	3.09	3.7	28=
Church focuses on being trendy	3.09	4.7	30
Greater flexibility	2.06	1.5	31
Lack of cohesiveness	2.06	2	32=
Less emphasis on discipleship	2.06	2	32=

Change	%	Mean Significance	Ranking
Less goal/project orientated	2.06	2.5	34=
Serious illness of leadership	2.06	2.5	34=
Move away from triumphalism	2.06	3	36
Availability of training courses	2.06	3.5	37=
Less access to elders	2.06	3.5	37=
Less emphasis on living in close proximity	2.06	3.5	37=
Emphasis on social justice	2.06	4	40=
Introduction of Sunday breakfasts at Soundwell	2.06	4	40=
Change in meeting patterns	1.03	1	42=
Homegroups continually changing/stopping	1.03	1	42=
Introversion & orientation to personal blessing	1.03	1	42=
Lack of leadership	1.03	1	42=
Church has become more like a business	1.03	2	46=
Emphasis on spiritual gifts	1.03	2	46=
Less emphasis on children	1.03	2	46=
Less opportunity to worship as a family	1.03	2	46=
Life based around meetings	1.03	2	46=
Committee leadership	1.03	3	51=
Involvement in arts/drama/politics etc	1.03	3	51=
Return of relational emphasis	1.03	3	51=
Tension between increasing maturity & others falling away	1.03	3	51=
Transfers from other churches	1.03	3	51=
Emphasis more on church than God	1.03	4	56=
Lack of risk	1.03	4	56=
Loss of prophetic/evangelistic slant	1.03	4	56=
Teaching/prophetic content mainly from outside BCF	1.03	4	56=
Conservative v radical ecclesiologies	1.03	5	60=
Emphasis on discipleship	1.03	5	60=

Alexander, L.C.A.

1993a   'Chronology of Paul', in G.F. Hawthorne, R.P. Martin and D.G. Reid (eds.), *Dictionary of Paul and his Letters* (Downers Grove/Leicester: InterVarsity Press): 115–23.

1993b   *The Preface to Luke's Gospel: Literary Convention and Social Context in Luke 1.1–4 and Acts 1.1* (SNTSMS, 78; Cambridge: Cambridge University Press).

1995   'Paul and the Hellenistic Schools: The Evidence of Galen', in T. Engberg-Pedersen (ed.), *Paul in His Hellenistic Context* (Edinburgh: T. & T Clark): 60–83.

Arnold, C.E.

1989   *Ephesians: Power and Magic* (SNTSMS, 63; Cambridge: Cambridge University Press).

1995   *The Colossian Syncretism: The Interface Between Christianity and Folk Belief at Colossae* (WUNT, 2/77; Tübingen: J.C.B. Mohr [Paul Siebeck]).

Aune, D.E.

1983   *Prophecy in Early Christianity and the Ancient Mediterranean World* (Grand Rapids: Eerdmans).

1997   *Revelation 1–5* (WBC, 52A; Dallas: Word Books).

Balch, D.L.

1981   *Let Wives Be Submissive: The Domestic Code in 1 Peter* (SBLMS, 26; Chico, CA: Scholars Press).

Barclay, J.M.G.

1987   'Mirror-Reading a Polemical Letter: Galatians as a Test Case', *JSNT* 31: 73–93.

1995   'Deviance and Apostasy', in P.F. Esler (ed.), *Modelling Early Christianity: Social-Scientific Studies of the New Testament in its Context* (London: Routledge): 114–27.

Barnett, P.W.

1993   'Opponents of Paul', in G.F. Hawthorne, R.P. Martin, and D.G. Reid (eds.), *Dictionary of Paul and his Letters* (Downers Grove/Leicester: InterVarsity Press): 644–53.

Bassler, J.M.

1984   'The Widow's Tale: A Fresh Look at 1 Tim. 5.3–16', *JBL* 103: 23–41.

1988   'Adam, Eve, and the Pastor: The Use of Genesis 2–3 in the Pastoral Epistles', in G. Robbins (ed.), *Genesis 1–3 in the History of Exegesis* (Lewiston, NY: Edwin Mellen Press): 43–65.

1996   *1 Timothy, 2 Timothy, Titus* (Abingdon New Testament Commentaries, Nashville: Abingdon Press).

Bauckham, R.
1988 'Pseudo-Apostolic Letters', *JBL* 107: 469–94.
1993 'The Acts of Paul as a Sequel to Acts', in B.W. Winter and A.D. Clarke (eds.), *The Book of Acts in its Ancient Literary Setting* (Grand Rapids: Eerdmans; Carlisle: Paternoster Press): 105–52.

Becker, H.S.
1963 *Outsiders: Studies in the Sociology of Deviance* (New York: The Free Press).

Berger, P.L., and T. Luckmann
1967 *The Social Construction of Reality: A Treatise in the Sociology of Knowledge* (Harmondsworth: Penguin Books).

Beverley, J.A.
1995 *Holy Laughter & The Toronto Blessing* (Grand Rapids: Zondervan).

Blasi, A.J.
1988 *Early Christianity as a Social Movement* (New York: Peter Lang).

Blau, P.M.
1963 'Critical Remarks on Weber's Theory of Authority', *American Political Science Review* 57: 305–16.

Campbell, R.A.
1994 *The Elders: Seniority Within Earliest Christianity* (Edinburgh: T. & T. Clark).

Chadwick, H.
1967 *The Early Church* (The Pelican History of the Church; ed. O. Chadwick; Harmondsworth: Penguin Books).

Collins, R.F.
2002 *I & II Timothy and Titus* (The New Testament Library; Louisville, KY: Westminster/John Knox Press).

Crouch, J.E.
1973 *The Origin and Intention of the Colossian Haustafel* (FRLANT, 109; Göttingen: Vandenhoeck & Ruprecht).

Davies, M.
1996 *The Pastoral Epistles* (New Testament Guides, Sheffield: Sheffield Academic Press).

DeMaris, R.E.
1994 *The Colossians Controversy: Wisdom in Dispute at Colossae* (JSNTSup, 96; Sheffield: JSOT Press).

Deming, W.
1995 *Paul on Marriage and Celibacy: The Hellenistic Background of 1 Corinthians 7* (SNTSMS, 83; Cambridge: Cambridge University Press).

Dibelius, M., and H. Conzelmann.
1972 *The Pastoral Epistles* (Hermeneia; trans. B. Buttolph and A. Yarbro; Philadelphia: Fortress Press).

Downes, D., and P. Rock.
1995 *Understanding Deviance: A Guide to the Sociology of Crime and Rule-Breaking* (Oxford: Clarendon Press).

du Toit, D.S.
1997 *Theios Anthropos: Zur Verwendung von θεῖος ἄνθρωπος und sinnverwandten Ausdrücken in der Literatur der Kaiserzeit* (WUNT, 2/91; Tübingen: Mohr).

Dunn, J.D.G.
  1975   *Jesus and the Spirit* (London: SCM Press).
  1977   *Unity and Diversity in the New Testament* (London: SCM Press).
  1998   *The Theology of Paul the Apostle* (Grand Rapids: Eerdmans; Edinburgh: T. & T. Clark).
Elliott, J.H.
  1995   *Social-Scientific Criticism of the New Testament* (London: SPCK).
Esler, P.F.
  1994   *The First Christians In Their Social Worlds: Social-Scientific Approaches to New Testament Interpretation* (London: Routledge).
  1995   'Introduction: Models, Context and Kerygma in New Testament Interpretation', in P.F. Esler (ed.), *Modelling Early Christianity: Social-Scientific Studies of the New Testament in its Context* (London: Routledge): 1–20.
  2000   'Models in New Testament Interpretation: A Reply to David Horrell', *JSNT* 78: 107–13.
Fee, G.D.
  1984   *1 and 2 Timothy, Titus* (A Good news commentary, San Francisco: Harper & Row).
  1987   *The First Epistle to the Corinthians* (NICNT, Grand Rapids: Eerdmans).
  1988   *1 and 2 Timothy, Titus* (New International Bible Commentary, Peabody, MA: Hendrickson).
Fiore, B.
  1986   *The Function of Personal Example in the Socratic and Pastoral Epistles* (AnBib, 105; Rome: Biblical Institute Press).
Fiorenza, E.S.
  1983   *In Memory of Her: A Feminist Theological Reconstruction of Christian Origins* (London: SCM Press).
Ford, J.M.
  1971   'A Note on Proto-Montanism in the Pastoral Epistles', *NTS* 17: 338–46.
Francis, F.O.
  1975a   'Humility and Angelic Worship in Col 2.18', in F.O. Francis and W.A. Meeks (eds.), *Conflict at Colossae: A Problem in the Interpretation of Early Christianity Illustrated by Selected Modern Studies* (SBLSBS, 4; Missoula, MT: Scholars Press): 163–95.
  1975b   'The Background of EMBATEUEIN (Col 2.18) in Legal Papyri and Oracle Inscriptions', in F.O. Francis and W.A. Meeks (eds.), *Conflict at Colossae: A Problem in the Interpretation of Early Christianity Illustrated by Selected Modern Studies* (SBLSBS, 4; Missoula, MT: Scholars Press): 197–207.
Friedrich, C.J.
  1961   'Political Leadership and the Problem of the Charismatic Power', *The Journal of Politics* 23: 3–24.
Garfinkel, H.
  1956   'Conditions of Successful Degradation Ceremonies', *American Journal of Sociology* 61: 420–24.
Georgi, D.
  1987   *The Opponents of Paul in Second Corinthians: A Study of Religious Propaganda in Late Antiquity* (Edinburgh: T. & T. Clark).

Goulder, M.
1996   'The Pastor's Wolves: Jewish Christian Visionaries behind the Pastoral Epistles', *NovT* 38: 242–56.

Grudem, W.
1988   *The Gift of Prophecy in the New Testament and Today* (Eastbourne: Kingsway).

Gunther, J.J.
1973   *St. Paul's Opponents and Their Background: A Study of Apocalyptic and Jewish Sectarian Teachings* (NovTSup, 35; Leiden: E.J. Brill).

Hanson, A.T.
1981   'The Domestication of Paul: A Study in the Development of Early Christian Theology', *BJRL* 63: 402–18.

Harnack, A.
1910   *The Constitution and Law of the Church in the First Two Centuries* (London: Williams and Norgate).

Hawthorne, G.F.
1983   *Philippians* (WBC, 43; Dallas: Word Books).

Heine, R.E.
1989   *The Montanist Oracles and Testimonia* (Macon, GA: Mercer University Press).

Heyob, S.K.
1975   *The Cult of Isis Among Women in the Graeco-Roman World* (Leiden: E.J. Brill).

Hirschi, T.
1969   *Causes of Delinquency* (Berkeley: University of California Press).

Hitchcock, F.R.M.
1940   'Philo and the Pastorals', *Hermathena* 56: 113–35.

Holmberg, B.
1978   *Paul and Power: The Structure of Authority in the Primitive Church as Reflected in the Pauline Epistles* (ConB, New Testament Series, 11; Lund: C.W.K. Gleerup).

Holmes, J.M.
2000   *Text in a Whirlwind: A Critique of Four Exegetical Devices at 1 Timothy 2.9–15* (JSNTSup, 196; Sheffield: Sheffield Academic Press).

Hooker, M.D.
1964   'Authority On Her Head: An Examination of 1 Cor. XI.10', *NTS* 10: 410–16.

Horrell, D.G.
1993   'Converging Ideologies: Berger and Luckmann and the Pastoral Epistles', *JSNT* 50: 85–103.
1996   *The Social Ethos of the Corinthian Correspondence: Interests and Ideology from 1 Corinthians to 1 Clement* (Edinburgh: T. & T. Clark).
2000   'Models and Methods in Social-Scientific Interpretation: A Response to Philip Esler', *JSNT* 78: 83–105.

Jefford, C.N.
1995   'Did Ignatius of Antioch Know the Didache?', in C.N. Jefford (ed.), *The Didache in Context: Essays on Its Text, History and Transmission* (Leiden: E.J. Brill): 330–51.

Johnson, L.T.
    1978/79   'II Timothy and the Polemic Against False Teachers: A Re-examination', *JRelS* 6–7: 1–26.
    1986   *The Writings of the New Testament: An Interpretation* (London: SCM Press).
    2001   *The First and Second Letters to Timothy* (AB, 35A; New York: Doubleday).
Karris, R.J.
    1973   'The Background and Significance of the Polemic of the Pastoral Epistles', *JBL* 92: 549–64.
    1979   *The Pastoral Epistles* (Dublin: Veritas Publications).
Käsemann, E.
    1964   'Ministry and Community in the New Testament', in *Essays on New Testament Themes* (London: SCM Press; Naperville: Allenson): 63–94.
Kelly, D.H.
    1989   *Deviant Behavior: A Text-Reader in the Sociology of Deviance* (New York: St. Martin's).
Kelly, J.N.D.
    1963   *A Commentary on the Pastoral Epistles: I Timothy, II Timothy, Titus* (London: A. & C. Black).
Klutz, T.E. (ed.)
    2003   *Magic in the Biblical World: From the Rod of Aaron to the Ring of Solomon* (JSNTSup, 245; Edinburgh: T. & T. Clark).
Knight, G.W., III
    1992   *The Pastoral Epistles : A Commentary on the Greek Text* (NIGTC, Grand Rapids: Eerdmans; Carlisle: Paternoster Press).
Kroeger, R., and C. Kroeger.
    1978   'An Inquiry into the Evidence of Maenadism in the Corinthian Congregation', in *SBLSP 14* (2; Missoula, MT: Scholars Press): 331–38.
    1992   *I Suffer Not a Woman: Rethinking 1 Timothy 2.11–15 in Light of Ancient Evidence* (Grand Rapids: Baker Book House).
Lemert, E.M.
    1972   *Human Deviance, Social Problems and Social Control* (Englewood Cliffs, NJ: Prentice-Hall).
Lewis, I.M.
    1989   *Ecstatic Religion: A Study of Shamanism and Spirit Possession* (London: Routledge).
Liefeld, W.L.
    1987   'Women, Submission and Ministry in 1 Corinthians', in A. Mickelsen (ed.), *Women, Authority & the Bible* (Basingstoke: Marshall Pickering): 134–54.
Lincoln, A.T.
    1999   'The Household Code and Wisdom Mode of Colossians', *JSNT* 74: 93–112.
Litfin, D.
    1994   *St. Paul's Theology of Proclamation: 1 Corinthians 1–4 and Greco-Roman Rhetoric* (SNTSMS, 79; Cambridge: Cambridge University Press).
Lofland, J.
    1969   *Deviance and Identity* (Englewood Cliffs, NJ: Prentice-Hall).
Lüdemann, G.
    1989   *Early Christianity According to the Traditions in Acts: A Commentary* (London: SCM Press).

Lührmann, D.
　　1980　　'Neutestamentliche Haustafeln und antike Ökonomie', *NTS* 27: 83–97.
MacDonald, D.R.
　　1983　　*The Legend and the Apostle: The Battle for Paul in Story and Canon* (Phila-delphia: Westminster Press).
MacDonald, M.Y.
　　1988　　*The Pauline Churches: A Socio-historical Study of Institutionalization in the Pauline and Deutero-Pauline Writings* (SNTSMS, 60; Cambridge: Cam-bridge University Press).
MacMullen, R.
　　1984　　*Christianizing the Roman Empire (A.D. 100–400)* (New Haven/London: Yale University Press).
Malherbe, A.J.
　　1980　　'Medical Imagery in the Pastoral Epistles', in W.E. March (ed.), *Texts and Testaments: Critical Essays on the Bible and Early Church Fathers* (San Antonio: Trinity University Press): 19–35.
Marshall, I.H.
　　1999　　*A Critical and Exegetical Commentary on the Pastoral Epistles* (ICC, Edinburgh: T. & T. Clark).
Martin, R.P.
　　1986　　*2 Corinthians* (WBC, 40; Dallas: Word Books).
Mathisen, J.A.
　　1987　　'Thomas O'Dea's Dilemmas of Institutionalization: A Case Study and Re-evaluation after Twenty-five Years', *Sociological Analysis* 47: 302–18.
Meeks, W.A.
　　1974　　'The Image of the Androgyne: Some Uses of a Symbol in Earliest Christian-ity', *HR* 13: 165–208.
Mott, S.C.
　　1978　　'Greek Ethics and Christian Conversion: The Philonic Background of Titus II 10–14 and III 3–7', *NovT* 20: 22–48.
Moule, C.F.D.
　　1965　　'The Problem of the Pastoral Epistles: A Reappraisal', *BJRL* 47: 430–52.
Mounce, W.D.
　　2000　　*Pastoral Epistles* (WBC, 46; Nashville: Thomas Nelson).
Murphy-O'Connor, J.
　　1991　　'2 Timothy contrasted with 1 Timothy and Titus', *RB* 98: 403–18.
Neyrey, J.H.
　　1986　　'Body Language in 1 Corinthians: The Use of Anthropological Models for Understanding Paul and His Opponents', *Semeia* 35: 129–70.
Niccum, C.
　　1997　　'The Voice of the Manuscripts on the Silence of Women: The External Evidence for 1 Cor 14.34–5', *NTS* 43: 242–55.
Niebuhr, H.R.
　　1929　　*The Social Sources of Denominationalism* (New York: Holt).
Niederwimmer, K.
　　1998　　*The Didache: A Commentary* (Hermeneia, Minneapolis: Augsburg Fortress).
O'Brien, P.T.
　　1982　　*Colossians, Philemon* (WBC, 44; Waco, TX: Word Books).

O'Dea, T.F.
1961   'Five Dilemmas in the Institutionalization of Religion', *JSSR* 1: 30–9.
Oropeza, B.J.
1995   *A Time to Laugh* (Peabody, MA: Hendrickson).
Payne, P.B.
1995   'Fuldensis, Sigla for Variants in Vaticanus, and 1 Cor 14.34–5', *NTS* 41:
            240–62.
Pervo, R.I.
1994   'Romancing an Oft-Neglected Stone: The Pastoral Epistles and the Episto-
            lary Novel', *JHC* 1: 25–47.
Pietersen, L.K.
1997   'Despicable Deviants: Labelling Theory and the Polemic of the Pastorals',
            Sociology of Religion 58: 343–52.
1998a   'The Mark of the Spirit?: A Charismatic Critique of the Toronto Blessing'
            (Carlisle: Paternoster Press).
1998b   'Women and the Pastorals, Part 1', *Anabaptism Today* 17: 8–16.
1998c   'Women and the Pastorals, Part 2', *Anabaptism Today* 18: 15–19.
Powell, G., and S. Powell.
1983   *Christian Set Yourself Free* (Altona, Manitoba: Friesen Printers).
Prior, M.
1989   *Paul the Letter Writer and the Second Letter to Timothy* (JSNTSup, 23;
            Sheffield: JSOT Press).
Quinn, J.D.
1978   'The Last Volume of Luke: The Relation of Luke–Acts to the Pastoral
            Epistles', in C. Talbert (ed.), *Perspectives on Luke–Acts* (Danville: Associa-
            tion of Baptist Professors of Religion): 62–75.
1990a   *The Letter to Titus* (AB, 35; New York: Doubleday).
1990b   'Paraenesis and the Pastoral Epistles: Lexical Observations Bearing on the
            Nature of the Sub-Genre and Soundings on its Role in Socialization and
            Liturgies', *Semeia* 50: 189–210.
Quinn, J.D., and W.C. Wacker.
2000   *The First and Second Letters to Timothy* (Eerdmans Critical Commentary,
            Grand Rapids: Eerdmans).
Roloff, J.
1988   *Der erste Brief an Timotheus* (EKKNT, 15; Zürich: Benziger).
Rosenmeyer, P.A.
1994   'The Epistolary Novel', in J.R. Morgan and R. Stoneman (eds.), *Greek Fic-
            tion: The Greek Novel in Context* (London/New York: Routledge): 146–65.
Rudolph, K.
1983   '"Gnosis" and "Gnosticism" – The Problems of Their Definition and Their
            Relation to the Writings of the New Testament', in A.H.B. Logan and
            A.J.M. Wedderburn (eds.), *The New Testament and Gnosis* (Edinburgh:
            T. & T. Clark)
Schlarb, E.
1990   *Die gesunde Lehre: Häresie und Wahrheit im Spiegel der Pastoralbriefe*
            (Marburger theologische Studien; 28, Marburg: N.G. Elwert Verlag).
Schmithals, W.
1983   'The Corpus Paulinum and Gnosis', in A.H.B. Logan and A.J.M. Wedderburn
            (eds.), *The New Testament and Gnosis* (Edinburgh: T. & T. Clark): 107–24.

Schneemelcher, W.
1965   'Acts of Paul', in E. Hennecke, W. Schneemelcher and R.M. Wilson (eds.), *New Testament Apocrypha* (2; London: Lutterworth): 322–51.

Schoedel, W.R.
1985   *Ignatius of Antioch: A Commentary on the Letters of Ignatius of Antioch* (Hermeneia, Philadelphia: Fortress Press).

Schreiber, S.
1996   *Paulus als Wundertäter: Redaktionsgeschichtliche Untersuchungen zur Apostelgeschichte und den authentischen Paulusbriefen* (Berlin/New York: W. de Gruyter).

Schur, E.M.
1980   *The Politics of Deviance: Stigma Contests and the Uses of Power* (Englewood Cliffs, NJ: Prentice-Hall).

Schweizer, E.
1961   *Church Order in the New Testament* (London: SCM Press; Naperville: Allenson).

Sohm, R.
1892   *Kirchenrecht* (I; Munich/Lepzig: Duncker und Humblot).

Spicq, C.
1969   *Les épîtres pastorales* (Ebib, Paris: J. Gabalda).

Stark, R.
1996   *The Rise of Christianity: A Sociologist Reconsiders History* (Princeton, NJ: Princeton University Press).

Stibbe, M.
1995   *Times of Refreshing: A Practical Theology of Revival for Today* (London: Marshall Pickering).

Still, T.D.
1999   *Conflict at Thessalonica: A Pauline Church and its Neighbours* (JSNTSup, 183; Sheffield: Sheffield Academic Press).

Sumney, J.
1990   *Identifying Paul's Opponents: The Question of Method in 2 Corinthians* (JSNTSup, 40; Sheffield: JSOT Press).

Tabbernee, W.
1997   *Montanist Inscriptions and Testimonia: Epigraphic Sources Illustrating the History of Montanism* (Patristic Monograph Series, 16; Macon, GA: Mercer University Press).

Theissen, G.
1982   *The Social Setting of Pauline Christianity* (Edinburgh: T. & T. Clark).

Thiessen, W.
1995   *Christen in Ephesus: die historische und theologische Situation in vorpaulinischer und paulinischer Zeit und zur Zeit der Apostelgeschichte und der Pastoralbriefe* (Texte und Arbeiten zum neutestamentlichen Zeitalter, 12; Tübingen: Francke).

Thiselton, A.C.
1978   'Realized Eschatology at Corinth', *NTS* 24: 510–26.

Thompson, M.B.
1998   'The Holy Internet: Communication Between Churches in the First Christian Generation', in R. Bauckham (ed.), *The Gospels for All Christians: Rethink-*

ing the Gospel Audiences (Grand Rapids: Eerdmans; Edinburgh: T.& T. Clark): 49–70.

Towner, P.H.
1987   'Gnosis and Realized Eschatology in Ephesus (of the Pastoral Epistles) and the Corinthian Enthusiasm', *JSNT* 31: 95–124.
1989   *The Goal of Our Instruction: The Structure of Theology and Ethics in the Pastoral Epistles* (JSNTSup, 34; Sheffield: JSOT Press).

Trebilco, P.
1994   'Asia', in D.W.J. Gill and C. Gempf (eds.), *The Book of Acts in its Graeco-Roman Setting* (Grand Rapids: Eerdmans; Carlisle: Paternoster Press): 291–362.

Trevett, C.
1992   *A Study of Ignatius of Antioch in Syria and Asia* (Studies in the Bible and Early Christianity, 29; Lewiston/Queenston/Lampeter: Edwin Mellen Press).
1996   *Montanism: Gender, Authority and the New Prophecy* (Cambridge: Cambridge University Press).

Troeltsch, E.
1931   *The Social Teaching of the Christian Churches*, 1 (2 vols.; trans. O. Wyon; New York: Macmillan).

Tucker, R.C.
1968   'The Theory of Charismatic Leadership', *Daedalus* 97: 731–56.

Van Broekhoven, H.
1997   'The Social Profiles in the Colossian Debate', *JSNT* 66: 73–90.

Verner, D.C.
1983   *The Household of God: The Social World of the Pastoral Epistles* (SBLDS, 71; Chico, CA: Scholars Press).

von Campenhausen, H.
1969   *Ecclesiastical Authority and Spiritual Power in the Church of the First Three Centuries* (London: A. & C. Black).

Walker, A.
1998   *Restoring the Kingdom: The Radical Christianity of the House Church Movement* (Guildford: Eagle).

Walsh, B.J., and J.R. Middleton
1984   *The Transforming Vision: Shaping a Christian World View* (Downers Grove, IL: Inter-Varsity Press).

Weber, M.
1968   *Economy and Society: An Outline of Interpretive Sociology* (ed. G. Roth and C. Wittich; New York: Bedminster).

Wedderburn, A.J.M.
1987   *Baptism and Resurrection: Studies in Pauline Theology against Its Graeco-Roman Background* (WUNT, 44; Tübingen: J.C.B. Mohr [Paul Siebeck]).

Wilson, B.R.
1967   'An Analysis of Sect Development', in B.R. Wilson (ed.), *Patterns of Sectarianism* (London: Heinemann): 22–45.
1973   *Magic and the Millennium: A Sociological Study of Religious Movements of Protest Among Tribal and Third-World Peoples* (London: Heinemann).

Wilson, S.G.
1979   *Luke and the Pastoral Epistles* (London: SPCK).

Wire, A.C.
1990   *The Corinthian Women Prophets: A Reconstruction through Paul's Rhetoric* (Minneapolis: Fortress Press).

Young, F.M.
1994   *The Theology of the Pastoral Letters* (New Testament Theology, Cambridge: Cambridge University Press).

INDEX

INDEX OF REFERENCES

BIBLE

Authors From Antiquity

Ps-Isocrates
Ad Demonicum
17　　　　21
38　　　　21

Strabo
Geography
7.3.3　　　130
10.3.7-17　112
10.3.23　　133

Theodoret
Haereticarum fabularum compendium
3.2　　　104

Thucydides
Historiae
1.21.1　　121